Jimi Hendrix and Philosophy

Popular Culture and Philosophy® Series Editor: George A. Reisch

For full details of all Popular Culture and Philosophy® books, visit www.opencourtbooks.com.

Popular Culture and Philosophy®

Jimi Hendrix and Philosophy

Experience Required

Edited by
THEODORE G. AMMON

OPEN COURT
Chicago

Volume 113 in the series, Popular Culture and Philosophy®, edited by George A. Reisch

To find out more about Open Court books, visit our website at www.opencourtbooks.com.

Open Court Publishing Company is a division of Carus Publishing Company, dba Cricket Media.

Copyright © 2018 by Carus Publishing Company, dba Cricket Media

First printing 2018

Jimi Hendrix and Philosophy: Experience Required

ISBN: 978-0-8126-9956-2.

Library of Congress Control Number: 2017954738

This book is also available as an e-book.

Contents

Johnny—James—Buster—Jimmy—Jimi . . . How Many Jimis?

Named **Johnny Allen Hendrix** by his beautiful mother who died of bad habits far too early. Subtitle: "But why wasn't Johnny Allen born in The South?" The simple answer is that he was born in Seattle.

So . . . . what, am I waxing philosophical here and proposing a sort of historical determinism, whereby if you play a certain type of music (blues, in this case) you have to be from a certain place? A Hegelian unfolding of The Absolute requires true blues musicians to have been born in The South, probably Mississippi? Oh nonsense, and pooh on Hegel.

Nevertheless, the Buster Hendrix experience of the blues came from somewhere, and lacking a crossroads in a delta, the young **James Marshall Hendrix** (His father returned from World War II and changed his son's name) picked up what music he could as a dirt-poor ever-hungry African-American child prowling around Seattle, of all places.

Fortunately his father, Al Hendrix, played saxophone, thus exposing his son to crucial musical influences. But the sax was not for James, and he played a broom until he finessed a cheap guitar. It's safe to say that no broom in the history of brooms has been as well-played as that of the Hendrix house in Seattle, Washington, USA.

Fast forward. James left high school and enlisted in the air force as a paratrooper, where he met Billy Cox, who became a life-long friend, musical companion, and bassist for Band of Gypsys. The story here is a bit murky, but it seems that young

Hendrix lost interest in the Air Force and: 1. hurt himself on a practice jump; or 2. convinced the camp psychiatrist that he was gay; or 3. both.

So he was discharged. And then began the serious music career, on the chitlin' circuit. This sojourn was fabulously important and infuriating at the same time. He was able to play backup for significant black musicians, such as The Isley Brothers and Little Richard, and likewise absorb the influences of T-Bone Walker, Albert King, Muddy Waters, Ron Isley, and Curtis Mayfield. All of these influences can be heard and seen in his compositions and stage performances.

But all the time poor, all the time hungry, and a trip to New York proved again both frustrating and life-transforming. Sleeping wherever he could, eating from the hands of strangers, having to pawn his guitar, he barely survived long enough to be "discovered" by Linda Keith, Keith Richards's girlfriend, and Chas Chandler, the bassist for The Animals. And sometime during that formative New York period he formed his own band, **Jimmy James and the Blue Flames**.

Easily persuaded to fly to London, Hendrix was introduced to a thriving WHITE music scene—no chitlin' circuit in England and Europe. No society divided severely along racial lines, but plenty of white guitarists—Clapton, Townsend, Mayall, Beck, and many others—who had already absorbed, in a fashion, American blues and hence were fascinated by Hendrix.

Hendrix represented more than American blues, however; his facility with the guitar was absolutely astonishing. And Chas Chandler saw to it, in his own managerial debut, that Hendrix got a rhythm section, access to a studio, and a contract. And the **Jimi Hendrix** experience poured into the hearts and souls of absorbent London and European instant fans.

So there were several Jimis along the way until his untimely demise at twenty-seven, just after the dissolution of Band of Gypsys; he was continually transforming. The question we all want answered is: If only he had stayed alive, what would his music have become?

Jimi was restless, even after the tremendous success of three brilliant albums in short order. Redding left, Mitchell stayed, Cox and Larry Lee, plus two percussionists whose contributions were laughably irrelevant, were added. So,

Woodstock saw Gypsy Sun and Rainbow, "nothing but a band of gypsies," Hendrix remarks.

Then the brilliant Band of Gypsys with Cox and Buddy Miles. The significance? An all-black American band and minimal foolishness on stage such as humping amps and burning guitars. But most importantly, the music morphed into a blend of rock, call&response, funk, and soul. The music had finally been pushed to the forefront and Hendrix was no longer interested in the antics of Monterrey.

So who was *this* Jimi? In four short years Johnny Allen Hendrix had become the undisputed master of electric guitar, of feedback, of the wah-wah pedal. But the question is what combination of musical styles would he prefer?

Unfortunately the release of *Valleys of Neptune* gave scant evidence or clues as to the direction of his music. The title cut has less in common with *Band of Gypsys* than with "Bold as Love" and some of the songs from *Cry of Love*. The more cautious ears will focus upon *Electric Ladyland* and the companion tunes "Rainy Day Dream Away" and "Still Raining, Still Dreaming," songs that wrap around the saxophone—a tip of his hat to his father?—and betray a clear jazz orientation.

It makes good sense to say that *these* two are the most important songs on the album, not the absurdly popular cover of Dylan's "All Along the Watchtower" and "Voodoo Child (Slight Return)." Rumor had it that Miles Davis was in the plans for a future fanfare. One can only imagine the two dominant musicians collaborating and struggling for musical control of the jams or compositions. It makes good sense as well to claim that Hendrix was incapable of leaving the blues. But jazz and blues are brothers, at least cousins. The "Rainy Day" duo on *Ladyland* proves the point, and establishes Hendrix as a probable first-rate jazz guitarist.

So what did we lose on September 20th 1970, besides the most important electric guitarist to date? Not more psychedelia, not more hard rock, not more R&B infused "pretty" songs, but rather an entirely new form of jazz blues, the likes of which the world will never know and had never heard. And which *Jimi* did we lose? Well all of them, but especially the Jimi we rarely saw on stage, if at all: the one who could "lay back and groove" for at least a rainy day, if not a week, month, years . . .

I

If 6 Was 9

1
I Stand Up Next to a Mountain

HANS UTTER

From video games to international air guitar contests, the meme of the "guitar hero" has taken on a life of its own, fusing individual stories into a collective mythology.

In our shared cultural environment, stereotypes and tropes can occasionally reveal grains of truth—once we peer beneath the surface. Countless songs celebrate the story of a musician who came from nowhere, beat the odds, and becomes a world-renowned rock star. Chuck Berry's rock anthem "Johnny B. Goode" tells the story of a country boy, born in poverty, whose guitar playing brought him to the peak of stardom and fame. Hendrix described his own journey in many songs, ranging from the down-and-out young musician trying to make it in the world ("Highway Chile"), the despair of "I Don't Live Today," to the heroic journey of "Voodoo Chile."

Jimi Hendrix's music and life were deeply rooted in a profound philosophical quest—his goal was to awaken his audience to the world around them and to share his personal journey of self-discovery.

The blues that permeates Jimi's music express both fatalism and freedom. In "Hear My Train a-Comin'," Hendrix invokes the classic blues symbolism of a train representing the inevitability of fate and mortality. At the same time, acceptance of the reality of death gives rise to an inner compulsion to seek freedom and self-expression. He vows to "leave this lonesome town" and "become a magic boy," and finally a "voodoo chile." Instead of acquiescing to the demands of the world, Hendrix believed in the possibility of individual freedom.

3

Embarking on the Hero's Journey

"I'm going to destroy a thing I really love!" Hendrix proclaimed, dousing his guitar with lighter fluid, fanning the flames like an ancient shaman during a sacrificial ritual. The searing flames that engulfed Jimi's guitar created an iconic image—instantly elevating him to a mythic status in rock history. Like the archetypal shaman, Hendrix continually challenged the expectations and prejudices of those around him.

The arrival of Hendrix in swinging London was an earth-shattering event, even for guitar legends like Eric Clapton and Pete Townsend of the Who. Hendrix was a living embodiment of the blues tradition, and highlighted their second-hand knowledge. After Hendrix jammed with Cream in London, Clapton famously lamented "you never told me he was that good!" The London tabloids described him as "The Wild Man of Borneo" and "Mau Mau," ignoring his virtuosity and originality.

His flamboyant stage antics, absorbed during his work on the chitlin' circuit, (venues open to African-American performers during the era of segregation) were light years ahead of what most British rockers were capable of. Hendrix took R&B and the blues to the next level, even influencing jazz icons Miles Davis and Gil Evans. He pushed the boundaries of guitar playing and performance antics into new territory, far beyond what the rock royalty of London had ever experienced. Shooting out lines of feedback-drenched blue notes, playing guitar with his teeth, and expressing primal emotions, Hendrix was the archetypal rock god. His lifestyle, infused with drugs, sex, and rock-'n'roll, seems to have been the embodiment of the Sixties psychedelic mantra "Turn on, Tune in, Drop out." Hendrix followed the first two admonitions, but did not drop out.

In our lives, we all make choices based on what we define as important to ourselves, and to our place in the world. Most choose to remain within the confines of the socially acceptable, living lives of "quiet desperation." Or, we can acknowledge our own mortality and accept responsibility for our own destiny. Hendrix proclaimed "I'm the one that's gonna die when it's time for me to die, so let me live my life the way I want to!"

The decision to pursue your dreams no matter what the odds requires a strong intention. Will, courage, and commitment provide the means to continue in the face of obstacles. Hendrix believed that music was one of the most potent avenues of liberation and happiness, if not the most potent, in a troubled and dark world.

The Hero's Journey

One of the aspects of the hero's journey, articulated by Joseph Campbell in his work *The Hero with a Thousand Faces,* is separation from the normal stream of day-to-day life, overcoming a series of challenges, and finally gaining special knowledge and power. The hero's journey is commonly broken up into three phases: separation, initiation, and return. This formula has been used in countless movies, novels, and songs.

Greek myths express psychological and philosophical ideas, and like music they can offer new perspectives and outline perennial concepts. The Greek myth of Prometheus recounts how he brought fire to mankind, but ultimately suffered for his transgression against the gods. Hendrix brought the fire of music to the world from the depths of his own past, his emotions, and the blues tradition. Like Prometheus, Hendrix struggled against the reactive forces that kept him down: against promoters who wanted him to change his sound, musicians like Little Richard who considered him a threat, and audiences who wanted his greatest hits, not his more complex later work.

Prometheus was a demi-god in Greek mythology. According to some accounts he also fashioned humankind out of clay. The goddess Athena brought these clay figures to life, thereby beginning the human journey on Earth. However, Zeus, the king of the Gods, disliked humankind and made life on Earth miserable for humans. Prometheus rebelled against Zeus and the heavenly hierarchy by stealing fire from the Gods and bringing it to humans. Fire was stolen either from Heaven itself or from the forge of Hephaistos (the Roman Vulcan), the blacksmith of the gods (*Handbook of Greek Mythology*, p. 54).

Prometheus instructed mankind in a wide range of arts and sciences, enabling the development of civilization. Zeus was enraged by this and plotted Prometheus's downfall by creating Pandora, a beautiful woman who seduced Prometheus's brother. She later opened a box that contained all the ills that beset mankind. Prometheus was taken to a mountain peak, condemned to endless suffering. Eventually, Prometheus repented and was released.

Hendrix's life and music embodied the hero's journey. The interconnected songs from *Electric Ladyland*, "Voodoo Chile," and "Voodoo Child (Slight Return)," clearly describe the mythic transitions of separation, initiation, and return. Of the two, the latter is most recognizable to most listeners; "Slight Return" became a concert staple, while "Voodoo Chile" was never performed live. The practice of voodoo, the summoning of spirits and trance, while found in blues songs such as "I Got My Mojo Working," is taken to another level by Hendrix. "Voodoo Chile" transports the listener on a metaphysical journey culminating in Hendrix's heroic rebirth. The music merges delta blues forms with blistering psychedelic guitar, the lyrics mythology and science fiction. Jimi's travels begin in an intimate live-performance setting, with the sounds and encouragement of an enthusiastic audience.

While Hendrix normally tuned the guitar down a half step, "Voodoo Chile" is tuned all the way down to D, giving the song an intense and otherworldly feeling. A powerful delta blues riff winds its way through Hendrix's unique variations on standard blues chord progression, culminating in a modal melody (*à la* Ravi Shankar)—transforming the blues into something new and unexpected.

The lyrics set the stage for Hendrix's mythological narrative: "Well I'm a Voodoo Chile, Lord I'm a Voodoo Chile / On the Night I was Born, Lord I swear the moon turned a fire red / Well my poor mother cried out 'Lord, the gypsy was right!' / And I seen her fall down right dead." Immediately, we're confronted with a loss that Hendrix suffered all his life—the death of his mother in 1958. This personal trauma sets the stage for travel into mystical and otherworldly realms, representing the *separation* stage of the hero's journey. The mythological aspects of his birth are revealed in the moon being transformed to a "fire red," and a gypsy fortuneteller's prophecies. Already in the first verse we are far from the usual rock mythology (such as "Johnny B. Goode," "Juke Box Hero," "Ziggy Stardust"). Although we could surmise that Hendrix is merely being pretentious, the track's instrumental intensity lives up to the lyrics.

The song continues further into the realm of mythology. Hendrix describes his rescue by mountain lions, after being presumably left to die, abandoned. This verse describes the *initiation* phase of the hero's journey, from which Hendrix receives a "Venus witch's ring." In the next verse, the supernatural powers that he has gained are described: the ability to travel in multiple dimensions of space and time, and in the realm of dreams. He is "a million miles away," yet "right here in your picture frame," floating "in liquid gardens" above "Arizona new red sand." At the base of this power is music, now a vehicle to traverse the universe and inner psychological experience.

The third verse outlines the *return* stage of the hero's journey: "Well my arrows are made of desire / From far away as Jupiter's sulfur mines." At the point when it appears that Hendrix has finally overstepped the boundaries of self-praise, he unleashes a powerful guitar solo that encompasses and transcends the blues-guitar tradition. The musical ambiance of this track creates a compelling, symbolic landscape, grounded in emotional resonance and embodied experience.

The second composition, "Voodoo Child (Slight Return)" begins with one of his most distinctive rock riffs. Growling percussive rhythms call to mind voodoo ceremonies; the distorted and wah-wah-soaked melody mimics a spoken ceremony. He again describes the power granted to him through music and his mythic journey. He can "stand up next to a mountain" and then "chop it down with the edge of my hand," finally creating an island. This proclaims his mastery and transcendence of the blues and R&B traditions, and the unique creativity of his music.

Like Prometheus, Hendrix returns from his voyages and brings back the fire of music to the world, but, like Prometheus, those in power and the masses do not understand his gifts. He embraces his personal tragedies and the social unrest of the Sixties, and heals them through the emotional release of music.

The Birth of Tragedy and Dionysian Art

The philosopher Friedrich Nietzsche (1844–1900) believed that music could transcend the human condition, considered as finite, fragile, and conditioned by society. For Nietzsche, suffering was a fact of life. The accepted values of society can serve to limit freedom, growth, and personal development.

In *The Birth of Tragedy,* Nietzsche posited that two polarities of Greek Tragedy, based on the gods Apollo and Dionysius represent the two fundamental modalities of all artistic expression. Apollo, the god of reason, symbolizes order, measure, and proportional beauty; Dionysus, the god of wine, symbolizes passion and excess—sex, drugs, and rock'n'roll! In his most intense moments, Hendrix and his band mates pushed the limits of blues and rock, of noise and intensity, creating a Dionysian ecstasy that pulled listeners out of themselves into a collective but totally individual experience. Nietzsche says:

> It is at this point that the tragic myth and the tragic hero interpose between our highest musical excitement and the music, giving us a parable of those cosmic facts of which music alone can speak directly. (p. 127)

This process is clearly visible in the mythic narratives and supernatural powers described in "Voodoo Chile."

One of the great frustrations of Hendrix's life was that he could not live down his image, and move beyond the rock-star persona. He wanted to create a new music, using orchestral instruments, for serious listeners. This parallels Nietzsche's exploration of how the Dionysian man "resembles Hamlet" because the experience of the transcendent cannot be reconciled with the world around them. The transcendence of art can be difficult to reconcile with day-to-day existence. Throughout his life, no matter what he was facing, Hendrix always found solace in music. Nietzsche explains how the contradictions are resolved through art:

> In this supreme jeopardy of the will, art, the sorceress expert in healing approaches him; only she can turn his fits of nausea into imagination with which it is possible to live. (p. 52)

The Tragic Hero

Hendrix's short life, with its almost mythological contours, is often described through the "live fast, die young" trope that surges through popular culture. Hendrix often alluded to his coming death. In this way, Hendrix embodies Nietzsche's description of the tragic hero.

For Nietzsche, "Tragedy absorbs the highest orgiastic music and in so doing consummates music," expressing the realities of life by confronting, not turning away towards an idealized world. The true artist is able to experience the whole range of life; "But then it puts beside it the tragic myth and the tragic hero," who, "Like a mighty titan, the tragic hero shoulders the whole Dionysiac world and removes the burden from us."

The tragic hero, through music, confronts the deepest aspects of life, including death, and thereby provides the audience with an emotional release. The function of myth is to provide understanding of life events in the broader context, outside individual social and historical constraints. The tragic hero, embodying and expressing transpersonal qualities, provides an aesthetic experience outside of daily concerns, and at the same time reveal a deeper significance to life: "At the same time, tragic myth, through the figure of the hero, delivers us from our avid thirst for earthly satisfaction and reminds us of another existence and a higher delight."

Catharsis

Hendrix expressed events from his own life through music, and hoped to give listeners emotional release. In the theories of ancient Greek drama, this is known as *catharsis*. Aristotle discusses the emotional effect of music on an audience, which include *sympatheia,* an emotional identification, and excitement or ecstasy that can create a catharsis, which purges the emotions and offers a more balanced state (*Politics* 8.7. 3–8).

For Aristotle, music was a central element that could bring about the cleansing of negative emotions and the eventual balancing of individuals. He explains how we all share certain basic emotions, but that some individuals are more profoundly influenced by their emotions:

> An emotion which strongly affects some souls is present in all to a varying degree, for example pity and fear, and also ecstasy. To this last some people are particularly liable, and we see that under the influence of religious music and songs which drive the soul to frenzy, they calm down as if they had been medically treated and purged. People who are given to pity and fear, and emotional people generally, and others to the extent that they have similar emotions, must be affected in the same way; for all of them must experience a kind of purgation and pleasurable relief. In the same way, cathartic (songs and) music give men harmless delight. (*Politics* 8.7.4, 1342a 5–24)

Those with intense emotions can experience a sense of calm and peace through intense artistic expression, which offers emotional release through identification (*sympatheia*) and catharsis. For Aristotle, this emotional release is beneficial to all. For audiences, rock stars can be larger-than-life figures who let the audience experience, if only briefly, an intensity of experience far beyond "normal" life.

Hendrix's later songs such as "Machine Gun" examine the horrors of war and violence. In this song, he creates a sonic tapestry of the cries of dying men and the explosive violence of modern weaponry, moving beyond notes and chords into pure sound. This provided an emotional release for the audience, and his sonic representation of war transformed violence into a cry for peace and justice. "I don't think they [the critics] understand my songs. They live in a different world. My world—that's hunger, it's the slums, raging race hatred and the only happiness is the kind that you can hold in your hands, nothing more!" Hendrix stated that his music was a release for both himself and the audience, "My music is my personal diary. A release of all of my inner feelings, aggression, tenderness, sympathy, everything" (*Electric Gypsy*, p. 161). Hendrix's ability to take everything he saw in the world, gaze directly into tragic reality of life, and finally offer an emotional release for himself and his audience is exactly the role of the tragic hero envisioned by Nietzsche, who "like a mighty titan, . . . shoulders the whole Dionysiac world and removes the burden from us."

Fly on Brother: Play on Drummer

On September 18th 1970, Hendrix's trip was over. I will not dwell on the details of his death here, but suffice to say that at the young age of twenty-seven, the world lost a unique musical voice. Hendrix's death was nothing if not tragic. Yet, his honesty, creativity, and genuine intention to make the world a better place live on in his music.

During his final years, he continued to develop as a composer, creating music with more harmonic complexity, drawn from flamenco, jazz, and classical music, as well as continuing to develop as a lyricist. He had scheduled recording sessions with Gil Evans, the jazz arranger best known for his work with Miles Davis, and was envisioning new musical vistas involving larger ensembles.

At the same time, Hendrix's image as a rock star was truly beginning to confine him. He believed that he was ready to do something else with his life, but was compelled to keep going to realize his creative vision, and to speak out against the injustices and suffering in the world around him.

We will never know what would have become of Hendrix's planned work with Miles Davis, or how his musical compositions would have developed. We can only go to the recordings that were left behind, albums such as *Nine to the Universe,* which show his jazz-influenced playing, and tracks from his projected album *First Rays of the New Rising Sun,* scheduled for release only a short time after his death. As a perfectionist, Hendrix would not have been happy with the release of incomplete tracks and demos, but that is all we have. The hero's journey was a work in progress for Hendrix—he was not content to live off past accomplishments, and refused to be locked into a specific genre.

The themes that he continued to develop remain as compelling as they did in the 1960s and his mastery of the guitar continues to inspire new generations. His life was a sacrifice to music. Just as he burned his guitar at the Monterey Pop Festival, his life and talent burned brightly throughout his short life. His personal sacrifice for music was not in vain, and remain a testament to the power of art guided by philosophical questions.

As long as human beings remain in the world, questions of the purpose of life and individual destiny will remain. The haunting words of "Voodoo Child (Slight Return)" still resonate: "I didn't mean to take up all your sweet time / I'll give it back, one of these days / If I don't meet you no more on this world / I'll meet you in the next one / Don't be late!"

2

Zen and the Art of Guitar Burning

RONALD S. GREEN

Zen Master Nansen heard two monks arguing over a cat in the temple courtyard. Each monk was saying, "This is *my* cat!" Nansen came out of his quarters, picked up the cat by the scruff of the neck with one hand and held a sword in the other. Poised in this way, he declared, "If either of you can say a word, you can save the cat." Dumbfounded, neither spoke. Nansen summarily cut the cat in half, ending the debate.

That evening, Nansen's top student, Joshu, returned to the monastery from begging for rice and asked the master what had happened during the day. After Nansen recounted the story about the cat, Joshu stood up without a word, put his sandals on his head and walked out of the room. Master Nansen shook his head as he left and muttered to himself, "Too bad, *that* would have saved the cat."

Zen is a Buddhist tradition that is transmitted from master to student outside of concerns with doctrinal arguments, but through direct experience. No argument could have saved the cat. Arguments discriminate between this and that, while Zen asks us to stop such internal and external dialogues and just experience life without adding or taking away from it.

Later, when a student asked Joshu to explain, "What is the Buddha?" Joshu replied, "Go have tea." Not understanding, the student asked Joshu to explain the complexities of Buddhist philosophy, the Dharma. Joshu responded, "Go have tea." The persistent student then asked, "What is the Sangha (the community of Buddhists)?" Again Joshu answered, "Go have tea."

Joshu was not avoiding the questions but responding that
direct experience is the Buddha, the Dharma, and the Sangha:
the Three Jewels of Buddhism.

He may just as well have said, "Go listen to a Zenmi Zendrix
lead." Although I would, without doubt, be struck by the master's stick of compassion to whack such discriminative explanations out of my head, I'll take the risk of offering one more.

Nansen's sword cut through the delusion of separateness
that the discriminative mind creates in order to make sense of
the world, even if that cognitive reorganization is ultimately
untrue and is the source of dissatisfaction and suffering. We
say, "I like this and I hate that" or "This is my cat and it's not
yours" and by definition, this is dissatisfaction (*dukkha*), wanting something we don't have and wanting to get rid of something we do have.

The shock of a Buddhist master killing a cat knocks this discrimination out of us and in the moment between breaths, *we
experience*. It is the same as if we had received a blow from the
master's staff or from Jimi's axe of compassion. In experience
free from discrimination, not only could six very well turn out
to be nine but in fact, it has.

An' Put It All in My Shoe (Might Even Give a Piece to You)

Zen has a foundation story telling how it began as a tradition
that does not rely on words or scriptures. The story says that
the Buddha once took his disciples to a quiet place. As they had
done many times, the Buddha's followers sat in a small circle
around him, and waited for the teaching. Such times were the
occasions when he gave the lectures that were later recorded as
the Buddhist sūtras, such as the famous *Lotus Sūtra* or the
Sūtra on the Foundations of Mindfulness. But this time he said
nothing. After a while, as the monks became puzzled, Buddha
simply held up a lotus flower and remained silent.

The disciples only became more confused. At last, a follower
named Kāśyapa or Mahākāśyapa (the Great Kāśyapa) suddenly understood and when he did, he smiled. In response, the
Buddha declared, "I possess the true Dharma eye, the mar-
velous mind of Nirvana, the true form of the formless, the subtle Dharma Gate that does not rest on words or letters but is a

special transmission outside of the scriptures. This I entrust to you, Mahākāśyapa." In this way, Kāśyapa became the second ancestor (after the Buddha himself) of the Zen tradition.

Let's think about what Jimi said in light of this. "Are you experienced? Have you ever been experienced? Well, I have." But more important than either these words or the Buddha's declaration is the Zen moment of pure involvement that comes before the words, in the flower of back-masked guitar sounds, a reversing of what is expected like stringing a right-handed Strat left and the whole Jimi Hendrix Experience. This pure experience involves letting go of the dualistic construction of the world that we cling to so tightly. Then, "We'll watch the sun rise from the bottom of the sea."

The Flower Hidden in the Big Muff

Jimi Hendrix's sounds and lyrics are a wealth of mad monk ecstatic wisdom pointing to expanded awareness beyond ordinary consciousness. But don't concentrate too much on the pointing finger, you guitar players, or you will end up imitating the style alone and lose the important Zen flower hidden within the flow of riffs.

There was a Zen master who used to raise a finger when he made a significant point. A young follower started imitating the finger with nothing behind the words it punctuated. Observing this, one day when the boy raised his finger, the master cut it off with his sword. The boy ran off crying but later, when he started to imitate the master without thinking, there was no finger there, only emptiness, and the boy was greatly enlightened. How will you play the guitar with no fingers? With your teeth?

Zeami Motokiyo (around 1363–1443) was the foremost writer and theorist of Japanese Noh drama. His plays and guidance in creating and performing Noh brought the art to its highest level of aesthetic achievement and appreciation. Zeami's teachings centered on Zen, particularly the story of the flower the Buddha held. His strongest motivation in producing Noh plays was to enlighten his audience through theatrical production. He maintained that the audience should not know this was happening to them, that the actors had to keep that hidden.

It was the task of Noh performers to hold up a metaphorical flower to the audience through acting, and at the same time to keep this flower hidden, perhaps even from themselves as it was happening. According to Mahāyāna Buddhism in general, the larger Buddhist tradition of which Zen is a part, this is also the task of a Bodhisattva, to attract people to the path of awakening clandestinely. A Bodhisattva is an "awakening being," a person who is not yet a Buddha but is both becoming awake (or enlightened) and is awakening others in the process. For Zeami, a performer has a particular set of tools or flowers for being a Bodhisattva.

The flower Jimi Bodhisattva held up was his guitar, Marshall, effects, voice, or lyrics leading to the pure experience of the unity of these elements within our lives and the world. Zeami speaks of one's flower as "essence," an essence that is an ongoing crystallizing of experiencing. The flowering of one's talent leads to an understanding of and direct experience of a Zen-like essence of the human and universal condition of sentient beings.

What is experienced, according to Buddhism, is *tathāta*, typically translated as "suchness" or "thusness" in English, even if English doesn't otherwise have these words. This means to experience life *thus*, just like it is, without internal dialogue narrating. It's opening the experiential window to the wind and letting pure experience blow in. Zeami taught that in the hands of a Bodhisattva, this can be transmitted in a single gesture, a turn of the head or, we can suggest, the feedback from a JTM-45/100.

For Zeami, in this way, Zen performance involves a mystic transmission to the audience. This requires an intuitive understanding on the part of the performer. Zeami thought that there is a fundamental rhythm basic to Noh and he points out that this is the same rhythm that is present in all of nature. Countless Hendrix fans have found this rhythm. Buddhists and others have offered ideas about how rhythm and mantra affect our brainwaves and consciousness.

One of the major principles of the flower in performance is that, to a great artist, one of the reasons a flower is beautiful is that it sheds its petals and eventually dies. That a flower undergoes constant changes in front of the viewer can be compared with the progression of Hendrix's famous set on the Monday morning that closed Woodstock as well as the Sixties.

Zeami said, "If hidden, acting shows the Flower; if unhidden, it cannot." Such a performance is pulled off through skill-in-means (*upāya*), that is, the ability to use one's talents and instruments as a means of awakening the audience to pure experience beyond and within the words and sounds, and thereby transmit the experience of thusness. As Jimi says in "Are you Experienced", "If you can just get your mind together then come across to me."

If You Meet Jimi on the Road, Kill Him

Zen art has a radical side, marked by extreme abbreviation, dynamic, and unconventional performance in painting and calligraphy. Chinese Zen (Chan) painters are famous for depicting images that might shock a person out of complacency and ordinary unenlightened thinking. The painter Liang Kai painted in a monochrome style like calligraphy. He painted Buddha suffering from the seasonal cold, emphasizing his humanity in keeping with the Zen understanding of an individual seeker of enlightenment. This approach of representing the historical Buddha directly, probably shocking to his contemporaries, is related to Zen's idea of non-duality, in this case, asserting a paradoxical non-differentiation between the pre- and post-enlightenment view of the world.

Zen painters used an outlandish style that was a pictorial metaphor for the irrational nature of sudden enlightenment. In many ways, Hendrix does the same thing, challenging the standing orthodox thinking about the war, America, and reality itself. "If the mountains fell in the sea, let it be, it ain't me," which can be a nice message also in the face of politics.

The same Chan painter, Liang Kai, also painted a depiction of the famous Zen master Huineng ecstatically tearing up a Buddhist sūtra. Although this might not have been historically accurate, it does fit the Zen ideas of non-duality, of shocking you out of your belief system, and of destroying the icon that might actually stand in your way of direct experience, whether this is a religious scripture, an image of an alleged saint, or the conventions of pop music. It may be the same as the person who can say, "Well, I stand up next to a mountain, I chop it down with the edge of my hand."

In Zen Buddhist tradition, when a new master succeeds the old, a robe or backrest is handed down symbolizing that the new master is fit to receive them, perhaps like stories of musicians giving their guitars to another, such as Johnny Cash to Bob Dylan. At the time when Chinese Master Linji was given the backrest by his master, Linji exclaimed, "Bring me some fire." This apparent disrespect for the iconic symbol of the Zen patriarchal lineage is perfectly in line with Zen ideals.

In doctrine- and veneration-based traditions of Buddhism, there is a long-accepted notion that we should always revere and preserve sūtras and images of the Buddha. However, in irreverent Zen fashion, Linji went as far as saying that burning a sūtra or a statue of Buddha could help us achieve enlightenment. From one perspective, this is like the Zen idea that we have to hit the bottom in order to rise.

Once we sink, as Jimi says, "We'll watch the sun rise from the bottom of the sea." When an outraged student asked Linji what he meant by burning the sūtras or an image of Buddha, the Zen Master replied, "When you realize that causation is empty, mind is empty, phenomena are empty, when your single thought is set to cut off, transcendent and you have nothing further to do, this is called 'burning the sūtras and the Buddha's image'."

The same destruction of the idols (or fingers) that, in our piousness, keeps us from the real experience that they should evoke, can be seen in Jimi's act of lighting his guitar on fire. The difference between Hendrix's act of destruction and that of Pete Townsend, who beat his guitar against the stage, is that the latter's is a proto-punk statement against the music establishment from the perspective of "My Generation." Hendrix's act is free from violence and means to involve the experience as opposed to the tool. It is a type of fire ceremony beyond the label of religion.

Master Linji said, "If you attain such insight, you will be free from the hindrances of such terms as 'secular' and 'sacred'." In a single thought, seeing an empty fist or a pointing finger, you mistake it for reality. You fabricate illusions within the six-senses field, and belittle yourself, saying, "I am a bumpkin, while he is a sage."

In the same vein, there is a well-known Zen *kōan* that says, "If you meet the Buddha on the road, kill him." Again, I'll risk receiving the feedback from the axe of compassion by venturing that this means we should get rid of the icons and symbols that we hold above us and thereby hold back ourselves.

Jimi Puts It All in His Shoe (and Might Even Give a Piece to You)

Jimi's song "Instrumental Solo" or "Instrumental Improvisation" later called "Villanova Junction" exemplifies his Zen-like attainment and bodhisattva-like offering of this experience to the world. It is well known that people talk about "The Star-Spangled Banner" at Woodstock as the culminating point of the Sixties. But, soon after it, Hendrix takes it to a new level of . . . not necessarily consciousness but experience. This can be related to Buddha holding up the flower for Mahākāśyapa, experience outside of doctrine or words, outside the meaning conveyed through his psychedelic interpretation of "The Star-Spangled Banner" or through "Purple Haze."

Hendrix says at the beginning of the set, "You can leave if you want to. You can leave or you can stay, we're just jamming." Most people had already left. At the beginning of the *Lotus Sūtra* too, many people in attendance leave before the Buddha speaks the highest Dharma. To this, similar to Hendrix's remarks at the beginning of the set, the Buddha comments, "Now I am free from twigs and leaves and have nothing but all that are purely the true and real. It is good . . . and now I will expound the matter for you."

It's the third day of Woodstock and Jimi is about to close out the Sixties and, according to some, address what Vietnam has done to America through the "Star Spangled Banner". People cried. Many who were there said as the sun rose and Hendrix conveyed the sounds of bombs dropping superimposed on the national anthem, they knew something was happening in that moment and that the Sixties were truly over. After the "Star-Spangled Banner", Hendrix transitioned seamlessly into "Purple Haze." A few months later there was Altamont.

A survey of the readers of *Tricycle: The Buddhist Review* found that 83 percent of American Buddhist converts have tried psychedelic drugs. Many subsequent surveys asked non-Asian Buddhists if they have used psychedelic drugs. The results showed that anywhere between 62 and 80 percent of the respondents report that they have. Among them, about half said that they believed that Buddhism and psychoactive substances were compatible. Many said that they continue to use psychedelics for spiritual purposes. However, most said that they believed using psychedelics is not the right path, but that they can provide a glimpse of the reality to which Buddhist practice points.

In interviews done by Douglas Osto for his recent book *Altered States*, many American Buddhist practitioners referred to psychedelics as the doorway or substance that opened the door to Buddhism. Perhaps, in the same way, "Instrumental Solo" can lead us beyond our national "Purple Haze", as Jimi said, "Not necessarily stoned, but beautiful." If so, something remarkable really did happen at Woodstock to change the paradigm, even if, as Abbie Hoffman suggested, it was, to the contrary, appropriated by the media and had been misrepresented to the public to this day as a stoned-out party.

According to this interpretation, Hendrix used the song "Purple Haze" as an eschatological gateway leading away from death and destruction signified by "The Star-Spangled Banner" and the age it represents, to a new Zen-like experiential beginning with his "Instrumental Solo". Thereby he takes us, in a sense, to "the land of the new rising sun," not Japan (the land of the rising sun) but one free of borders, internal, external, both, and neither.

Even if the name "Villanova Junction" is not one that Hendrix gave the instrumental, it is perhaps accidentally appropriate in terms of Zen. Because, accordingly, the song is the junction to the new world just as the Latin origin of the world "Villanova" gives it the meaning of "new town." From a Zen perspective, in performing "Instrumental Solo" or "Instrumental Improvisation" at Woodstock, Hendrix proved he really was the Axis, just as he says in "Are you Experienced" when he stops talking and only plays, "Let me prove it to you." By using his Stratocaster axe as the Zen stick of compassion he serves as the axis of the world and universe, thus the double entendre (kind of) of "axis" and "axe-ist."

But how can we say whether this is the case or not without, ourselves, discriminating between what is and what is not? About Jimi and Zen, we are like the man up a tree in the *kōan*. You're up a tree. You're holding onto a branch by your teeth.

Your feet can't reach the branch below and your hands can't grasp the one above. Someone comes along at the bottom of the tree and asks, "What is the meaning of Zen and who was Jimi Hendrix?"

If you don't answer, you fail to help the person. But if you do, you will have to let go of the branch and crash below. What do you do? Play the guitar with your teeth?

3
Mermen and Dismemberment

Jerry Piven

Jimi Hendrix is clearly known for his ludic pyrotechnics. He's known as an innovator, and also as one of the innumerable 1960s hippies who dropped lots of acid, invoked psychedelic images, and famously died after taking drugs and asphyxiating.

Jimi's lyrics are often surreal, and if he isn't singing about mauve hazes and waving his freak flag high, he's hammering on about love and passion. But beyond the pyrotechnics and amp-humping, Jimi could also demonstrate immense sensitivity and evoke poignant images of despair and death.

Beyond any clichéd 1960s doggerel about peace, Jimi also wrote of the anguish caused by violence, the way it destroyed the soul, and tore people apart. He also evoked some surreal images of Thalassal immersion, death, and rebirth, to escape a world so battered and torn. Beyond the wish for oblivion and salvation, Jimi assails us with sonic discord to force us not to look away from human misery, but to engage with our anguish in the depths of our being. Only then can we understand the pain enough to cease slaughtering others.

> Music is sexual, magical, emotional, spiritual, logical, scientific, and a living, moving force. So if any of those things frighten people, then they're not human in the first place.
>
> —Jazz virtuoso Victor Jones

Opening

The 1960s gave birth to a new vision of peace, love, and protest against worldwide injustice. It was an impassioned revolt against the military actions in Vietnam, the stultifying values of previous generations, and the horrific violence toward ethnic minorities. Agent Orange and racism would recede before the summer of love and the Age of Aquarius.

And there were the usual disjointed clichés about peace and love, awash in enough acid and bong resin to inspire years of raucous mockery of these unwashed hallucinating hippies with munchies and bloodshot eyes floating through clouds of their own herbal haze. So there would be no paucity of Sixties songs about the horrors of war, the joys of peace, and how we would all live together in a utopian commune of harmony and understanding once Jupiter aligned with Mars. (Then love would rule the stars . . .).

The question is whether we can glean anything philosophically from all this acid reflux, especially from a musician like Jimi Hendrix, who immolated his guitar and waxed lysergic about kissing the sky.

While flamboyant performances and ludic pyrotechnics may have launched Jimi into the stratosphere as a rock icon, his music also reflects a vision of excruciating pain, despair, and visceral repugnance toward social injustice and racial violence, our national history of ethnic cleansing, and a war machine that marches gluttonously toward death.

Exposition: Death in Life

The song "I Don't Live Today" is avowedly an anthem about the plight of Native Americans, uprooted, slaughtered, infected with disease, and "sitting at the bottom of a grave" in their current ghostlike despondence. But Jimi isn't just arguing that it was morally wrong of the invading soldiers to murder and ravage the native population. He's eviscerating the feelings of meaningless and despair that emerged from those despicable events.

It's one thing to read in a history textbook that soldiers killed people, stole their lands, and gave them smallpox. It's another to evoke the existential misery of the aftermath, of the current lives of people who live like gravid corpses in life, who see no light but even yearn to be rescued to die once and for all. The line "I wish you'd hurry up 'n' rescue me / so I can be on my miserable way" suggests a life so excruciating that you yearn to be delivered into death.

Jimi is evoking a desolation so soul-destroying that we're rendered motionless and prostrate, where we long, not even for joyful rescue, but for a redeemer to yank us from the bottom of the grave, so one can be on their "miserable way," in bitter resignation, toward nothingness.

For there's no hope here, no vision of transcending that state of death in life, no glimmer or possibility of joy. Jimi has evoked an image of existential death that won't even allow us the peaceful repose of dying. If Jimi didn't read the Sisyphean ruminations of Albert Camus or the holocaust writings of existential psychologist Victor Frankl, he surely shows us another portrait of the person so devastated by hopelessness that he's rendered a living corpse. It's not just a story of our shameful past, but the bleak wasteland of the survivors.

Jimi's musical accompaniment instills this wasteland with disharmony and cacophony. Words on a page may keep the events at intellectual and historical distance. Jimi creates a sonorous meditation on death so that our bodies can be breached by misery and despair, so we may actually feel the existential nausea, bitterness, bleakness, and anguish that may move some to beg for release in death. In sum, Jimi is creating dissonance for his listeners not just to limn the plight of those suffering from historical events, but is doing *philosophy as discord*, as a rejection of the intellectual distancing that keeps such things safely away from lacerating us emotionally.

Jimi similarly evokes such despair and imagery of death where we might succumb to the usual platitudes, rationalizations, or even patriotic sentimentality. Consider his rendition of "The Star-Spangled Banner." The song is usually sung at sporting events, where fans cover their hearts with their hats and become momentarily sentimental about the great sacrifices and suffering endured for our freedom. Talk about cliché.

Ritually weeping a tear of sadness before ball games is a way of avoiding actual thought or meditation on the ravages and injustices of war. People die. Their bodies are blown into bloody fragments. Their intestines spill out into the mud. Human beings are melted and mutilated in a holocaust of

chemical and incendiary weapons. Rituals of empty sentimentality before entertainment may be the most asinine
insult to the horrors of war, and may actually be ritualized
ways of *avoiding* any moral or emotional contamination by
such atrocities.

Make appearances of being sentimental and patriotic for two
minutes before the first pitch and you can pretend to really care
about freedom and the sacrifice of human life, and then go on to
gorge yourself with crackerjacks and hot dogs while screaming
"kill the ump!" and forgetting all about who was sliced ear to ear
or blown into blood vapor in the carnage of our wars.

Hence Jimi bombards us with the shrill sounds of bombs
raining down and exploding, of deafening ambulance sirens, of
the misery and chaos that war actually is. The National
Anthem shouldn't be a shallow excuse for people to affirm their
thoughtless patriotism, but a moment to mourn the horrors of
war. If we wanted to rekindle patriotism during that anthem,
we would consider just how much death, just how much bloodshed and misery, war breeds. To be sentimental in the face of
bombs tearing people to shreds is inane. It's why F. Scott
Fitzgerald could write that 100-percent real American = 99-
percent village idiot.

Patriotism doesn't have to entail impassioned imbecility. It's
what we've made it when we refuse to internalize just how horrific slaughter is, when we parrot self-righteous, thought-termi-
nating clichés about freedom and loyalty as a defense against
moral culpability, when it all becomes a substitute for existential engagement with the appalling atrocities and devastations
of war. And that breeds callousness toward those who are mur-
dered, tortured, and raped, the contemptuous malice that
scorns dissimilar human beings (wherever they are) as lives
that don't matter, a celebration of national or ethnic dominance
where we're quick to bark about bombing people into the stone
age but slow to experience humane concern for others.

To be affected to the core of our being by the incomprehensible horrors of massacre and suffering that soldiers and civilians—human beings on *every* side, all victims, all dismembered
physically or emotionally—that's what Jimi wants to evoke
with his cacophony when playing our national anthem.

When asked why he made such noise, Jimi once said he
thought it was beautiful. Let's not trivialize this: Jimi was say-

ing that a song about death shouldn't arouse mindless patriotism or sentimentality. The beauty is in the deep recognition of how much suffering people endured. It doesn't glorify war in a stupid display of egotistic nationalism. It awakens us to how horrific it was. And that pain is the source of humble gratitude. Again philosophically: Jimi's sonic evocations of death and horror are counterpoint to hollow nostalgia and ethnocentrism. His cacophony is a lacerating sonic detonation that disrupts the saccharine avoidance of moral culpability or willingness to really experience the despair and anguish of war.

His argument is that war is abominable, not trivial, not something to be reduced to trite clichés and sentimentalities. Beauty comes from the recognition of that sorrow, from an awareness of what human beings suffer and endure, not from its avoidance. Jimi is echoing Nietzsche's *The Birth of Tragedy*, and Baldwin's *The Fire Next Time*, and Du Bois's *The Souls of Black Folk*. Du Bois and Baldwin are speaking primarily of the sorrowful songs and jazz that emerged in response to the agonies of slavery and bigotry. Du Bois's *Dark Water* is also a poignant meditation on slavery, suffering, death, and beauty.

Interpolating the sounds of death disturbs our saccharine glorification of war, and rather forces us to see the monstrosity of children and our own youth turned into corpses. Beauty comes *not* from pretending suffering doesn't exist, or glorifying our soldiers dominating evil, but from recoiling in dread and thanking the stars that human beings persevered.

Beauty *can't exist* when you sentimentalize war, or pretend that the enemy all deserved to die, or when you refuse to confront just how horrific all that bloodshed and barbarity really are. That's lobotomy, not beauty. It's the sheer foolishness of the person who euphorically chants his country's name on the 4th of July but has no remorse for innocent children or grandmothers who are liquefied or crippled in war, because they are evil or worthless . . . *Lebensunwertes Leben*, "life unworthy of life" (the Nazi term for people who deserve to die). That's the epitome of ugliness, not beauty.

Rainbow Bridge: Death, Despair, and Rebirth

One of Jimi's most hauntingly beautiful and existentially anguished songs is "1983 . . . (A Merman I Should Turn to Be)."

Here again, Jimi evokes imagery of detonation and death in an impassioned song on the sadness of war. ? "O say can you see it's really such a mess / Every inch of earth is a fighting nest / Giant pencil and lipstick tube shaped things / Continue to rain and cause screaming pain / And the arctic stains from silver blue to bloody red / As our feet find the sand and the sea . . ."

Ironically echoing "The Star-Spangled Banner" in the second verse, Jimi ensures that we understand just how horrible war is. Amid the mellifluous orchestration of melodic layers and accompanying sounds of gulls and water, Jimi again evokes images of destruction and death. He paints an image of missiles bombarding the earth, of people screaming and dying, or their blood staining the ocean red.

In this composition, however, Jimi interpolates not cacophony and chaos but images of the sand and sea. He creates a thalassal image of walking with his lover away from the devastation of war into the lifegiving sea. The word Thalassa relates to the primeval Greek goddess of the sea, but also to the psychological fantasy of returning to the waters of the womb in some sort of mystical rebirth. Jimi seemed to gravitate toward oceanic visions, and here the ocean is the silence that insulates from the harsh bedlam and discord of war, immersion in enveloping peace, a womb of life, amniotic fluids.

Where Jimi's "I Don't Live Today" and "Star-Spangled Banner" are disruptive, upsetting, discordant pieces (even if melodic), "1983" is again hauntingly melodic. While Jimi creates imagery to awaken us to the horrors of how war rains death upon its victims, his elegy here focuses on the way to escape that ugliness through enwombed immersion in love. This idea of amniotic rebirth also echoes the yearning to be delivered from pain and death that we saw in "I Don't Live Today." Similar imagery can be found in "Valleys of Neptune," where Jimi sings of the ocean swaying him and washing away all his wounds. Amid psychedelic chromatic imagery of rebirth, the sunrise will cleanse the world with rainbow hues, and the new tide will see the Valleys of Neptune arising.

While Jimi envisions the waters of life and rebirth in "1983," the imagery descends into dark silence. Rebirth here is still a fantasy of oceanic immersion sequestered from the world of chaos, movement, wakefulness, and violence. While the womb gives birth, seclusion in the womb is a fantasy of uterine slumber that avoids being born back into the world. To be reborn, in Jimi's vision, is not to be reborn into this world at all. In that sense he's creating an image of rebirth that remains on the mythic, or poetic fantasy level, akin to a religious dream of paradise where one refuses entry back into the world.

It's a comforting and seductive image, but it also illustrates Schopenhauer's idea that metaphysical visions of paradise, heaven, and bliss are existential escapes from pain and suffering. If they remain fantasies, then they are merely consoling dreams, a mode of soothing the self when the world is too much with us. When taken literally, they can become illusions of salvation from this world and rebirth in some heavenly paradise. The consequences are not only the yearning for deliverance from the realities of this world, but the actual belief in world-denying fantasies and illusions.

Beyond metaphysical comfort, this may also entail what Nietzsche considered a mode of "Socratism" and "hangman's metaphysics" that extolls the beyond and condemns the real world and life itself. Should we resist the temptation to scorn or forsake the world in favor of illusory paradises, we still risk succumbing to a world-repudiating, life-negating despair. We may withdraw from life, from its conflicts and struggles, seeking oblivion and cessation of pain. We may retreat from life into emotional closedness, what Heidegger terms an inauthentic mode of being, where we're no longer present in the world and are emotionally withdrawn, away from those things battered and torn that cause emotional agony. And thus we've turned away from life itself, having gated and interred the emotions, submerged ourselves in that womblike emotional retreat. And further, we will never confront injustice or change anything. Bombs will continue to rain and cause screaming pain, and stain the Arctic with blood.

Ritornello (Slight Return): Fear, Fantasy, and Metaphysical Mirage

Metaphysics morph into myriad protean seductions and consolations. Some ache for the oblivion of chemical forgetfulness, the lethic forgetfulness of the poppy field, any pill or potion or vapor that obliterates distress, anxiety, or memory.

If certain chemicals ostensibly amplify aspects of awareness or heighten the senses (or even enable a deeper descent into our own buried thoughts and crises), we also dilute our pain with so many medications. We forget ourselves, arrest relentless thoughts that arouse anger and fear, blunt the agony, become comfortably numb, and sink into sensations of oceanic bliss. Or we more surrealistically shatter self-awareness, our minds blown so psionically that we don't know if it's tomorrow or just the end of time.

Whether through drugs (recreational *and* pharmaceutical), television, social media, games, porn, hedonism, wealth, or what have you, we find all sorts of ways of blotting out pain and awareness. Jimi seems to have sought diverse modes of euphoric forgetfulness and bliss, as we know. For Jimi (as with so many of us) music itself could be a form of ecstatic transcendence that reached into the depths of pain and momentarily provides some kind of cathartic release and oblivion.

When "manic depression" touches Jimi's soul, sweet feeling drops from his fingers even as the despair captures his soul. Beyond mere oblivion or the need to be rescued passively, Jimi seeks resolution by experiencing the pain and burning through it musically. In this piece the lyrics of love and music coalesce, so he can sing "music sweet music / I wish I could caress, caress, caress." Jimi's resolution to despair is his art, creation itself, sonorous expression of that turmoil, and some way of reaching the person he desires. Jimi may sometimes sing about oceanic silence but he rails against nihilistic renunciation with unrelenting musical intensity. Jimi expresses his strife and (manically) seeks solutions that *engage* with the world and human beings, not merely quiescent oblivion.

Innumerable others yearn desperately for some form of metaphysical belief that rescues and redeems them from the agonies and injustices of the world. They clamor for meaning, answers, salvation, and redemption. Some are reborn through religious reawakening, prostrate themselves before heavenly powers, and surrender themselves to ritualized rebirths cleansed of pain and sin. They immerse themselves in blissful fantasies of celestial beings who love and care for them, who will nurture and guide them from misery into the gates of heaven.

Jimi's thalassal imagery of immersion by the sea is a timeless fantasy of uterine bliss that has recurred in myth, religion, and poetry for millennia. The waters of redemption and surrender to God all evoke the wish to be loved and cradled by a protective mother, a being of eternal warmth and tenderness.

While the beloved god is often male, the fantasy evokes aspects of powerful protective fathers but also loving mothers who cradle and succor the child. Even if the conscious fantasy is male it often contains imagery and characteristics that suggest that the overt male imagery actually conceals the wish for the nurturing mother. The father subsumes the maternal imagery and functions, and there's some psychological work suggesting that the masculine imagery conceals troublesome wishes for refusion with mother. (See for example Ruth Stein's book *For Love of the Father*, or Piven's *Terrorism, Jihad, and Sacred Vengeance*.)

Whether this thalassal wish manifests itself through rituals of purification and rebirth, or through visions of God welcoming us into a nebulous paradise, or even through the idea of ascending to heaven through apocalyptic destruction of self-immolation, there are innumerable religious fantasies that recycle variants of the idea that we can surrender the self to a more sublime power that will deliver us from ignominy, injustice, and pain into an enwombing world of love and delight.

Again, however, Jimi doesn't offer us metaphysical consolations. While he sings of the desire for oblivion, and the wish for oceanic submersion, Jimi doesn't exhort us to forsake the world, relinquish life's pleasures—or its struggles—so that we could be nestled in the bosom of an underwater goddess or rescued by a redemptive god in heaven. Jimi's metaphysical allusions are fantasy, not doctrine or dogmatic theology.

When Jimi sings "if I don't meet you no more in this world, I'll meet you in the next one" there's nothing to suggest that he's condemning this world as so irredeemably corrupt and loathsome that it should be forsaken. He's not calling for renunciation of the world or repentance, or calling for us to genuflect before God, confess our sins, and adopt a life of prayer so we'll get into some sort of actual afterlife.

Rather the opposite: In "Voodoo Child (Slight Return)" Jimi is resigning himself to the reality of pain and suffering rather than offering metaphysical or theological consolations and platitudes. He may sing about meeting someone in the next life, but he's not offering that with the pitiful hope that all sorrows will be dissolved in some blissful hereafter. Jimi is rather reconciling himself to the reality of finitude and loss, accepting with grace the possibility that people are torn apart and may never embrace again before death.

It is acceptance of the turbulent chaos of this world, and it is this world he embraces in its stark madness. It gives rise to adamant existential defiance, standing his ground in the present, not metaphysical consolations and hopes for a better world beyond. When Jimi slowly speaks "I'm the one to die when it's time for me to die. So let me live my life the way I want to" in "If 6 Was 9," the chaotic musical din quiets around him as he bluntly asserts his freedom to live and die on his own terms. This is acceptance of the stark reality of death, and resolute determination to embrace this world with existential intensity, not pleas for solace or fantasies of divine deliverance.

As intimated earlier, religious imagery can be taken literally or figuratively. Taken literally it drives belief in divine or demonic entities, a set of sacred and profane realities, specific moral commandments to follow, modes of existence, consciousness, harmony or suffering beyond death, and so on. Taken figuratively religious imagery evokes the grave and constant in human sufferings, and the deepest of human yearnings, but it doesn't offer consolations in the form of "actual" paradises or gods. As suggested, metaphoric evocations express suffering and desire but instead of pacifying us with mirages of other benign worlds or redeemers in the beyond, they enjoin us to contend with misery and injustice here and now. Jimi's "electric church" inspires sonic euphoria, an intense feeling of being members of a congregation bonded not by belief in a god or savior but by messages to love, to live together, to mourn and fight tragic suffering, in human community.

Epistrophe: Opiates, Illusions, and Art

So, rather than positing metaphysical solutions to suffering, Jimi beseeches us to engage with humanity. As Davis says in his book *Art and Politics*, the religious longing for divine redemption constitutes "the flight from both historical understanding and historical responsibility" (p. 68). Looking outside ourselves, outside *our own* capacity for hatred and violence, outside our responsibility to engage with problems in the here and now, leads to fantastical solutions that solve nothing in the real world, and dreamscapes that won't help is understand ourselves.

That's again why Davis could say that "religion has always been a barrier to historical consciousness" (p. 63). It's *not* that religion can never amplify self-awareness. It's that the positing of literal gods to whom we must pray, whom we must obey to avoid hellfire or enter heaven, are metaphysical alternatives to this world. As Marx tells us in his critique of Hegel, certain religious dreamscapes disguise our chains as flower garlands.

Metaphysical figments aren't only delirious distractions, but again as Schopenhauer wrote, they are born of fear and inspire all those visions of a loving divinity to ward off dread and despair. So they immerse us in fictions and fantasies as thalassally unreal as Jimi's aqueous oasis, which sadly drown us in irreality if we believe them. Imbibed to rescue us from horror and anguish, our piety means the belief in mermaids and smiling starfish—choosing to live in mirages analogous to acidic hallucinations that wash away reality.

The infamous opiate of religion is its power to soothe us with promises of salvation and bliss in some other existence, and the consolation that our suffering serves some divine yet unknown purpose. So we convince ourselves that it's part of God's celestial plan instead of a horrific injustice that needs resolution now.

That's why Nietzsche could warn us to beware of superfluous teleological principles—the fatuous assumption that everything serves a purpose (*Beyond Good and Evil*, p. 21). We engage in theodocies, tortured straw-grasping bids to reconcile evil and suffering with the idea that God is actually good (instead of a sadistic bastard, or that he doesn't even exist at all). But again, as Nietzsche tells us, God's only excuse for all the ceaseless injustice and evil and suffering, is that he doesn't actually exist (*Ecce Homo*, p. 244).

And for Jimi, it's not that there can't be a god. (In "Midnight Lightning" Jimi does sing "you got your god and so do I," though what that god may be is a mystery.) It's that nothing is really accomplished by singing his praises or genuflecting till the starfish come home. (As his contemporary Jim Morrison said, you can't petition the Lord with prayer.) And a palpable danger here is not only remaining ensconced in reality-obliterating fairytales to escape our paralyzing dread, but that all too often, we've been willing to ignore actual tyranny and misery in the real world while coercing others to believe our fantasies, or massacre them when they believe something else. We've shown ourselves willing to let people die from plagues, burn them alive, or wage holy wars against nonbelievers to preserve our holy hallucinations.

So Jimi's constant pleas were for us to stop the suffering and injustice *here*, not just chalk it up to God's mysterious plan or barf out clichés about the importance of faith, but engage both socially and emotionally. Jimi sings of shattering our mirrors so we can get beyond ourselves, our egotistic concerns, our own self-preoccupations, and our petty prejudices, so we can love others in the world. This is the message voiced in the twentieth chapter of Conrad's *Lord Jim*, exhorting us "in the destructive element immerse." If it opens up a vast and uncertain expanse, a crepuscular horizon, so be it. That is the "traumatizing and questioning" power of art, that we may shatter our mirrors and cocoons, immerse ourselves in the reality of atrocity, and rage against it.

Recapitulation: Anguish and Dissonance as Existential Engagement

Hence Jimi was not singing the praises of metaphysical illusions, suicidal resignation, or retreat from life. He may have been portraying the seductions of such blissful amniotic escapes, which are so tempting when the world is consumed by violence and death. But Jimi knew the world couldn't really be eclipsed by fantasies of submersion. The middle of "1983" enters a world of chaos. It could have stayed with gulls and gurgling oceanic sounds, but the fantasy of uterine gestation gives way to discord. More aggressive guitar runs, drum fills (many quoting the great Elvin Jones), and psychedelic fluting give us an idea that the ravages of the world wake us from soothing dreams, and finally we return to the realization that the thalassal descent into the depths is a poignant wish for retreat from the killing noise.

If only giant foams could greet us with a smile. If only we could flee on flying dragonflies and eat cotton candy clouds. We could bind ourselves in a Spanish Castle and count ourselves kings of infinite space. But those are only fantasies.

The *dangers* are succumbing to the monstrous murder in the real world, surrendering to metaphysical illusions, or emotional withdrawal from life. If Jimi were merely herding us toward some insipidly utopian vision of Neptunian valleys or turquoise mercury beds or amniotic bliss, he wouldn't interrupt our placid drift into the ocean with disharmony and noise. He wants us to be aware that the world is rife with horror and pain, especially when we're tempted to benumb ourselves with literal (or littoral) consolations.

As much as Jimi may slip into some of the psychedelic clichés of his time, he isn't offering metaphysical platitudes or naive optimism about the age of Aquarius. Love and aquatic imagery of blissful rebirth are soothing, but injustice and death must be confronted, *cacophonously* if we try to avoid these stark realities with the usual avoidances intoxications, homilies, or hippified blather.

Jimi invokes similar images of pandemonium and destruction elsewhere in his corpus, as when he writes of the "sirens flashing with earth and rockets stoning" in "Earth Blues," and in the song "Somewhere Over the Rainbow" imbued with visions of cities burning and weapons "barking out the sting of death." Here again people "pray desperately" and yearn for deliverance. This is conjured with sustained despair in "House Burning Down," where Jimi summons the image of infernal flames turning the sky red, the ghostly whine of the burning timber, and the wailing of innocent victims.

Reputedly inspired by race riots, Jimi again eulogizes the grief and desolation caused by senseless violence. Nowhere is this as hauntingly sustained as in "Machine Gun," where Jimi again invokes images of bodies being torn apart while the snare resounds like gunfire. As with Jimi's other dirges, these compositions use aggressive disharmony and sounds of weaponry to induce inner despair and distress.

Coda: Anguish, and Awakening the Humanity in the Crypt

If Jimi could be at times playful or romantic, or tender, or even frivolous, in these epic arias he plants us within the chaotic maelstrom of death and dolorous anguish. If Jimi can sing about escape or salvation, he offers no platitudes or facile consolations. If Jimi did exhort us to love one another, he didn't pretend that love was the panacea that would magically solve pandemic inhumanity and slaughter.

With the cries of his guitar and impassioned pain Jimi wants us in the present to force us into an encounter with that injustice and despair. What he enjoins is *existential engagement* with wailing torment. Cheap thrills, flowers, and truisms can't diminish our propensity for massacre, and nor can detachment and isolation. Philosophy itself serves this avoidant, evasive flight from anguish when it pontificates abstractly, at the expense of immersing oneself in the torturous dread and horror of our helplessness and despair of death.

With Jimi, we might rip through that ethereal retreat, and suggest that only a discord that anguishes to the core can catalyze intensely human concern for the plight of others. He seeks to awaken "the vitality buried in the crypt," as Davis writes in *Deracination*. Jimi evokes the passion of Rimbaud, a poet who sought to unveil and reveal by disordering and deranging the senses. Jimi is our own poet of cacophony and dissonance, the seer who sears us with excruciating realities we strive to escape.

Don't be fooled. Jimi's antics and discord weren't just a flamboyant artifact of his era. We need his dissonant mirror-shattering now. We need to fracture our measly little worlds and scrutinize the absurdities and injustices we live in, our own oceanic daydreams that keep us so submerged from the horrors of the world that we don't realize we live in castles made of sand, dissolving and deliquescing though we imagine them eternal.

For some of us, the world is rife with atrocity. We've invaded countries and slaughtered hundreds of thousands of innocents under utterly false pretenses. We've rained down depleted nuclear shells to poison their lands for generations. We've tortured thousands of innocents—not terrorists, but civilians. We've used drones to assassinate and annihilate. We've also seen vicious, sadistic violence against our own citizens. Against those protesting injustice. Against those whose skin color is different. It goes on.

And for many people, all the victims deserve it. For many people a mendacious, sleazy impressario should rule the nation, and they're thrilled when he calls our Latin neighbors murderers and rapists, boasts about grabbing pussies, appoints corrupt white supremacist, evolution-rejecting, climate-denying executives to his cabinet and promises to dissolve environmental protections, eradicate affordable care, expel millions, refuse refugees, ban a religion he despises, or create a federal registry of everyone belonging to the wrong faith. All in the name of making our country great again. We need Jimi's dissonance more than ever. Someone's house is burning, and it's ours.

Choking on our angry spittle isn't the answer, however. (Or our own vomit, or even someone else's vomit . . .) It's all too easy to fume and choke on unfairness, but maybe something else can be done. Jimi reached out to people, and moved us. So while we need to shatter those mirrors, and break our chains, and sow discord to lay bare all the injustice around us, we can also follow Jimi's other leads.

We don't want to remain underwater, or drifting on a sea of forgotten teardrops. Like Jimi we can immerse ourselves in joy and create arresting beauty in response to pain. We can retain some optimism and humor as we get the brothers (and sisters) together.

Find yourselves. Come alive. Our freedom is a chance to give. Keep on pushing. Straight ahead.[1]

---

[1] I'd like to thank Howard Johnson, Victor Jones, T.S. Monk, George Rossi, and Michael Wolff for reading this chapter and sharing their thoughts.

4
Hendrix—Freedom and Love

THEODORE G. AMMON

It is difficult to begin a chapter about Jimi Hendrix without throwing roses, and just as difficult to end one with any other conclusion than a superlative such as "The best who ever was and who ever will be."

For many of us the alignment of our respective *chi* hinges upon Hendrix being declared and recognized as "the best." But let's whittle down the matter. Hendrix is not considered the best acoustic guitarist, nor the best slide guitarist, nor the best pedal steel guitarist, nor the best musician ever nor even the best in the twentieth century.

On *The Dick Cavett Show*, Hendrix himself, when confronted with Cavett's accolade "One of the best electric guitarists in the world," responded that perhaps he was the best currently sitting in his chair. And indeed he was. But what else?

He was the best upside-down Fender Stratocaster player of the twentieth century, from 1965 to 1970. And this claim I would say is indisputable. So I have located his "bestness" in time, but my claim does not certify Hendrix as especially good, because next to no one plays guitars upside-down just because they are left-handed. Even if he played horribly he would most likely still be the best during 1965–1970 for the upside-down Strat. I haven't thrown a rose yet, and "the best in Dick Cavett's guest chair" is not much of a compliment.

So wherein lies Hendrix's bestness?

"Fire" was the first song I heard penned by Hendrix, not his already famous version of Billy Roberts's "Hey Joe" released in

the UK, backed by "Stone Free." However I didn't know that
"Fire" had been composed, performed, and recorded by
Hendrix. A cover of the song was released shortly after *Are You
Experienced* by a worthless group entitled 5 x 5. The group's
other hit wonder was "Apple Cider" and then blessedly they
disappeared. So the timeline of Ammon was: local garage band
played "Fire" at a school function, I betook myself to a local
45 record store ASAP and asked for it but was handed the
cover by the no-name group, overheard some kids at school
talking about a musician named Hendrix, checked the credits
on the 45, then went on a mission from God to find the
composer.

And there he was in the local record shop, but only in the
album section. No 45s by Hendrix there or elsewhere in my
town. Very odd, but then I grew up in Mississippi. "Oddities" is
a polite way of describing the wretched goings-on of my state
during the 1960s (see numerous history books for the nightmarish particulars).

I trembled when I played the album on my piece-of-shit
stereo and by the end of "Purple Haze" was not merely moved
or satisfied, I was fundamentally changed. "Fire" is a rock'n'roll
song with a pulse, but "Purple Haze" spoke to my soul, and then
there were "Manic Depression," "The Wind Cries Mary," "Love
or Confusion," "I Don't Live Today," and the almighty "Are You
Experienced?"

Well, was I?—experienced? Depends upon who's asking, yes?
I was not experienced way back when, when Jimi asked of me
an ultimate question; and he did it with such joy and mystery:
"But first / are you experienced?/ Have you ever been experienced? /Well I have / Not necessarily stoned, but beautiful."

"Beautiful," I thought.

What Is Beautiful?

Had I ever been beautiful? Was I then beautiful ? I was not
sure I understood the issue. At first I thought he asked
whether I had ever dropped acid—a naïve response, though not
entirely irrelevant. Other groups and people were much more
explicit about the benefits of taking drugs. Grace Slick for
example: "Feed your head. . . ." and Timothy Leary encouraged
us all to "Turn on, tune in, and drop out."

And many did, believing they had found a doorway to an alternate and more profound reality. LSD was the alleged key to the potential of the mind and to understanding the human condition, and the key to living a life free of corporate America and the military-industrial complex, free of greed and the nine-to-five routine, free of war-mongering and of 1950s values about sex, race, gender, and music.

Yes, many did turn on and drop out, and the many included Charles Manson and his devoted band of murderous outcasts. No, "Beautiful" was not restricted to the hippies and happy druggies. Nor, of course, did it mean physically beautiful, I surmised. Eventually I stumbled upon a Zen-like answer, though I didn't know Zen at the time: If you have to ask whether you are, then you aren't.

Another tease I found in the lyrics of "If 6 Was 9": Hendrix doesn't care about mountains falling into the sea, about hippies cutting their hair; and "go ahead on Mr. Businessman / you can't dress like me" and then: "I know I gotta die when it's time for me to die / so let me live my life the way I want . . . to."

Easy to say, but do we know what it means to live your life the way you want . . . to? Can we *feel* it and *act* it? And finally: "Sing on brother / play on drummer." Music trumps all other considerations. The paradox is that Hendrix was haunted and harassed by producers, managers, contracts, fans, and earlier by hunger both physical and artistic. Recall Little Richard's strict rules of compliance that no one could upstage him in antics or dress. Hendrix sweltered under such confines. But when he was "discovered" by Linda Keith and then Chas Chandler of The Animals and wooed to London, given a white rhythm section, and turned loose in a studio he gave birth to a series of songs that rivaled the most provocative on the scene in London and elsewhere.

Consider other "first albums": those of the Beatles, Rolling Stones, and in America, groups such as The Shondells, Paul Revere and the Raiders, and, God help us, Sam the Sham and the Pharaohs. To America's credit it did produce some first albums of note: those of the Doors, the Allman Brothers, and Jefferson Airplane, and even some one-hit wonders such as The Music Machine had respectable first outs. But it took the Beatles how many attempts to produce a *Rubber Soul*, *Revolver*, and *Sgt Pepper's*? Whereas Hendrix's first album was

larger than its influences and spoke to the human condition as
none other at the time, as well as to music itself: "Never hear
surf music again," whispers "Third Stone From the Sun." No
more surf music. Considerable irony there, since Brian Wilson
finally detoxed, has gained a sense of sanity and happiness and
has been touring to play his famous *Pet Sounds* album in its
entirety, simultaneously with a travelling Hendrix tribute
review, featuring Dweezil Zappa and others. (At the shows I
attended, gray-haired white boomers predominated in Wilson's
audience, but the Hendrix audience was mixed, with consider-
ably more hair on average.)

Was Hendrix Free?

One answer to the question of living your life the way you
"want . . . to" is to assert a robust sense of free will—even if it
is a harmless myth we tell ourselves. For example during the
time of this chapter thus far, I have had two pots of coffee. I
should be wired enough to zip right through it, given a robust
sense of free will in procuring the coffee.

The fact is, I have a serious caffeine addiction, as well as a
jones for coffee, especially espresso. So maybe I am *determined*
to write. And Hendrix asks to be *allowed* to live his life the way
he wants to—he does not clearly assert that he can do so. In
"Stone Free" he allows that every week he is in a different city,
so he isn't tied down. He doesn't want to be "tied down" and
wants to ride the breeze. Even in the song "Freedom" he asserts
that he needs freedom "so I can live." "Freedom, That's what I
need" and . . . "set me free." No claim that he *can* do what he
wants—his resolve is to "keep on pushing, straight ahead."

And "Ezy Ryder": "We got freedom coming our way." In song
after song Hendrix asserts the right to be free or the desire,
even the desperation, to be free. But we don't find in Hendrix
any claim that the human condition is one of freedom. It perhaps should be, but we have to struggle for it. And "it" obviously
differs for Blacks and Whites of the time. And the "it" is still not
clearly defined. We find the standard stuff: I want to be able to
cut my hair as I please, dress as I please, ride the breeze at will,
and so forth. Well, maybe that's "it"—either the liberty to move
about unimpeded or the liberty to move about without serious
consequences.

To be blunt, I can walk down the street wearing whatever, with my hair however, and still be guaranteed health insurance and police protection. *That* would be freedom of a sort. Making choices unimpeded, without serious consequences. Let the white-collared conservatives walk down the same street to their nine-to-fives, pointing their plastic fingers at me, but leave me the hell alone for all that and let me raise my freak flag! HIGH!

Maybe, maybe, just maybe.

If I live my life the way I wanted to, as Hendrix would have me live my life, then I really would be free of corporate management, ne'er-do-wells of all stripes, and for him the Jim Crow attitudes of the American South, throngs of clinging white fans, even if I enjoy the excessive sex and free drugs of fandom.

Creative Freedom?

But the real point is creative freedom. Without creative freedom the rest of the accoutrements of fame and fortune ultimately fail to satisfy. Did Hendrix have creative freedom? His lyrics are mainly written on hotel stationery—suggesting a man continually on the road, which is precisely what he claims in "Stone Free"—although he touts this moving about as freedom, as not being tied down, there is no evidence that he was able to relax at a palatial home in the rolling hills of Connecticut or anywhere else.

Once he left his "home" in Seattle, he lived on the street, with alleged family, would-be family, with would-be friends or in motels and hotels with the band du jour. Relaxing was not among Hendrix's luxuries, in short, neither before nor after Chas Chandler and London. The paradox of London is that he was thrust into fame and that fame wound the clock on his untimely demise.

Hendrix, a kind and gentle soul, his wretched beginnings as a child in Seattle notwithstanding, virtually gave away whatever pittance of freedom he had enjoyed to date when he surrendered to the tutelage of Chandler. But at least Hendrix had the opportunity to experiment in the studio, his one true home, and the albums he produced in the remainder of his life were nothing less than astonishing. Not surprisingly then, freedom—both having it and not—became a major theme in his work.

As his music developed and changed, and his band became the all black Band of Gypsys, he dropped the pyrotechnics, sexual antics with the guitar and amps and in general focused intently on getting it right—no longer did the audience dictate his on-stage persona, and no longer did he allow the audience to demand specific songs. Hendrix asserted some minimal freedom to be a musician first-and-foremost, and the *Band of Gypsys* album proves it.

One of the greater ironies of his music however was his infamous "Star-Spangled Banner." ". . . over the land of the free / and the home of the brave." He was not free but was Hendrix brave? I suppose, in a manner of speaking. He pushed against the limits of his instrument and the possibilities of rock and the blues. But free? Again, no. He sang continually about what he was not and would never be.

One could ask the same question of Mick Jagger and Keith Richards and imagine the same answer. Once the duo went for a walk in Manhattan. Before they had processed a few blocks, thousands of people lined the street to see whether it could be true. It was simply a walk, for heaven's sake, but the problem here is obvious. At a certain level of notoriety and fame, there is no such thing as "simply a walk."

Yet Jagger and Richards have a bevy of homes and apartments between them where they may recline and, as it were, take the phone off the hook. And that feat takes business savvy, a trait Hendrix utterly lacked. For the promise of recording a song Hendrix would sign most any piece of paper thrust in front of him, resulting in contractual entanglements that haunted his entire professional career and posthumous fortunes.

In spite of his fame, even making the money he was promised and deserved was not always a given. And unlike the insular lives of many superstars his pond was actually a swamp of leeches. One early case in point was a hotel room he trashed in Stockholm—an act he was goaded into by a hanger-on—which cost him and the Experience nearly one third of their earnings from the tour. Granted trashing hotel rooms is as common as it is stupid in the music business, nevertheless one third of his tour earnings . . . really? And who exactly handled this exchange of funds? In some ways Hendrix was as free as the thirteen-year-old girl who "freely" engages in sex with older men. She could just say no, yes? And likewise the sex "addicts" of the world could simply refrain from acting upon their desires. Unfortunately it doesn't work that way, and, yes, the world is worse off for it.

What about That Freak Flag?

And so our earlier view of freedom is exposed as inadequate. Freedom as the liberty to move about unrestricted and without serious consequences is again the stuff of dreams and philosophical fantasies. Unrestricted movement, even if prudent, must be coupled with moral sense. Did our beloved Jimi have good and practical moral sense?

If we focus severely upon his wanton lifestyle then the drugs, alcohol, and sex may offend moral sensibilities. However, wanton behavior is not clearly immoral. Suppose then we shift focus to his music, and glean what we can from, say, his very first hit, "Hey Joe." "Hey Joe, where you goin' with that gun in your hand? / Goin' down to shoot my old lady / you know I caught her messin' around with another man / and that ain't too cool." Then Joe will go "way down south" where he can be *free*! from the hangman's rope, in Mexico. So as the song portrays him, is Joe a moral man?

The immediate philosophical answer is that we need to know what moral principles are in play. If we abide literally by the Hebrew scriptures, for example, then adultery and fornication would be punishable by stoning to death. Joe is therefore within his moral rights surely by substituting one form of death for a more immediate and less painful one. Yet there must be a trial by a competent body of authorities, and Joe alone cannot justly be judge, juror, and executioner, you say. So the song is about a *crime* actually, even if a crime of passion, but nevertheless serious legal and moral harm would result.

Not so fast, no such facile conclusion should predominate. Joe has been seriously wronged, and Joe is not clearly acting rashly out of passion; his act as portrayed is one of premeditated murder. Had Joe stumbled upon his wife in the throes of adulterous acts then perhaps a court would show leniency; but as it stands the song relates a premeditated murder and at that a misogynist one. Why not have Joe shoot the cuckolding man making whoopee with his "old lady"?

Hey Joe, What's Up with That Gun?

The song uses a well-worn trope of the innocent man wronged by his woman, who then extracts a tragic revenge. Consider *Othello*. Although we know that Othello falsely suspects Desdemona of infidelity with his trusted lieutenant Cassio, in the play we are privy to the secret machinations of Othello's servant, "honest, honest Iago," who suspects his own wife of sexual shenanigans. So Iago conspires against the gullible and righteous Othello, so that Othello sees only what he is led to see by Iago.

Desdemona thus wrongly dies at the hands of Othello as a result in part of Iago's treachery. Yet Shakespeare does not direct Othello's murderous and vengeful wrath towards Cassio. *That* would not make for tragedy; whether Desdemona is guilty or innocent matters little from one perspective, that of the historical trope. Women must pay, so goes the story, and in spite of Western society's sordid history of discrimination against women, they are the ones whose abuse or death make for tragedy in male-female relationships, they are the temptresses, the ones who must be covered from head to toe, the ones responsible for the original sin, the ones who live in red houses. Or so some say . . .

Yes, "Hey Joe" uses a common trope, but the situation of Joe nevertheless is a tragic one, and not simply the stuff of a traditional blues song. And as tragedy "Hey Joe" presents a fundamental moral problem. The question I suppose is whether we can glean from "Hey Joe" and perhaps other songs something of Hendrix's own moral sentiments. By a circuitous route, I will say "Who knows?" And then contrast "Hey Joe" with "Wait Until Tomorrow," admittedly an apparent random pairing.

The basis for comparison is that of the bond of love and the question of who protests that bond; in the case of the latter song the girl's father. "Click bang, oh what a hang, / your daddy just shot poor me." She was unsure that they should run away together and so balks at the last minute while the trap is set involving the father. The same theme reappears in the Zevon-Springsteen tune "Jeannie Needs a Shooter," in which the male lover is shot by the father, who rides away with Jeannie. And the last line: "Jeannie needs a shooter." Hendrix needed his own shooter.

The problem with attempting to glean moral commitments from art, especially literature and music with lyrics, is that fabricated narrators tell the tales. Were Hendrix and Hendrix's life to have unfolded along the lines of "Hey Joe" he would have slipped off to Mexico many times over, or been shot many times over. Shooting an ordinary bloke is one thing, but killings at the level of Hendrix's fame are not only the stuff of tabloids, they make for TV movies and much more.

Witness the sordid affair of the O.J. Simpson trial, for one example, and compare it to *Othello*. To state the obvious, the artists are not their narrators. Ice-T was not and is not a cop killer. He was making a point that actually did play out recently in Ferguson, Missouri, and elsewhere. White cops kill black males for next to nothing, such as broken tail lights, and get away with it. And the law enforcement outrage over Ice-T's point resulted in Warner pulling the album, replacing the song "Cop Killer" with "Freedom of Speech", and deleting the words 'COP KILLER' from the chest of the nightmarish figure covering the front of the album.

Two ironies here: "Freedom of Speech" is more poignant than "Cop Killer" and Ice-T landed a role as a cop on the famously popular TV show *Law and Order: Special Victims Unit*. Even so, he found time to rap with the death metal band Six Feet Under on at least one track. The lyrics will test the sensibilities of even the hardcore, but again he is not a psychopathic killer who relishes torture and snuff. His narrator in the rap, however, would be electrocuted by the justice system were he real. We create personas, and sometimes live within them on stage for a while (as Bowie seemed to do), but Hendrix engaged in harmless antics onstage, and offstage he was frequently a somewhat shy and retiring personality. Both on- and off- the music was the absolute.

So did our beloved Jimi have good moral sense, the question with which I began this digression? We can't determine the matter from his songs, and his lifestyle gives few clues, except to those adamantly opposed to drugs, alcohol, and copious sex.

The Power of Love

So wherein lies his bestness? Hendrix is quoted as having said: "When the power of love overcomes the love of power, there will be peace." Freedom occupies a central role in his thematic development, but no less than love. Hendrix's facility with a Stratocaster is the stuff of legend, but the complexity of his life's explorations of love? Not so much. What comes to mind is his proclivity for sex and more sex. Reckless and immoral behavior? I have effectively sidestepped the issue and will again here. From "The Wind Cries Mary" to "Red House" to "Wait Until Tomorrow" to perhaps his most beautiful love song "Little Wing" to "Burning of the Midnight Lamp" to "Power to Love" to "Message of Love" and others, we find myriad views on love and its power. In spite of what Hendrix's reputation rests upon, the sophistication with which he handles the theme of love in his work is on a par with his technical facility and with the absorption of influences. Add the two and the most powerful spokesman for the human condition of love, not freedom, emerges from the sixties.

And I am out of time for now, alas. Have to wait until tomorrow. Click bang, what a hang.

II

I Know I Gotta
Die When It's Time
for Me to Die

5
Jimi, Janis, and Jim

RANDALL E. AUXIER

Everyone knows the "27 Club," founded by Jimi Hendrix, Janis Joplin, and Jim Morrison. We can extend it back a year to include Brian Jones of The Rolling Stones, and indeed, there is a convincing theory that Keith Richards also died at twenty-seven and has been *undead* since that time. But that's a chapter for a very different book.

Some people trace the problem back to Robert Johnson's Deal with the Devil at the crossroads of Highways 49 and 61. Immortal fame, and the world bows down to you as a genius, in exchange for your soul, at twenty-seven? There are some who would take it.

There's no important statistical evidence to back up the idea that virtuoso musicians are more likely to die at twenty-seven than any other age. We noticed "twenty-seven" because of the close proximity of Jimi's and Janis's deaths. Jimi died on September 18th 1970, and before anyone could recover, Janis bought the farm on October 4th 1970. People observed, in passing, they were both twenty-seven. Then, when Jim Morrison took a dirt nap beginning July 3rd 1971, people said "Hey, he was twenty-seven too . . ." Then they noticed Brian Jones a year earlier, and then they started counting, eventually making their way forward through Kurt Cobain and Amy Winehouse. They ignore anyone who died at twenty-two (Buddy Holly) or sixty-nine (David Bowie), or even an embarrassing seventeen (Ritchie Valens). I'm guessing the "69 Club" is larger and growing faster. But there's something about the number twenty-seven itself, isn't there?

Are we just superstitious? If so, you would think that the mortality rate among The Ramones would give rise to a cult club. Come to think of it, I guess it has. There's no reasoning with a cult. People *want* to be superstitious. They *like* how it feels, especially when their consciousness is . . . err, umm, "enhanced." These feelings and their cults go far deeper than coincidental numbers, like seventeen, twenty-seven, or sixty-nine, however interesting they are. The numbers are a gateway drug for a deeper suspicion that the world makes a kind of sense we can't really understand. And, people *like* the feeling that something is unexplainable or still beyond the reach of common sense and science. They want to believe that some great secret roils beneath the boring crust of daily life, some spirit, some spark, some random finger that rises from hell or descends from heaven and says "You, young man, *you* shall be different."

Voodoo Children

In one way, the joke is on *all of us*, but the one who laughs last, or never at all, is the one who got touched by that unexplained finger. "You, Edgar Poe, shall write like none before and shall have the power to disturb the psyches and ruin the sleep of every future generation." And "You, Charlie Chaplain, shall be the funniest human being who never said a word," and, importantly, "You, Jimi Hendrix, will play the electric guitar like no one ever has before or ever will again." The critics widely agree on this last point. His Rock and Roll Hall of Fame Biography actually says:

> Jimi Hendrix was arguably the greatest instrumentalist in the history of rock music. Hendrix expanded the range and vocabulary of the electric guitar into areas no musician had ever ventured before. His boundless drive, technical ability, and creative application of such effects as wah-wah and distortion forever transformed the sound of rock and roll.

Note that they said "instrumentalist," *not* "guitarist." Yes, they qualify it with "arguably," but then they amplify it with "instrumentalist," removing him, intentionally, from comparison with merely other guitarists and insisting on the broadest field. We come to the point of our exercise: Jimi Hendrix was a *genius*.

That, I want to say, is a great part of why we're knee deep in hoopla, not only over Jimi, but over twenty-seven.

There is a cult of genius deeply ingrained in our Western collective consciousness, and we demand sacrifices, human sacrifices, of young originals, and in particular, we destroy them with our adoration. The true genius must *never* understand what we see when we see him or her. And if our genius lives fast, dies young, and leaves a beautiful body, well, we feel satisfied that it was necessary for the sake of beauty, or art, or handing us a depth in passion and suffering that makes our lives matter, just a little bit, by proximity.

There is something mysterious about this "originality" we demand. Where did the cult of genius come from? What is a genius anyway? Einstein? Mozart? I will get behind that question here. You'll see why Jimi, Janis, and Jim really were geniuses in the fullest sense of the word, even if it isn't the way we use the term today. But it will raise more questions—good thinking always has that effect. I think we can get at why the young geniuses, the true ones, medicate themselves. Some survive it, but many don't. Their genius, their "gift" exiles them from our company and also from any serious shot at self-understanding. It's a chastening thought to consider that "Gift" is the word for "poison" in German. Perhaps it's more than a linguistic accident to say that Jimi was "gifted."

Let Me Stand Next to Your Fire

Until about 1774, the word "genius" was used in a generic way to describe anyone who did something well *on a given occasion.* The genius was a *genie* (same word) who lived *in* the creative art itself, and individuals were possessed by that genie sometimes. "He has the genius of music tonight!" they would say, meaning only that the spirit that animates music, or painting, or sculpture, or drama, alighted and left.

Genius was always related to an *art*, not to sciences, not mathematics, not crafts. The general idea, reaching to ancient times, was that a muse was responsible for each art, perhaps a different one on each occasion, especially with what we now call the fine arts. This spirit would pour itself over favored individuals and bring the art to life. It could be as specific as a given instrument, or a given part in a classic tragedy, or it could be as generic as the whole art form. But the genius lived *there*, wherever "there" was. Individual people were *not* "geniuses," they just sometimes *had* a genius. And not on every occasion. The genius came when it wished and departed without ceremony, leaving the bereft artist with only the drab ordinaries.

All this changed in 1774 when a German fellow named Johann Wolfgang von Goethe (1749–1832) published a novel called *The Sorrows of Young Werther*. Goethe was a mere twenty-five when he joined the pop culture eighteenth-century literary movement in Germany. It was called "Sturm und Drang," which, believe it or not, translates quite passably as "rock and roll." His book was a sort of simpering tale of star-crossed love, resulting in the protagonist's suicide. If that sounds familiar, well, yes, and Goethe is to the German language what Shakespeare is to English. Is the book "good"? No, but it is *great*. (It is possible for a book to be great without being very good. I would offer Robert James Waller's *The Bridges of Madison County* as an analogy. Awful. Terribly written, overwrought, silly. Great book.)

So Goethe put his finger right onto the popular pulse and suddenly he was a rock star. In the minds of his readers, he *was* Werther. The novel convinced people that the shallow sentiments and ardent passions of his otherwise listless protagonist had come from the deepest depths of his young heart. So all the young men started imitating everything "he" did. Goethe goes for a year of wandering to Italy, and half the young men of Northern Europe go to Italy. Goethe writes a travel journal, they start writing travel journals. He studies plants, they study plants. He studies the physics of light and color while serving in the military . . . you get the picture. And an alarming number of these young fools commit suicide for impossible love. And every woman wants to be Goethe's female lead, Lotte, except that they wouldn't have denied the advances of this amorous hero.

Goethe went, however, from being rock star to being really the first "genius." His talents were so numerous, so diverse, and so extreme, that people began to think of him as a person who had no creative or intellectual limitations. He didn't seem to have merely *a* genius of poetry—or drama or history or philosophy or science—on one night or for the duration of a work. He seemed to have *every* genius, *all* the time. This was not true, of course, and Goethe knew it very well. He did his very best to explain to people that there were lots of things he could not do. He was only average at mathematics, or music, he pointed out. No one wanted to hear it. He tried to tell them, he failed to convince them, and then just settled into letting them say whatever they wanted to say.

Goethe's cultural standing was a lot like Bob Dylan's, but his range of abilities was far greater. Goethe decided just to do whatever good he could in the world, talk to whoever wanted to see him, and write his works. His honesty about his full humanness frustrated the romantic youngsters who wanted to shoot for the stars. But Goethe wasn't headed for the twenty-sevens' club. That was reserved for Shelley, Keats, and Byron (and his vampire lover John Polidori), even if they did not have the decency or foresight to die precisely at twenty-seven. There was death enough to go around in 1821–22. It looked a lot like 1970–71, to be honest. Goethe watched it all, about like Bob Dylan did, and died at a ripe old age, with all his prizes on the mantelpiece, like Dylan will.

If 6 Was 9

I'll resume the story about genius, but we've already opened up a vein. Let's let it bleed a little—that's probably what killed Byron, by the way. He got sick, they *bled* him (fucking idiots), with unsterilized knives, and he died of sepsis. Not so romantic, but neither is asphyxiating on your own vomit, when you think about it. For now, let's note that not everyone who achieves fame has the constitution to survive that achievement. Fame is not genius. Genius can go unrecognized. Consider Van Gogh. He couldn't sell a painting. I would love to think I would have bought one if I had been around back then, but I doubt it. Still, look at them! Surely I would have noticed that! But people didn't. I am people. So are you. Fame, on the other hand, is a snowball on a downhill slalom. Everybody notices, no one is driving.

The sort of detachment that leads to a song like "If 6 Was 9" is very much a product of having to preserve your distance to keep your sanity, while everything else is on the downhill. Jimi had a thousand people pulling on him, wanting a little piece of his energy, his fire, his vitals. It appears to me that what *Jimi* wanted to do was *play the guitar*. That's about all he ever wanted to do. It got him in trouble of course, because people didn't understand, and they never, ever do *get* that you're actually, really, truly, honest-to-god, *different* from other people. Goddammit. If you tell them you're different, they say "Yeah, sure, you and everybody else." If you show them (and this was Jimi's tack), a few may get it, but the very fact that you *are* different keeps them from understanding *what* you're doing.

On the other hand, there's the handful who *do* get that you're different, and who want a *piece* of that feeling. Not being able to create such experience themselves, they want to try to guide you, control you, profit from you, make love to you, anything and everything. It is draining as they pull you away from what you really do (I suspect; it's not like I know). And then, if and when *more* people start to notice what you do and *can* do, the sharks move in for feeding. Not many people in their twenties are psychologically, fiscally, or emotionally prepared for all the pressures. People in their twenties will try to escape, detach, push back; they'll make mistakes and lose the center of their creative powers. If they survive, they end up having to go in quest of that "center" again later. Mozart didn't live that long. Beethoven did. You don't want to be either one of them, unless perfect misery is what you crave.

When Jimi was doing okay, Jimi was focused on the guitar. The rest of the world could turn upside down as far as he cared. Was he counter-culture? Yes, but only as a matter of circumstance. These hippies were the people who listened. But he wasn't buying their bullshit any more than he was buying the stuff spread by the establishment. He was looking for sounds, feels, experiences, and the sonic stylings were the Holy Grail, not the approval of the mavens of the counter-culture. He tried to tell them that 6 could be 9 for all he cared. They weren't inclined to listen to what he was actually saying. They were inclined to hear what they already believed. It wasn't Jimi's problem. Except that it was. Art doesn't get to segregate itself from life or from the Zeitgeist.

The Zeitgeist

That brings us back to the story of genius. The term "Zeitgeist" was created during the era of German rock and roll (*Sturm und Drang*). Something was in the air, or the water, or both, from

Frankfurt to East Prussia, and it spread to Britain very quickly. Goethe translated Shakespeare into German and corresponded with Walter Scott, and a new era of cultural cross-fertilization ensued. Never, ever forget that when The Beatles couldn't make a living in England, the Germans were willing to pay them to play. And they came home with German instruments, Rickenbackers and Gretsches and Hofners and Ludwigs, far superior to anything being made in the UK, and then they rocked that Island. That was Jimi's opinion too. There's a reason he went there to find his fortune and there he died. But *they* would listen when *we* wouldn't. It was the same with Howlin' Wolf and Willie Dixon after all.

The Germans and the English (the Scots never wholly bought it, but they bought Goethe) went on a forty-year experience called "romanticism," and the world has not recovered from it. *You*, my friend, haven't recovered. *You* believe in romantic love. *You* have silly ideas about whether your willpower and inner self are sufficient to make the world bend to your aspirations. If you are over that part, from your youth, *you* are disillusioned *because* the world wouldn't yield to the power of your personality and individual uniquities. That's still romanticism.

The only thing more annoying than a romantic is a disillusioned romantic. The USA is full of them. One of them is writing this chapter. Another is in possession of your body reading it. Yes, yes, we both wanted more, didn't we? Fuck us, I'm tired of us. And most of all, we romantics believe in "genius." It is one of our triedest, truest—and tiredest—characteristics. That's why I can't stand us. But Hendrix was a genius, you know?

Goethe is interesting too. He didn't become a romantic. He got over being so strung out on twenty-something emotional overload at just about the same time that people started killing themselves to be *like* him. Such *Werther wannabe's* didn't want to be reminded that Goethe didn't kill himself. By 1792, the people of good sense had suffered enough of this unbridled youth culture, and a spokesman for "the establishment" stepped in. His name was Immanuel Kant (1724–1804), and he is the third greatest philosopher in Western history (behind only Plato and Aristotle). He said, "About this 'genius' thing, let me tell you what's up with that." I'm paraphrasing. "There is something to it," Kant admits, but it has to be put in a human and historical context. He allows that there are individual people who are geniuses. So if Goethe is sort of like Bob Dylan, Kant is saying "I like Bob Dylan; I'd give him the prize." But . . . hold the phone, as we used to say back when there were actual telephones.

Kant *did* like Goethe's writing, and Goethe liked Kant's philosophy. It's sort of like Dylan saying that he digs John Dewey, and Dewey saying "yes, that young Robert Zimmerman has some genuine poetic ability . . ." (which I believe Dewey would admit). Dewey died when Dylan was twelve, so this couldn't really happen, but you get the idea. Famous philosopher dude says young poet dude is good; young poet dude lives long enough to read some philosophy and says "Cool." (By the way, Dylan flunked out of college because he was reading Kant instead of what the profs assigned, or so he claims.) Kant has more to say about genius of course. It's easier to illustrate it than explain it.

Pearl before Swine

Janis Joplin was not beautiful, but she was plenty sexy, and when sober, wicked smart. Too smart. She was emotionally uneven, temperamental, and most of all weak-willed in the face of her infinite need for affirmation and sadly, love. These things killed her at twenty-seven, whether on purpose or by accident. We will never know because *she* probably didn't know which she had done. It may be fair to say, as we did when we were kids, that it was accidentally on purpose. But there was this one thing she could do: strut on stage and transform an audience into putty with her soulful voice. Sure, she had influences, such as Bessie Smith, but Janis didn't sing like anyone before her. She wasn't imitating anyone. Have you heard her version of "Summetime" with Jimi Hendrix on guitar? How did she do that? Her own explanation, as told to the *Rolling Stone* writer David Dalton went like this:

> I'm a victim of my own insides. There was a time when I wanted to know everything . . . It used to make me very unhappy, all that feeling. I just didn't know what to do with it. But now I've learned to make that feeling work *for* me. I'm full of emotion and I want a release, and if you're on stage and if it's really working and you've got the audience with you, it's a *oneness* you feel. (*Piece of My Heart*, 1991)

Kant says that a genius dips into her (or his) own *nature* and produces something she cannot possibly understand. The reason she can't understand it is that it comes from beyond the forms and conditions of human understanding. To understand anything, we humans have to take our intuitions of both the world and our own inner life and conform them to the "universal categories" of knowing. These intuitions must be somewhere, somewhen, and they must have some definite qualities, quantities, ways of being and relations to other things. That's how we manage to put our finger on a thing and say "Just this, and not something else." You do all that every time you recognize a friend, or identify a Mercedes Benz, or remember a night on the town (if you *can* remember it).

But the truth is that nothing in our experience ever quite fits into all those categories and conditions. We are never one hundred percent sure that this friend is really what she seems to be, and most of all, that we, ourselves, are exactly what we take ourselves to be. Jim Morrison wrote a nice tune about it, strange man that he was. And who do you think the killer on the road is, anyway? It's *you*. He had probably been reading Camus rather than Kant. But at some level we are all strangers to ourselves. For most of us, it's just an annoyance. But for some people that confrontation is their undoing. Sweet family dies.

When You're Strange

Geniuses confront in themselves as strangers, and it seems to happen alone, for them. Their brains squirm but won't deliver an insight into what they do. They just do it. That works fine for a while. I think the stranger pops up when faces come out of the rain and start taking an intense interest in how those geniuses do that *something* no one has ever done before. If you are the most original artist in a generation, in some way, and if you're doing something that everyone afterwards will imitate, something they'll all have to incorporate into their understanding of that art, you are a genius, Kant says. You "give the rule" to the future of the art from your very nature. But faces look ugly and women are wicked when you're alone.

If you also happen to catch the zeitgeist, then people might start pressing you to explain *how* you are doing what you do. But it can't be *explained*. You just reach into your own primal nature and enact the result. The genius has no possibility of understanding it, and if pressed too hard, she may become a victim of her own insides, to use the phrase Janis chose. It must feel like, since you're the one *doing* this thing, you *should* be able to say how you're doing it. But Kant says no, that isn't going to happen. A genius never knows how it's done and cannot teach anyone else to do it. But works of a genius "give the rule" to all future works, because they pull some pure product, some unforeseen combination of otherwise familiar elements, straight from the bin of natural, human possibilities and place it before us, in full bloom.

There Must Be Some Way Out of Here

Our first response is "astonishment," Kant says, which is unpleasant for many people. We don't know how to believe what we are experiencing and can't quite incorporate it into our experiences. This experience of the work of genius stands out. We don't have a template for it, you might say. So we have to step outside the box and re-imagine our own experience so that this thing we are hearing, when Janis sings, when Jimi plays, when Jim performs, was always *possible*, just never actual. Gradually we begin to assimilate it to our past experience, with further listening and watching, and we begin to "get it." But never entirely. That's how most people do it. Their unpleasant astonishment, with time and effort, becomes what Kant calls "admiration," which means we *accept* what our senses are conveying to our understanding, but still can't quite believe it because we can't fully categorize it.

Since Jimi and Janis and Jim simply *do it*, they have no trouble at all *believing* it. It pours out of their separate natures without mediation, and all the thought and practice and effort and repetition is just a matter of deepening their access to the way this possibility is actual in their natures. No amount of thinking will enable them to draw a circle around this thing and explain it to themselves or anyone else. If you're beginning to think that Kant is saying "It kinda sucks to be a genius," you're getting the drift. A genius is always a misfit. Yes, some geniuses pretend to understand themselves. Edgar Allan Poe was like that. Most are well aware they don't understand how they do what they do. That includes Jimi, Janis, and Jim.

The Art World

Most people are annoyed by having to rethink their whole understanding of human possibility, as geniuses force us to do. That's why geniuses are often not recognized in their own times. It's too hard to see it, too much work. But some people are thrilled by that experience. It's the sort of people who are emotional daredevils, or, most importantly, the artistic *avant-garde*. At any time, Kant's as surely as our own, there are people out there trying things that we've never heard of, *yet*. There is a thin slice of our fellow humans who are drawn to whatever is just now surfacing in the domain of human creativity. These people like the rush they get from being on the cutting edge. And among these people, there is a tiny, tiny handful capable of recognizing genius. Linda Keith was, evidently, one such person. Chas Chandler was another. These are the people who were able to understand why Jimi Hendrix really was different.

There have been numerous tales of such visionaries, and they often take the role of managers—Colonel Tom Parker, Andrew Loog Oldham, Brian Epstein, John Hammond. They are the ones who overcome the resistance in the avant-garde itself, which is usually swimming in mediocre creativity, and who find a way to say to it "Look, now here's something you should really pay attention to . . . introducing Jimi Hendrix." In the movie based on Jimi's life, *Jimi: All Is by My Side*, they depict the moment when Jimi has *The Experience* learn the song "Sgt. Pepper's Lonely Hearts Club Band" five minutes before they play the biggest show of their lives—with The Beatles in the audience, with the album *Sgt. Pepper's* having been released just *three days* prior. Fortunately someone had the foresight to film this performance. You can look it up. But unlike the actual performance, the biopic shows Chas Chandler (Jimi's manager) watching in horror as Jimi strikes into this song as his opening number, at least until he looks around and realizes that the musical and artistic *avant-garde* is ready to embrace this.

So what kind of moxie does it take to play The Beatles' new song back to them three days after its release, and to do so in front of all the people who can make you or break you? Well, yes, that takes balls. But I feel like I know what Jimi would say, which is something close to the depiction in the biopic. Jimi's band is stunned when he announces they will open with a song they've never played, and it's cut number one off the Beatles brand new album. They resist. Jimi says, "It's a cool song, if we don't fuck it up." He has musicians who are capable of this (on one hearing of the record), and he thinks the song is cool. No, this isn't *done*. But it was always *possible*. So how confident are you that your artistic vision will be embraced? Jimi would say: "It doesn't matter. It's just a thing you do." I think that's what Jimi said and what he believed. He knew "people" don't *do* this. But *Jimi* does. This is a part of genius.

Riders on the Storm

Sometimes the *avant-garde* fails. Even a genius fails. Andy Warhol was one of those people with an eye for talent, but talent is not quite genius. Kant says that "genius is a talent for producing something for which no determinate rule can be given . . . hence the foremost property of genius must be originality." But he continues, "Since nonsense too can be original, the products of genius must also be models . . . exemplary." Through the models—as possibilities for human originality—a new rule comes into our experience. "Play it like Jimi," or "Sing it like Janis" becomes a universally recognized direction, even if no one can quite do it.

But a genius may also be loose among the avant-garde, and may misuse genius to try to do what he can't really do any better than anyone else. If a genius, like Warhol (who most definitely fits Kant's profile), says "Hey look at this guy," the rest of the art world may follow and hail someone as a genius who really isn't. I am still trying to decide about Jean-Michel Basquiat. Talent? Definitely. Greatness? I am not seeing that. Genius? No. But a member of the twenty-sevens' club? Yes. I wonder if we would know about him if he hadn't died at twenty-seven. People say Warhol never recovered from his death. I want to believe it matters, romantic that I am, but that's because I am convinced *Warhol* was a genius.

I know my opinion doesn't matter, but I am trying to be intentional about the way I use the term "genius," to know what I really mean by it. Basquiat doesn't seem to be "giving the rule" to future creators of art. He shows us a highly developed version of a possibility we already knew, which is where graffiti can lead as art. Banksy is doing more to give the rule to the future, really changing the art world in ways it can't ignore. "Paint it like Banksy" is more likely to stick than "paint it like Basquiat." But "That painting is like Warhol" is utterly pervasive and everyone knows what it means.

On the other hand, Basquiat did seem to pull his artistic vision from his own immediate nature, and not to know quite how he was doing what he did. Were people responding to him as to Warhol, with the astonishment that *becomes* admiration? Maybe. I don't think so. I think that his art made a kind of sense to people already, so they liked it—they didn't have to struggle to grasp it as an artistic possibility. Having a squirming brain that calms itself with drugs and alcohol is not enough for genius. And sometimes these toxins (drugs, alcohol, popularity) will impair even a genius. Definitely Jimi, Janis, and Jim all did things that betrayed their very human inability to handle their odd situations. Among the masses all of these, including Basquiat, were talented riders on the storm, but not able calmers of themselves.

Mr. Mojo Rising

Jim Morrison found out in New Haven, Connecticut, on December 9th 1967, that even being a natural genius doesn't get you through every storm. I mean to call to memory his decision to go on a tirade against authority from the stage. He had reason to do so, having just been maced by an off-duty police officer. It got him arrested, on stage, for inciting a riot. The charges were dropped, and a legend was born. But it's not something that people hail as "a genius behaving like a genius." It stands in sharp contrast to Jimi's brilliant move of playing "Sgt. Pepper's" for the Beatles. Jim had been backstage, and instead of demanding that his band learn a new song on one hearing, he was engaging in one of the vices common to genius, which is using the divine energy to get sex, and expecting privileged treatment when it went south with the police.

But bad behavior of all sorts has been a feature of the cult of genius, from Mozart to Michael Jackson. It's the dark side.

Not knowing the boundaries is also a common condition. Kant allows that the genius is usually socially deformed, due to being too closely in touch with that roiling world of nature. Its laws are *not* our social conventions. And so the genius, for all that creative (and often intellectual) prowess, is a little closer to animal ways. This creativity belongs not to imagination alone but to nature's own variety, and the way imagination out-runs thinking and becomes a kind of immediate interaction with possibility—nature's possibilities for human action, com-pletely apart from the restrictions of convention.

Kant's greatest disciple (and critic), Arthur Schopenhauer (1788–1860) was someone who knew the dark side. He says that "Men of genius . . . have more mind than character—are often not only awkward and ridiculous in matters of daily life . . . but they are often, from a moral point of view, weak and con-temptible creatures as well." He also adds that geniuses "can-not bear solitude" because they only see what relates to their own wills. "With objects which have no such bearing there sounds within them a constant note: *It is nothing to me*, which is the fundamental base in all their music." The will of the genius is "so violent in its demands that it affirms its own life by denying the life of others" ("Genius and Virtue"). And there it is, in a nutshell. Geniuses draw other people to themselves in order to use their energy. Others are drawn to geniuses for the same reason, but the relationship is unbalanced and almost always unhealthy for one or the other, or both.

Most of us are on the outside. We don't know a genius and wouldn't want to. It isn't surprising that the ordinary human has to be shown repeatedly that a genius *is* a genius before we can believe it. To us, it's all a bad case of codependent users and abusers. This brings us to Jim Morrison's arrest in Miami in 1969 for allegedly exposing his willie to a concert crowd. Boundary issues? No one denies that, by then, Jim was very far gone into drugs and alcohol. But conventional people struggled with more than that. They struggled with his dark thoughts as connected with his poetry and his very sexualized self-presentation. The latter they had seen from Elvis, but not this kind of mix of existentialist poetry with the hyper-male, aggressive, self-conscious, predatory animality, whipped out for their wives and daughters to see.

Jim's father speaks for all of us, although he is not *like* us. George Morrison was a Rear Admiral in the US Navy. That's about as "establishment" as you can get. He was obliged to write a letter attesting to his son's upstanding character as part of the legal proceedings against Jim. Here, in part, is what he wrote:

Admiral Morrison's letter to the Fla. Dept of Corrections: (dated October 2, 1970)

Thank you for your letter of September 30. I appreciate this opportunity to comment on my son Jim.

I saw him last about 5 years ago during his senior year at UCLA. He was successfully completing his fourth year of college. As in all his academic work through grade school, high school, and college, he was an excellent student. While he had always been an intellectual rebel, he had always obeyed and respected authority. . . .

While in London, I was called by an old friend in California who had been approached by Jim for a loan to finance his first record. Concerned by his appearance, particularly his long hair, the friend called me. I, in turn, wrote Jim a letter severely criticizing his behavior and strongly advised him to give up any idea of singing or any connection with a music group because of what I considered to be a complete lack of talent in this direction. His reluctance to communicate with me again is to me quite understandable.

Since returning to the United States I have on several occasions made an effort to contact him. One time I was successful in talking with him by telephone. Our conversation was quite pleasant and I congratulated him on his first gold album, but nothing of consequence was discussed. We have had no direct contact since that time. . . .

While I obviously am not a judge of modern music, I view his success with pride. Based on my knowledge of Jim through his twenty-first year, I firmly believe that his performance in Miami was a grave mistake and not in character.

I will always follow his progress with the greatest of interest and concern and stand ready to assist him in any way, should he ask. Thank you again for this opportunity to affirm my conviction that Jim is fundamentally a respectable citizen.

Very truly yours,

G.S. Morrison, Rear Admiral USN

I saw the original of this displayed at the Rock and Roll Hall of Fame in Cleveland—it's on US Navy letterhead. The irony is that it's probably exactly the truth about all of us in relation to someone like Jim—or Janis or Jimi—until enough time has passed to provide perspective. The Doors were an epoch-making band and their music stands up very well to our later expectations and sensibilities.

Take Another Little Piece

The music of Jimi and Janis and Jim really is more than just popular or hip, or representative of a zeitgeist. It's truly giving the rule to subsequent music-making. Otherwise Janis and Jim and Jimi wouldn't still be icons on such a broad scale, *for their actual work*, not just their images and their deaths, for their work, unless they were 1. doing something genuinely original, and 2. doing it in such a way that everyone afterwards has to take account of it in creating art within that sphere. They made the rules.

We don't love their stories as much as we love their work. The mystique is all well and good, but when it comes time to listen to some actual music, I don't want something current. I have to take another piece of Jimi, Janis, and Jim. Or we could get some cheap wine and just listen to the full version of "LA Woman." The essence here is not the twenty-sevens, or the tragedy, or the romantic darkness, it's the freaking music.

Our geniuses were not after money or fame, even if they reveled in success. It isn't why they did what they did. There's "a peculiar kind of instinct, which drives the genius to give permanent form to what he sees and feels, without being conscious of any further motive." It's like a tree driven to bear its fruit, says Schopenhauer in "On Genius."

Still, it's a tree and a fruit you've never seen before. Wanna taste? Admiral Morrison speaks for those who first encounter that weird tree. Sometimes, often in fact, genius doesn't even look like talent to Admirals and nurses and insurance salesmen, and such. What can the Admiral say? He knows his son is an intellectual rebel, and, well, quite a songwriter and performer, as it turns out. The Admiral is looking at a gold record. Half a million stoned kids can't be wrong, right? Well, we'll follow his career with interest *and concern*. (Gotta love that part.)

What else can we do? Jimi's father was the same. *His* son was no genius. Until he was. But it was too trippy to be believed.

Jimi Lives

Jimi Hendrix played the guitar like no one before him, and with the one possible exception of Prince, like no one after him. (And make no mistake where Prince learned it.) The clarity and precision, the utter perfection of Jimi's fretwork, with fingers landing precisely in the sweet spot of every single note, rhythmically perfect; the originality of his licks and tones, the aggressive artistry of all his decisions, well, let's just say that it equals or exceeds any other *instrumentalist* of the rock era, just as the Hall of Fame claims. There were some pretty amazing instrumentalists in that half-century. The lead guitarist is a beast who never existed until they electrified the instruments, so there were no rules. There are now. And if you want to play any instrument plugged in, Jimi is your ruler. He was able to fold this true genius as a player into a stage persona that served his legacy. His music will always be studied by scholars of rock, and there will always be such. So Jimi lives.

But he isn't still *alive*, which begs the question *why* people say that some of the dead are still alive (as they say about Jim and Elvis). When some people say Jim is alive, they mean as in, with heart still beating somewhere in space and time. But no one says Jimi and Janis are still alive (or Joey and Dee Dee and Johnny and Tommy, as far as I know). Something is different here, with Jim and Elvis.

I admit that I made the pilgrimage to Jim Morrison's grave in Paris. It looked to me like he's probably there. If not, a lot of people have wasted a lot of pints of cheap whiskey by leaving them on his grave. (I'm sure someone gathers them, and I'll bet they ain't put down the drain.) Maybe Jim comes at night and . . . I don't know, drinks it or sells it or moves it to Chopin's grave twenty yards away. So, remember, I think he's dead, but I did go and check. What is it in us that brings on doubt in his case? Remember what I said about how we love superstition.

It can't be the circumstances of death—just like Jimi and Janis, Jim and Elvis overdosed. They didn't do an autopsy on Jim, it's true, but in Elvis's case, there isn't much doubt about how very dead he was. Yet, people say Elvis is alive, physically.

All of them had roller-coaster emotional lives and careers. It's true that Jimi and Janis were still on the rise, while Jim and Elvis were on the downhill and may have wanted out. But all of them wanted out sometimes. The same for Kurt and Amy and Brian Jones. Lost souls, lonely while adored, the same story throughout. It's the story of celebrity and fast living, but in only a few cases, also a story of genius. Can we find in genius a difference that leaves us with "Jimi lives" but "Jim is still alive"?

Touch Me Babe

Schopenhauer may help a little. He says that the "simple man," including even "the ordinary professor," will look "upon genius much as we look upon a hare, which is good to eat after it has been killed and dressed up. So long as it is alive, it is only good to shoot at." ("On Genius") But if we are the Elmer Fudds of the world, there are certain hares that never become Hasenpfeffer. We just never seem to get a clean shot at them. We think we've got 'em and then they pop up behind us and say: "Ehhhh, what's up Doc?" Their rabbit holes seem endless.

This is my experience of Jim Morrison's combined work and persona. There is no question that Jimi said profound things, on a pretty regular basis, but then he smiled, toked, and rejoined us all. Apart from being a guitar genius, he was goodness and decency and light and love (so long as he wasn't drinking). I feel that I understand what he wanted. Same with Janis. She was brilliant and funny and delightfully scattered, and also it was about love, when she was sober, and in her case, often even when she wasn't. Yes, they both went to a dark place sometimes, but their dark places feel familiar to me. I know that rabbit hole. I feel like I've been there, and I'm guessing you feel the same. At their core, they feel like family.

But Jim and Elvis never felt like family. They drifted away from us and their dark place was alien, scary, dangerous, primal. And there is the key, perhaps. Schopenhauer says that in the genius exists the will to live that runs through the whole species, and finds a moment of clarity. We both envy and fear this pure life that runs through geniuses from nature itself into music and painting and sculpting and acting and performing. We want to touch that pure *élan*, but we're afraid. And I may be wrong, but I feel in my guts that Jimi and Janis were afraid too—afraid of what *they* were. I think Jim and Elvis were not afraid of what they were, they were just bored of what *we* are. I think Jim meant it when he said "C'mon touch me babe, can't you see that I am not afraid?" And this is actually the very opposite of "Let me stand next to your fire."

6

Quicker than the Wink of an Eye

DARYL HALE

The story of life is quicker than the wink of an eye.
The story of love is hello and goodbye.
Until we meet again.

—JIMI HENDRIX, "The Story of Life," September 17th 1970

These lines, from Jimi's last poem, cryptically capture so much of Hendrix's views of music, love, and his colorful though compact life. Its very concise, crisp form captivates us—Jimi's short sketch of a briefer life—dead at twenty-seven.

So why should we care, fifty years later, about what was in that wink? And the same is true of the witty, simple lyrics to his songs—pithy poetic homages, which modern cynics might see as shallow consumerist "hooks." Can those scribblings offer us any enduring insights into that wink of an eye? Some would simply dismiss Hendrix as a mere sign of the times, yet another drug-induced death as the ultimate price for a life of hedonistic pursuits, musical degeneracy, and arrested adolescence.

However, Jimi was an icon of an era, and so we might polish the dust off the image, not to bask in the glow of a long-lost ideal, but so we can recover a bit of goodness we may have lost in too quickly dismissing that wink. Jimi's right that his life went quicker than the wink of an eye. And his lessons in love also were, as he confessed, a whole lot of hello and goodbye. But perhaps after these fifty years, our distance from the heady days of Monterey, Woodstock, and Vietnam is now deep enough that we can meet Jimi again, perhaps now truly for the first time.

Later in the 1980s, we began to hear a lot of dismissive reactions from traditionalists about mistaken directions they saw American culture moving in the 1960s. Under the banner of Freedom, many promoted free love in practicing unrestricted sexual couplings, free thought in trying out mind-expanding drugs, and free expression in exploring new musical forms like rock'n'roll. The myriad loves, drug experiments, and musical explorations of Jimi Hendrix follow this typical pattern of 1960s counter-cultural expressions.

Critics saw only a destructive pattern of sexual libertinism, psychedelic deaths, and cultural demise, tracing it to individualist self-exploration. One critic traced this self-expressionism to a failure of moral nerve of the Academy. Allan Bloom's *The Closing of the American Mind* argued that this self-discovery approach to culture, and constant openness to new forms of expression merely resulted in a deafness to the older, traditional forms of education, expression, and cultural wisdom. Accordingly, these new counter-cultural forms of expression were merely self-absorbed, flattened, and *decadent*. For such critics, Jimi's demise from a drug-induced stupor seemed fitting, especially for a counter-culture that sought only self-aggrandizement.

Bloom's judgments were a bit harsh, but more importantly, they overlooked some depths to the counter-culture he condemned. Charles Taylor's *The Ethics of Authenticity* captured those depths in his notion of authenticity. Beneath these expressions of self-fulfillment, no matter how debased or travestied its outward forms, is a genuine moral ideal of being true to oneself. Self-determining forms of Freedom are those that are based on being in touch with our deepest needs. In earlier ages, humans thought they needed an ideal form of the Good, as specified by the wise (Plato), or constant civic engagement in a vibrant State (Aristotle), or a life devoted only to God (Aquinas) for their source of authenticity. But modern culture stresses self-determining Freedom—that we each can pursue our own good in our own way, and this requires that we break the hold on us of those previous external sources, that we decide for ourselves.

Certainly, Jimi Hendrix lived a life of self-determining Freedom. So we can take him as an exemplar of what it is to discover this kind of modern authenticity, and we can see how he develops over time his own authentic voice and talents musically, personally, and culturally. Though he wrote no book for us to peruse, his understandings of Freedom, and his own unique sense of authenticity, emerge from his song lyrics, interviews, hotel stationery scribblings, poems, and diary entries. Even if his life was lived quicker than the wink of an eye, all of those jottings are perhaps symbolic of the fast-paced 1960s, and therein we might find insight into that eye. Perhaps we can recover his synoptic vision of a humanist authenticity that made up Jimi Hendrix.

Early Years of a Highway Chile

Jimi was born in Seattle, Washington, on November 27th 1942. According to Jimi's own poetic recollection, the night he was born, the moon turned *"fiery* red" ("Voodoo Chile"). Maybe it was lightning outdoors—if so, that cosmic event captures the disquiet that haunted his younger years.

All recall that his parents were constantly having family struggles in Jimi's youth. Both loved their drink, and they broke up regularly, resulting in Jimi and his brother Leon being carted off to other family members. So he remembers regular trips to a grandmother's place on an Indian reservation (she was full-blooded Cherokee) in Vancouver, British Columbia. His parents divorced when he was eight; his mother died when he was fifteen; and his father was given to fits of violence. This disruptive background, and inherited anxieties about relationships, Jimi captured pointedly in his song, "Castles Made of Sand" (on *Axis: Bold as Love*, October 1967). In it, a woman slams a door in her drunk partner's face, and he responds by wondering where all their sweet love had gone. "Against the door he leans and starts a scene. / And his tears fall and burn the garden green. / And so castles made of sand, fall in the sea, eventually."

Later in the song, he imagines himself a young Indian brave who would soon become a fearless chief, a fierce protector of a crippled young girl (undoubtedly his mother). But as Jimi recreates these scenes from his early life, we find he has also constructed a mythic world that interweaves much of his lived experience: the Native American heritage presents him as a young brave, the young girl crippled for life symbolized his mother. But not content with these concrete realities, Jimi envisioned a mythic world that captures gems of wise reflection on the transience of human life—castles made of sand fall into the sea eventually.

Though Jimi started the world at zero, his next major challenge came at age seventeen when he decided to drop out of high school. In the meantime, when he lived at home, he often heard music from his father's parties, and he came to appreciate the sounds of Muddy Waters, Elmore James, Howlin' Wolf, and Ray Charles. Tired of working for his dad, Jimi began hanging out with a crowd of hooligans who occasionally got into trouble with the police, and he was arrested for riding in a stolen car. But his sentence was suspended when the judge heard that Jimi was enlisting in the armed forces.

Undoubtedly, Jimi saw military service as his path to Freedom, and away from a home that never really brought him fulfillment. He had run away from home several times to escape the miseries at home, but this trip, to Fort Campbell, Kentucky, was more permanent. Here, his dream of becoming a Screaming Eagle was dashed by his injured ankle in paratrooper jump practice. But he had already grown tired of the constant strain under orders from army commanders, and his music was being ignored. Still, now that he was dismissed from the Army, he had Freedom to find his own niche. "He left home when he was seventeen . . . / A rollin' stone gathers no moss . . . / He's a highway chile."

It was in Clarksville, Tennessee, that he met a bass player, Billy Cox, also an ex-soldier which gave them an added bond. Even more, this theme of walking on—being a traveling musical gypsy—would give him a sense of fulfillment that his home life had never done. It's no surprise then that one of Bob Dylan's songs, "Like a Rolling Stone" would become one of Jimi's favorites to perform.

Many critics of the 1960s saw this mobility as rootlessness, but Peter Clecak put his finger on the right note when he described it as part of *America's Quest for an Ideal Self*—rock music and its potential for presenting dissent, personal quest, and hope for fulfillment gave this generation an empowerment denied others. If the 1950s were a time of conformity and upward movement, and the later 1980s became more self-absorbed, materialist, and reactionary, then the 1960s and

1970s were the centerpiece of more hopeful, optimistic, and spiritually liberating movements in American culture.

Clecak nicely captures this cultural moment by calling it a rapid democratizing of personhood—many extensions of self-fulfillment were pursued, along with increases in personal and socio-political rights. So it's no surprise that rock festivals, with youth traveling cross-country, became popular events. And the lyrics of songs like Dylan's "Like a Rolling Stone" became anthems for the youth movement, relics in time capsules echoing their new-found and wide-ranging mobility. For Jimi, even more, these lyrics recalled his own quest for a new self-determining Freedom. Dylan's powerful poetic voice simplified the common experience of the young well-to-do having to learn new skills in this national quest for a better life. Fancy prep schools never prepared them for living on the streets. "How does it feel, to be on your own? / With no direction home! / A complete unknown / Like a rollin' stone!"

Perhaps this rootlessness was really a call for belonging, since the conventionally defined ways of belonging passed on to the children of the 1950s—material possessions, home ownership, upward mobility in the professions—were not deemed as worthy by the youth of the Sixties and Seventies. And though Jimi began to find a cultural home for his own musical style in America, he tired of always being a backup guitarist to some great soul or rhythm and blues bands—Isley Brothers, Little Richard, Curtis Knight and the Squires, and Sam Cooke. He was told to conform—in dress, guitar style, and performance—to be subordinate to the main performers. However, he had paid his dues in too many package tours. So when the chance to try out a new direction came his way, he took it. Chas Chandler, former bassist for the Animals, now turned producer, heard Jimi perform in the Village in New York and offered him a chance to form a group in England. As Jimi put it, "Chas rescued me."

Have You Ever Been Experienced? Well, I Have . . .

Almost as soon as his plane landed, Jimi got introduced to the British royalty of rock and blues. He sat in with Cream, and really dug the way Eric Clapton played the blues, reminding him of the great Albert King. And Ginger Baker's octopus-like antics on drums really hooked him. So when Jimi and Chas held auditions, they decided on Noel Redding, a gutsy rock-'n'roller who played bass like it was lead guitar; and Mitch Mitchell, who was a spirited funky R&B drummer, and self-confessed jazz addict. And Jimi's reason reveals his synoptic spirit—he did not want a group that simply could play "The Midnight Hour" but one that synthesized different styles. If all of them were bluesmen, they would get locked into the same old style of playing. But they needed no rhythm guitarist, since Jimi could do that quite seamlessly in ways that led naturally into his signature blues-style lead-guitar solos.

The Jimi Hendrix Experience really was a synthesis, a fusion of funky rock, folk blues, a bit of soul, and even jazz orientations. This meant that, as the *Are You Experienced* liner notes put it, the trio aspired to create a wider Experience, not an older one. And Jimi's wider experience was captured by himself in this spread-out way in all the interviews on television (*Dick Cavett Show, Tonight Show*), with radio station disc jockeys, music writers, guitar magazines, and music critics (*Circus, Melody Maker, San Diego Free Press, Disc and Music, Jazz & Pop, Rave, Rolling Stone*), as later was collected chronologically by Steven Roby in *Hendrix on Hendrix*. All these diverse fragments that comprise Jimi's Experienced eye—his vision—also taught us how to listen with new ears.

A large part of the reason that we have to listen with new ears is that Jimi, along with a guitar technician and sound engineer, tweaked his guitar in ways that got new sounds from it. He became a master at manipulating feedback distortion ("Wild Thing," "Wind Cries Mary"), fuzz-tone pedals ("Foxey Lady"), sound phasing (end of "Bold as Love," where his Stratocaster is phased through a Leslie speaker), wah-wah pedal in "All Along the Watchtower" (which aurally, electrically reinterprets Dylan), the amazing sustain on "Voodoo Chile," and all of this wider Experience was embellished through that mountain of Marshall amplifiers. Also, *our*—the listeners', the audience's—experience of music is expanded by all the novelty tones from Jimi's spontaneity on his Stratocaster. Jimi creatively, in the moment, evinced eerie sounds by tapping the Fender's body with his ring, or blowing across the strings, and turning a dial or pulling a lever.

By his very nature, Jimi was a performer. While touring with American R&B bands, this side of Jimi had been discouraged. Famously, Little Richard fined anyone in the band who wore flashier outfits than he; so a standout backup guitarist, with a flair for showmanship would not get so far under that leadership. But now in England, Jimi found that his guitar expertise could hold its own. He was now in jam sessions with Eric Clapton and became close friends with Eric Burdon of the Animals. After a short eight days in London, Jimi played Howlin' Wolf's "Killing Floor" in a concert hall, and he left Clapton and others in the audience in awe. Jack Bruce observed that if Eric was *God* (so reported the press), then *God* just got burned by some unknown. Not only that, but Paul McCartney became an instant fan of Hendrix after his first gig in London; and the Beatles were absolutely blown away by Jimi's rendition of the title cut of *Sgt. Pepper's Lonely Hearts Club Band*, when he played it at the Saville Theatre in early June 1967. It was McCartney who recommended Hendrix for the Monterey Pop Festival later that summer. Clearly, Jimi was no longer riding in the back of the musical bus, as he had in America.

One of his most well-known tunes from *Are You Experienced* —one that got immense airplay—was "Hey Joe," a classic blues number, which made the Jimi Hendrix Experience a huge hit in England. In America, the radio stations quit playing the song because of the lyrics. Were the honest lyrics of a blues song—"I'm gonna shoot my old lady 'cuz I caught her messin' 'round with another man"—too racy for the times?

The song that really got airplay was "Purple Haze." Everyone took this to be an homage to the psychedelic age and to experimental drugs, like LSD, though Jimi explained it as another song in which he explored a science-fiction fantasy (recall his imaginary mythical universe he was prone to create), but it got edited down to the short version, and the lyrics seemed to fit with a current youth experience. Jimi's real favorite from this LP was a somber blues ballad, "The Wind Cries Mary." In it, he describes the cosmic outcome of a breakup—a queen is weeping, and a king has no wife; the traffic lights will turn blue; his bed will be empty. Then at the conclusion of the song, he wonders whether the wind will remember the names it has blown around over the years; and we get this winsome retort: "And with its crutch, its old age, and its wisdom, / It whispers, "No, this will be the last." / And the wind cries Mary."

Given Jimi's somewhat unstable upbringing, it is tempting to read these lyrics as reflections on his own broken home. He insisted that it's merely a story about a breakup between a boy and a girl, perhaps his latest girlfriend. Probably it's a bit of both. But it certainly underlines, again, the brevity of life and relations. In the aural content, we can hear the sound of raindrops reversed or echoed and phased, which captures and underlines the wind's actions, moving from whisper to cry to the crescendo of a scream, and then resolved back into a gentler cry at the end. Of course, it does not hurt either that Jimi's voice encapsulates his best Dylanesque folk-electric sound. And his guitar work is subtle, underlying but not overwhelming the lyrics, keeping the somber tone of a folksy electric blues ballad. As Jimi described the ideal song, it was a "complete marriage" between words and music.

Of course, a key part of the Jimi Hendrix Experience included much more than soft blues ballads. He became renowned, especially after the Monterey Pop Festival, for his guitar theatrics onstage. At Monterey, at the end of his performance, he lit his guitar on fire, an act he called a sacrifice. Prior to that, he had painted his guitars for the offering. And on some occasions, he mimicked sexual intercourse between his guitar and the amplifiers.

These sorts of theatrics became almost a defining part of Jimi's role as performer. While traveling on the Chitlin' Circuit, as it was then called, Jimi developed the knack for playing guitar with his teeth. And the Experience pivoted around Jimi's guitar histrionics—playing guitar with his teeth, humping the amps with his guitar, and the sacrificial pyrotechnics—all while parading around in decorative outfits. Certainly, Jimi was an accomplished entertainer as well as musician.

Still, he tired of the continual audience expectation that the guitar be burned. In reality, by Jimi's count, he only burned the guitar a total of three times out of three hundred concerts. Nonetheless, too many concert-goers expected, even demanded, the stage theatrics. So by the time he ended his Experience, he was done with the theatrics, moving in new directions. Jimi hoped to move towards more deeply felt intuitions, more honest expressions in his art.

Let Us Not Talk Falsely Now, the Hour Is Getting Late!

Throughout his career, Jimi was pressured into doing more touring than he really wanted. He enjoyed much of the live performances and interactions with audiences, but life on the road also has its drawbacks—little time alone, and so Jimi often used hotel stationery to write down lyrics for songs, playing sequences for their performances, or directions for album covers. However, he was also bound up through a bad, coercive contract with a recording company to quickly produce an album right after *Are You Experienced*. At the same time, he was committed to far too many concert dates, with very few breaks between them. It was while the Experience was still on tour, in April 1968, that they began recording sessions for *Electric Ladyland*. The compressed nature of his time shows up on the album and CD covers for *Ladyland*. Inside, we discover Jimi's picture suggestions and design for the album, the sequence of songs, more creative poetic mythology, along with a list of fellow musicians who contributed to various songs on the album. What is telling in the *Ladyland* liner notes is that all these directions are in Jimi's own handwriting on hotel stationery while on the road—from the Cosmopolitan in Denver and the Newhouse Hotel in Salt Lake City. This explains how pressed and stressed Jimi was to get out this album, to meet a contract obligation.

Though contractually obligated, Jimi had clear ideas about what he wanted on the album design—photos by Linda Eastman, his jotted liner notes he entitled "Letter to the Room Full of Mirrors" (his way of describing life as a rock superstar). However in the UK, a photo shoot of twenty-one naked women was pasted on the cover, which Jimi actually hated; and in fact, many record shops refused to carry the album due to the risqué cover. Still, it showed even more how contracts restricted artists as to what they actually could control. But given these limits, *Ladyland* hinted at more new directions for Jimi and his cohorts.

On this new album, Jimi insisted on Steve Winwood playing organ on "Voodoo Chile," since Stevie had impressed him with his soulful playing with Spencer Davis and Traffic. Accordingly, we get to hear that amazing duet of euphony, as Stevie's organ answers Jimi's blues guitar, yet each fills out nearly a whole orchestra in giving us a full sound onstage. This song has to count as one of the best full-band blues numbers ever recorded. Now, Jimi was expanding his band's sound beyond the trio to show what a more comprehensive musical Experience might include. Toward this end, Traffic's Chris Wood also supplied his unique flute sound on the song "1983," displaying the wider aural vision of the Experience.

Yet another Dylan tune gets covered in Jimi's "All Along the Watchtower." Jimi tells us his main reason for returning to Dylan songs is that he emits true feelings, genuine honesty in his lyrics. Jimi even felt like "Watchtower" was the kind of song he might have written. As we hear the lyrics, it seems obvious also (given the timing and pressure to produce an album) that this combination of "Dylan, Clapton, and James Brown" (as advertisements for his shows in England put it) is also replying to the corporate studio owners: "Businessmen they drink my wine / Ploughmen dig my earth / None of them along the line / Know what any of it is worth."

The record producers have a response. The "thief" cautions us not to get excited, since after all, many "here among us" think that life is but a joke. Still, the narrator notes the value of speaking honestly, authentically—"let us not talk falsely now"—since the hour is getting late. Might this Dylan song not be Jimi's reply to the studio corporate heads to be patient, that they will get their money? Upon their chance meeting on the street in New York, even Dylan mused that he didn't know that anyone had done his songs better. And on top of that, it was released as a single, and soared to the top of the pop charts in both Britain and the US.

Even more amazingly in his soloes on "Watchtower," Jimi demonstrates the full range of what he can do on guitar—straight guitar licks, but also slide, wah-wah, and echo chamber effects. A very short tune it is, but Jimi displays a whole array of wizardry that he has learned over the years in playing the Strat. Might this not be yet another way of Jimi's reminding the moneyed producers that he can play guitar in ways that no one else does, that his creative genius, his authenticity, is not really for sale?

Jimi's guitar magic must have still been working, since the two-LP *Electric Ladyland*, though produced rather hurriedly to get out of debt, soared immediately to Number One on the *Billboard* charts. And the album showed all the earmarks of

Jimi's producer's genius, down to the detailed album design ideas and sequence of songs, along with Jimi's tell-tale mytho-poetic narratives.

Did Jimi Have Soul?

Some black critics of the day accused Jimi of race desertion. After all, he abandoned American rhythm and blues or soul groups, fled to England, and hired two white musicians to play bass and drums for him in the Jimi Hendrix Experience. Was his Experience culturally diverse enough? Did Jimi have soul?

True, Jimi's well-attended rock concerts were staged in wealthy, white, middle-class settings, typically an immense athletic stadium. Undoubtedly, concert promoters targeted these areas for both arena size and for audiences that could afford ticket prices. But also, Jimi himself noticed that the Jimi Hendrix Experience was not being played on R&B stations. Jimi found in his own apprenticeship with the R&B-soul circuits in the States that those leaders had no room for a virtuoso blues guitarist who also showed a flair for showmanship. So, some of this criticism is self-insulating.

However, there may be some deeper reasons for arguing that Jimi had soul. Jimi promised to do a free show at the Apollo Theater in Harlem (where he had premiered earlier). And Jimi also recognized that too many in the music world got hung up on musical categories, classifying one style as soul, another as hard rock, yet a third as jazz; and crossover artists were not easily categorized by critics, radio stations, and the general public. Jimi's music crossed over so many musical boundaries—his influence from the folk blues masters, like Robert Johnson and Muddy Waters; his driving hard-rock sounds, such that Clapton and Cream were in awe of his expertise; and his drifting off in jazz directions, as drew in Buddy Miles. Add on to that his amazing technical mastery of extracting sounds from a Stratocaster (especially in that upside-down signature Hendrix performance motif), never quite executed before, and it is no surprise that his music was hard to categorize. When militant critics insisted that whites could not play blues, Jimi gently coerced some "brothers" simply to sit and listen to a Cream album. The reaction (as given by an interviewer in *Teenset* magazine): the listeners were amazed at how three white boys got all that done. Jimi saw the power of music as one for healing divisions and transforming cultural differences and attitudes.

Perhaps the deepest reason for Jimi's soul, though, was his later movement towards music that dealt with social problems and justice. At a soul concert in New York, Jimi contributed about $5,000 to a scholarship fund for impoverished students. Jimi committed himself to perform at the Watts Summer Festival in 1970. The criticism that Jimi had deserted his race even sounds hollow in light of Jimi's own reply—that he was a mixture himself of most races, and so could not desert anyone. Even more powerfully, Jimi wrote a song, "Voodoo Child (Slight Return)" that was dedicated to the Black Panthers. And one of Jimi's most telling responses to the Detroit riots of 1967 showed his activism, "House Burning Down." It begins with his noticing the sky turning hell-fire red as a house is burning down; in the song, he asks "why someone burned his brother's house down?" A leader from the crowd shouted that they were tired and disgusted with their treatment by the white majority. Jimi offered in reply: "I say, "The truth is straight ahead, / So don't burn yourself instead, / Try to learn instead of burn, hear what I say!""

Clearly, Jimi wanted to clear up some of the social problems and injustices that confronted him. On top of racial injustice awareness, Jimi also moved toward an environmental consciousness. So, in a number of Jimi's comments in his last year, he recognized the need for harmony between humans and Earth. He saw too many warning signs in tidal waves, earthquakes, and the solar system. Even the sun, he remarked, hesitated to shine: "Through slag-filled clouds / That come from crowds / Of factories coughing waste, grit and grime."

In his last major concert at the end of the decade, December 31st 1969, Jimi introduced his new "Band of Gypsys" (Billy Cox on bass, Buddy Miles on drums) to a sold-out crowd at the Fillmore East in New York. In this concert, Jimi finally captured on stage the extended, after-hours jamming techniques typical of R&B bands, what he had excelled at in his studio hours with his bands over the years. But, with such songs as "Earth Blues," he also continued to present his worries for the planet. And with "Machine Gun," and the precise staccato drumbeats marking out the tempo of a machine gun in war, he symbolized musically the dissent against the whole Vietnam war, one that was tearing "my body" and "our families" and the nation apart. This war protest song envisioned a mother who dreaded a son returning in yet another body bag: – 'over yonder stands a mother, I'm her only baby boy'. Surely, this live version with the added lyric is Jimi's tribute to his mother but also a snipe at the sins of Mr. Nixon's War.

Finally, though he always cautioned listeners to resist getting upset, his rendition of the "Star-Spangled Banner," delivered so memorably at Woodstock, did revolutionize the way we hear it. It was a new, technically astute version of an old classic we thought we knew. Jimi had been playing it as part of his repertoire for about a year. But for the forty thousand still in the crowd at Woodstock, it became a defining moment of the 1960s, since now the young learned that they could love their country, but hate the government currently running their country.

Jimi's Quick Departure but Long-standing Legacy

Even if Jimi's life passed quicker than the wink of an eye, his musical legacy remains. Guitar players still scour issues of *Guitar Player* and *Melody Maker* to get clues about exactly how Jimi got all those unique sounds out of that Strat. Clapton and Stevie Ray Vaughn are just a couple of the many great blues guitarists that learned from Jimi. And Jimi, in his own spiritual journey—from the Experience to the black Dylan to the soulful dissenter—had yet one more stage to complete. He sought to go beyond the realm of dissent to a new Axis, one that keeps love following music, as the night the day.

As Jimi matured, he moved from wanting to be heard—in which case, he was then willing to play the clown, with pyrotechnics on stage—to discovering in his own words "the wisest way to be heard." Even further, he moved from offering protests to moving towards solutions to what was being protested, which implied new directions. Already on *Electric Ladyland* and *Band of Gypsys* (Buddy Miles on drums), we find him dropping hints about the jazz orientation of his "Earth music." Now, on his more recent album, *AXIS: Bold as Love*, Jimi painted in more detail some of the ethereal directions for his music, based in an imagined mythos of a new Earth to replace the "smell of a world that has burned" ("Up from the Skies"), or travel by a dragonfly to a daydreamed world ("Spanish Castle Magic"). Musically, also it is expansive, towards jazz. The deceptively simple lyrics of "If 6 Was 9" point to the freedom of the musician, as opposed to the businessman, with his three-piece suit straitjacket. And the ending is phenomenal: his lyric, "Sing on Brother, play on drummer" drastically understates the jazzy flute work that concludes the piece.

More poignantly, Jimi's own lyrics in "Little Wing" captivate us with a cherubic imagery. While in England, he once lived in Handel's house, and was mesmerized by the cherub with a broken arm on the ceiling. Is his fascination with cherubs an experiment in ideal love? Jimi's own love life had been one of many women, with no permanent attachments established, though in his later years, he conceded a deeper need for lasting companionship, well beyond the groupies (Electric Ladies) with whom he was continually surrounded. No wonder then that "Little Wing" underlines his ideal love: she is "walking through the clouds" and "riding with the wind." It also seemed timely for him, given all the recent stress and strain associated with producing more records, to imagine a woman who when he is sad would come to him and give to him a thousand smiles *for free*. And her parting words, both idyllic and idolizing, captivated Jimi—"Take anything you want from me. Anything."

Axis ends fittingly with "Bold as Love," which walks us through the entire gamut of human emotions. And he recognizes in this authentic humanist manifesto that we need not defer to our lesser emotions, like anger or jealousy, nor should we parade trophies of war. Rather, we can be daring and bold in chancing Love as the best response to the fragilities of life, romance, and conflict.

Now, Jimi began to see the musician as a messenger, perhaps from God, but one who has returned to his childhood, before the fingerprints of parents made an imprint on their minds, and before school or standards of progress smudged up the child's mind. As a number of his comments suggest, Jimi could not buckle under to the social pressure to fit him into one particular style of music, or to see love as any more than "Hello" and "Goodbye." Nobody could cage him. Still, we have learned to appreciate Jimi for his genuine authenticity as a musical artist and person. Contrary to the condemnations of

Bloom and black militants, Jimi left us with some real gifts—authenticity, simple lyrical honesty, technical virtuosity, and dissent as central to democratic discourse. Given our recent public discourse that lacks in all of these areas, might we not return to those?

At his tragic end, Jimi was haunted by his own demons—too many drugs, too many "yes people" surrounding him, mismanagement, and increasing debts—and all multiplied by loneliness and even abandonment, due to his association with the Black Panthers. Still, given Jimi's penchant for humor—well-noted by all, interviewers, friends, and musical partners—perhaps his final role was that of a "tragi-comic poet," as Cornell West pithily put it in *Race Matters*. West's examples are usually jazz greats, like Billie Holliday, but Jimi fits the role just as well.

If Cornell's conclusion is correct, that we should keep our eyes on the prize, not on the perpetuators of our oppression, then Jimi kept his aural vision fairly well-aimed at a target in the distance. His new aim of creating a jazz fusion band with Miles Davis showed his far-ranging musical synopsis; and he never lost sight of the prize. As Jimi would remind us from his late work, the real power of soul is found in our burning desire to reach our hearts and hands across our divides of race, earth blues, romantic encounters, and wars, and agree to work towards love, peace, and hope.

Fly on Little Wing!

7
A Life Along the Watchtower

CHRISTOPHER KETCHAM

Jimi Hendrix covered Nobel Laureate Bob Dylan's "All Along the Watchtower" and in doing so he made it his own. Charles Cross reports that even Dylan commented to Jimi, "I don't know if anyone has done my songs better" (*Room Full of Mirrors*, Chapter 22). It became one of Hendrix's signature works because he made the lyrics and music come alive in a way quite different from Dylan.

At the Watchtower

It is a cloudy, blustery day. Hendrix's guitar opening bodes the heaviness of the weather and then soars higher as does the wind when it whistles through ramparts.

We feel drawn into the grotesque, the stories of Rabelais and the Medieval feast where Joker and pickpocket both worked the crowds. The *carnival*, the *feast of fools*, the *feast of the ass* and other assorted festival entertainment upturned the regular order: where royals ruled and serfs obeyed. During festivals, the Joker made the fool of the local aristocrats and commoners alike. Commoners dressed like royals, albeit with cocked crowns, bulging codpieces, and other disrespectful garb. They spoke profanely, as was common in the marketplace. While music played, people danced, frolicked, ate, fucked, and drank for the duration of the feast. The pickpocket worked both the standing crowds and the inebriated fallen. Such was the respite from the order of existence imposed by class and ecclesiastical hierarchy. In life, the monarch owned your body; in death God owned your soul. There was no escape from this hegemony.

In Mikhail Bakhtin's account, even the monks could be seen driving an oxcart down the street, slinging dung at the crowd (*Rabelais and His World*). After the mirthful festival, all returned to their regular social order, hung over of course.

The Joker says to the Thief in the song "All Along the Watchtower," "it's all so confusing." Hendrix's guitar accompanies the Joker much like the festival background music, rich, melodic, but complex, as Hendrix riffs usually were. It's to this circularity that the Joker asks whether there is a way out of here, this hegemonic society that seems to drink up the fruits of his labor and plows away what he has sown. Yet, says the Joker to the Thief, "nobody seems to know what any of it is worth."

The Joker brings us face to face with Jean-Paul Sartre's nothingness. This is not the nothingness as in the void, but the idea that humans are both being and nothingness. We can ask a question, and be in question of ourselves—of what anything is worth? We are not static beings; we continually remake ourselves through our thoughts and actions. To put this in a Sartrean form that the Joker might to trip up lesser intellects, "Thus he is not what at any instant we might want to say that he is, and he is that toward which he projects himself but which he is not yet" (*Being and Nothingness*, p. xix). One is both there (being) and not, or not yet (nothingness).

We have stepped into Heraclites's river, never to step into the same river again, but as we step into the water . . . we leave no footprint, so how could we ever know that we have stepped . . . It's all so confusing.

The Thief brushes away the nihilist talk from the Joker. He suggests that rather than take the attitude that life is a joke, we must, as his profession surely does not countenance, tell the truth about the way things are.

So much confusion: a depressed Joker; an honest Thief. The double oxymoron shows the yin and yang of existence for what it is, without permanence either in definition or in duration. The Thief does not disabuse the Joker of his explanation of being and nothingness, but adds a wrinkle from Martin Heidegger, that, oh by the way, truth is, we are beings towards death. This is in response to the Joker's deeper concern, "If we are to be plowed under into moldering nothingness, then what is being worth?"

"Bah," says the Thief, "we've been through that discussion before. Life is not a joke." This isn't a jab at the Joker's profession, but the idea that there is meaning to life. It isn't all just a nihilistic waste of time. Then Hendrix's guitar takes off like a paper blown into the wind: soaring, dipping, flipping.

"But is there some way out of this mess?" the words of the Joker hang in the air like the blown paper. Martin Heidegger responds with, "What if it is only in the anticipation of death that resoluteness, as Dasein's [the human] *authentic* truth, has reached the *authentic certainty* which belongs to it?" (*Being and Time*, p. 351). Our resoluteness to persist for as long as persistency is possible and the care we have for being in the world itself bring about the possibilities of both being and nothingness that the worries the Joker. We are on a journey with an uncertain duration but definite conclusion. It is Heidegger and the Thief telling us, "Let us best use what we have for what time we have for it."

Can we say that Jimi Hendrix maxed out his life, however abbreviated it was? Hendrix asks in "The Wind Cries Mary," whether the wind will remember the names from the past, but the wise wind says no, this will be the last time they are heard. How brief is this life and then we are gone and mostly forgotten. Was Hendrix, the prodigy who died at twenty-seven, the authentic anticipatory resoluteness of which Heidegger spoke?

We're fascinated by the prodigy who soars high and fast like the youthful Icarus but then plunges too soon into the abyss: Hendrix, Amy Winehouse, Janis Joplin, Jim Morrison, to name a few. What could they have brought into the world had their anticipatory resoluteness not been cut short by personal demons or addictions? And the wind whispers, Jimi.

So, we enter this discussion with the Joker and the Thief wondering just what authenticity is. With Jimi Hendrix, the issues of authenticity and care loom large, as we will see.

About Buster

Charles Cross explains that Buster Hendrix left Seattle after a brush with the law, but not into music. The army's 101st Airborne and its Screaming Eagle called to him. However, the army wasn't for Buster so he pulled a Corporal Klinger from MASH, though not as a cross-dresser. Buster convinced army doctors that he had homosexual tendencies. It was all a ruse. But it worked. Buster was discharged.

Then the kid once known as Buster slung his guitar over his shoulder like Johnny Guitar, and began his long journey from Tennessee, into the deep South and the chitlin' circuit, to New York, and finally London where he became Jimi Hendrix.

Buster's first guitar was a broom. As a child, Buster was the proverbial guitar hero. Then he bought a single string broken down guitar for five bucks. When he got his first real guitar he taught himself by listening to and playing with other musicians and asking them how to play riffs and other routines. Jimi could never read music (*Starting at Zero*, p. 163).

Cross explains that Buster's youth was confusion. His mother and father were alcoholics and his father was abusive. He had brothers and sisters, some who became wards of the state. Buster was often taken in by relatives and friends or relatives or friends moved in with Buster and his father until they couldn't stand living with his father anymore. Yet, we can see Jimi's determination not to dwell on his difficult childhood in the lyrics to "Rainy Day Dream Away" where he says it's a rainy day, that's all. Nothing to get uptight about, let the rain drain your worries and lay back and dream what you might dream.

Charles Cross says that Buster's younger brother Joe was born with physical deformities. His father had him committed to foster care. We can wonder whether Hendrix's own "Hey Joe" with a gun in his hand is also going after his own mother who let his father abandon him to the state.

Buster flunked out of high school. He wasn't stupid, far from it; it just wasn't for him. Music was for him. Sure, we know all this and the fact that he invented his own sound and became a true guitar hero, not one who just strummed straw.

In early 1968, Jimi Hendrix said, "I felt like 'All Along the Watchtower' was something I had written but couldn't get together. I often feel like that about Dylan." Why "Watchtower"? I suggest that the Joker and the Thief represent the struggle for authenticity that waged within Hendrix. The lyrics rang for Hendrix as if he had written the words himself. (*Starting at Zero*, p. 136)

The Order of Things

After the Joker and the Thief stop talking, Dylan and Hendrix shift us to the scene of the watchtower. Princes watch atop the tower; women and servants go about their business: the order of things. Then two riders approach amid the howling of wind and a wild beast and Hendrix's growling guitar. Then, Hendrix's guitar soars into higher crescendo as if to announce a coming.

Change is coming to this wary place. This harbinger of change is Hendrix himself. He knows it. Music itself has led to Hendrix's spiritual awakening and he has changed music. Even as he covered Dylan, he changed the song forever. Listen to Dylan sing "Watchtower" today, and you will hear Hendrix.

Substance over Style

Hendrix was an omnivore when it came to guitar music. He didn't much take to jazz because it favored the brass instruments, but he loved the improvisations (*Starting at Zero*, pp. 165–66). He liked the crooners like Sinatra and Martin, and dove headlong into the Delta blues on the chitlin' circuit but didn't quite get it. Cross relates an anecdote: "He hadn't rubbed elbows with someone who had mud on him, like me," said Johnny Jones of the Imperials (*Room Full of Mirrors*, Chapter 9). Like other prodigies, Hendrix tried as many other styles and techniques of guitar playing as he heard and wanted to imitate. Then, and only then, could he make his own sound. He went through the stages: novice (broom), learner (one string guitar), apprentice (real guitar, listen, and imitate other professionals), accompaniment (early bands), rebel (he was fired from many gigs for being too wild), and finally into a place where he could be the master of his own way of playing: The Jimi Hendrix Experience.

He combined playing competence with showmanship and flamboyant dress. He became the Joker. Cross recounts the story of Jimi in a British bar in 1967 where he was denied service. At first, Jimi thought that it was because he was black. Turns out it was his manner of dress which the barkeep took as being clownish. Barkeep posted 'no clowns' on the door when the circus came to town (*Room Full of Mirrors*, Prologue). The circus was in town. Hendrix became the Joker, not by dress alone, but because he wanted a way out of that which had been him; that which had come before. In "Love or Confusion," Hendrix asks, "Is this love, baby, or is it just confusion?"

There was so much confusion in the music business. He commented once, that someone had taken a studio tape he had done when he was quite stoned and produced a record that Hendrix had not authorized. Then again, he was often at odds with producers who wanted to do things their way but not what he thought was right—the businessmen were drinking his wine and plowing his work into fields they took to be their own. Nobody knew the worth of these things . . . but did Jimi?

Cause

The middle Sixties were a time of turmoil. Civil rights became the watchword of the African-American community in the US, while Vietnam was America's watchtower. Hendrix went to schools that were quite diverse in Seattle in the 1950s. However, his father, a World War II vet, still faced discrimination in work. Hendrix experienced the Jim Crow of the South while touring there. Yet, in London, he felt somehow disconnected from all the issues and problems facing African Americans back home. He said:

> I don't feel involved. I feel almost completely lost now, sometimes almost from everything. I feel sorry for the minorities, but I don't feel part of one, I am for the masses and the underdog, but not for trying to get the underdog to do this or that, because I tried before and got screwed so madly millions of times. So now I'm just for anyone who can do the job. (*Starting at Zero*, p. 175)

Hendrix had reached a different place. He knew more of being than nothingness at this point in his life. He could have become a victim or a revolutionary, but he transcended what had gone before him. His dismissive approach to his past freed him for his authentic being-towards . . . towards what he described as a kind of spirituality through the production and performance of music. He was offering a third approach, different from revolutionary or victim.

His was the idea that we can become the authentic *being-towards* of Heidegger. We can let go of the baggage of oppression: of becoming fine-tuned players within the hegemony, or even lashing out against it. If we become stronger being-towards our own authenticity . . . what else is more important? Hendrix saw that there is a way out of the hegemony, and it is to walk back from it to a point in existence where one does not know or understand the meaning of hegemony, or what the hegemony is worth.

Hendrix didn't just preach this, he turned it into personal ritual like a Buddhist monk does towards his own meditative efforts. He practiced between sets. For some, he took too long to tune his instruments before playing live. There was purpose to all of this.

Electric Church Music

He called his brand of music "Electric Church Music," not church in its common meaning, but spiritual, metaphysical, a freeing of the soul to be more than what we have been told to be (p. 166). In this, Hendrix had become the Thief, the Thief who dismisses the idea that life is nothing more than a joke. The anticipatory resoluteness of his music is directed towards spirituality and a deeper meditative state. Hendrix's transcendental axe was his music. He said as much:

> There's other moves I have to make now, a little more towards a spiritual level, through music. We concentrate mostly on sound. It is a very hard and harsh and primitive sound, not necessarily good or bad or stoned. You get the feeling you're going to get something out of it if you let your mind flow with it. It's more than music. It's like church, like a foundation for the lost or potentially lost. (*Starting at Zero*, p. 167)

Who are the lost? His generation, fighting for meaning in a world of change? Wondering about nihilism in the face of anticipatory resoluteness, wanting to gain a higher plane of existence through mind altering drugs? Perhaps, but let's return to the Watchtower for a moment.

There are some who see Dylan's words as a play on the biblical verses Isaiah 21:5–9:

> 5. Prepare the table, watch in the watchtower, eat, drink: arise, ye princes, and anoint the shield.
>
> 6. For thus hath the Lord said unto me, Go, set a watchman, let him declare what he seeth.
>
> 7. And he saw a chariot with a couple of horsemen, a chariot of asses, and a chariot of camels; and he hearkened diligently with much heed:

8. And he cried, A lion: My lord, I stand continually upon the watchtower in the daytime, and I am set in my ward whole nights:

9. And, behold, here cometh a chariot of men, with a couple of horsemen. And he answered and said, Babylon is fallen, is fallen; and all the graven images of her gods he hath broken unto the ground.

Hendrix wanted to do the same, grind the Babylonian craven images of nihilism into the ground. He explained:

We try to make our music so loose and hard-hitting that it hits your soul hard enough to make it open. It's like shock therapy or a can opener. You hypnotize people to where they go right back into their natural state, which is pure positive—like in childhood when you get your natural highs. And when they come down off this natural high, they see clearer, feel different things. It's all spiritual.

Hendrix the Thief has stolen into the mind and wrung from it the defeatism, the nihilism, that life is nothing more than a joke, and returns the listener to a more primitive state of being to where one is attuned to both being and questioning thereof (nothingness). Then he sends the listener back, back onto the path of anticipatory resoluteness to see and feel like they did as a child, unencumbered by the baggage of that which they have been told they cannot be and what they must be. This approach is neither defeatist nor revolutionary, but a denial of the hegemony altogether in order to chart one's own course. Antonio Gramsci said that both the oppressor and oppressed buy into the message of the oppressor. Hendrix simply denied the oppressor's message altogether to forge his own authentic path.

He's saying: it all can be if you have the right attitude. This is remarkable for a young man who endured so much in early life. I believe that what he was saying to us is that he never wanted to let go of the freshness of being a child, of searching for meaning through music, and when he got there, sharing the same with others. He didn't want to look back into the problems of his youth and that which others of color of his generation were dealing with. Sending one back the being of a child is not a regression, but a letting go of baggage one learns to cling, grasp, and crave as one meets the exigencies of existence.

However, Jimi wasn't so sure of his craft. "I think I am a better guitarist than I was, but I never was good" (p. 232). About melodies, riffs, and tunes that came to him he said, "On guitar I just can't get them out. I can't play guitar well enough to get this all together." However, he then went on to explain all the things he wanted to do, like writing Greek or Norse tragedies and composing the music for them. Then, he said about his success, "I'm not sure I will live to be twenty-eight years old, but then again, many beautiful things have happened to me in the last three years. The world owes me nothing" (p. 235). What are we to make of Hendrix's confessions?

In the verse of Isaiah, "watchman" is someone you trust to tell the truth of what he or she sees, which the Thief advocates that he and the Joker do. Hendrix becomes this watchman who says what he sees, albeit in the guise of the Thief, the Thief that razes Babylonian false idols, the Thief of nihilism and defeatism, and the cure to the sickness unto death that plagues the Joker. Yet he is also pragmatic. He knows he's a good guitar player, but he is searching for more, a different, more meaningful sound.

Hendrix also becomes the approaching riders, the twin representatives of a return to childhood innocence and a renewed spirituality of openness to transcendence. He said about his performances, "I play and move as I feel. It's not an act, but a state of being. My music, my instrument, my sound, my body are all one action with my mind" (p. 56).

The resetting of the clock, so to speak, brings to the fore Heidegger's idea that we are principally beings of care, care about the world, care about being, care about everything about us. Heidegger says, *"Being-in-the-world which is falling and disclosed, thrown and projecting, and for which its ownmost potentiality-for-Being is an issue, both in its Being alongside the 'world' and in its Being-with Others"* (*Being and Time*, p. 225).

Heidegger is saying that we are thrown into the world, pushed out of mother's womb into a fantastic place of sights, smells, and other people. We take the world in full grasp of our little fists and begin to learn how to become with others. We are the embodiment of care, care about the world and others. Yet, we turn away from ourselves. Heidegger explains, "Dasein's falling into the 'they' and the 'world' of its concern, is what we have called a 'fleeing' in the face of itself" (p. 230). Rather than pursue our own truth, our own authentic being in the world, we fall into 'they' thinking, wanting to be more and more like the other, the "they." It is comfortable, less taxing, and thoroughly inauthentic.

Hendrix believed in the idea of rebirth. He saw death as something not to fear but, "The idea is to get your own self together, see if you can get ready for the next world, because there is one. Hope you can dig it" (*Starting at Zero*, p. 236). His being-towards isn't towards death, but towards the continuity of self-improvement and renewal, leading to rebirth and a better life. However, he worried about others who will be born into this world.

Hendrix said, "Sadness is for when a baby is born into this heavy world, and joy should be exhibited at someone's death because they are going on to something more permanent and infinitely better" (p. 236). From inside the womb, in his song "Belly Button Window," Hendrix looks out of the belly button window but all he sees are frowns. He wonders whether these frowning people want him to be born at all. He's not saying that he will not be born, but he wants to be born to people who will want him. If not, he can wait where he is, in spirit land.

However, he says in the song, that if they don't say no, he's coming down regardless of love or hate. He will be born into this world on his own terms, not anyone else's . . . it would be much nicer if they wanted him. The frowns are the frowns of the hegemonic world of his own parents who drowned themselves in drink. Even from the womb, Hendrix is saying that he brings his own anticipatory resoluteness into the world and he will attain his own authentic being his way. Through his idea of rebirth, Hendrix is telling Heidegger that he will not be thrown into this world. He will throw himself into this world under his own terms. Even before he is born, he is fighting the 'they' world of Heidegger towards a Hendrix world of anticipatory resolution.

We become jaundiced by the hegemony: 'they' thinking and being like others rather than becoming ourselves. Electric Church Music was a way of cutting off the 'they', to return Heidegger's Dasein to authentic thinking and being, the towards-which, the anticipatory resoluteness that escapes the 'they' towards what one can truly become until one can no longer be. The intense introspection to get into the state of being where he could create and perform to his satisfaction also caused Hendrix great angst.

The move from inauthenticity to authenticity produces anxiety because it turns us away from the 'they' thinking we have come to lean on. Our becoming 'they' is difficult to unbecome. Heidegger well understood this anxiety, *"The turning-away of falling is grounded rather in anxiety, which in turn is what first makes fear possible"* (*Being and Time*, p. 230).

In "A Room Full of Mirrors," a song that Hendrix never released during his lifetime, this reflection becomes so deep and disturbing that the protagonist smashes a mirror to get relief from the anxiety such anticipatory resoluteness brings. In this room full of mirrors, he sees only himself, the self he has come to know, his hegemonic self, his 'they' self. By smashing the mirrors, he has let go of this inauthentic being.

Can we ever see beyond the hegemony that is out there in the world? In his "Castles Made of Sand," Hendrix speaks of relationships that are castles made of sand that eventually fall into the sea. We make our own world whether it be sandcastles or like the third pig in the fairytale the *Three Little Pigs*, build our house of brick to keep the big bad wolf from blowing our house down . . . and the wind whispers, Jimi.

There's a price to be paid for authenticity, just as much as there is a price to be paid for inauthenticity—being 'they'. Both played out in Jimi. Cross found a shattered mirror sculpture made by Jimi in the basement of Jimi's father's home. The struggle for Hendrix was emerging from the room full of mirrors, a sanctuary of self-full-ness, of continuous reflection about what he has been, into the hegemonic world, without losing sight of himself, his originary authentic self, his child-like self, full of wonder. The shattered mirror still reflects, but its shards reflect the hegemonic confusion of the 'they' world of which the Joker speaks and into which the being-towards-authenticity must venture. This same struggle (anxiety) plays out in all of us.

Jimi built the mechanism, Electric Church Music, for returning us to a moment where we can see the world through child eyes. He says in "Electric Church Red House," "Yeah, it's about the time we'd like to present you to the electric church." For Hendrix, as he says in the song, the music itself is freedom, the freedom to see the world anew, just like the child.

In his performances, Jimi cared about his audience and their spiritual wellbeing as a child would, carrying out a fantasy play with a favorite teddy bear. But more than this, as a child views the world . . . this is what Jimi wanted to share with us and have us return to: that seeing we so desperately need, that reflection that bodes authenticity and anxiety at the same time (being and nothingness). Shattering the mirror brings forth the world, but also the angst of being in the world and the struggle against becoming the hegemonic 'they'.

Yet we know that Hendrix, himself, used psychotropic drugs to both enhance his child-like reflection and escape from it. Such experimentation requires a returning to an equilibrium of sorts and this is purportedly what killed him as he mixed too many uppers and downers to level himself. The very real issue of being and nothingness played out to end Hendrix's life, just as he began to explore that which could bring him and his audience greater authenticity of being and becoming. However, to gain the greater measure of Hendrix, we must look towards what Hendrix was trying to accomplish even though he ultimately failed himself in this effort. Prophetically, he said shortly before he died, "There's so many songs I wrote that we haven't done yet, that we probably will never do" (*Starting at Zero,* p. 233).

In his performances and words, Jimi explained to us that he had and always would be Buster, the authentic anticipatory and resolute child thrown into the world, but who sees the world always through child's eyes. In this countenance, Buster's Jimi saw himself as the someway out of here. Yet, Buster promised no easy path through this because there is, deep down, the notions that we are drawn to, and these are child-like authentic reflection, but also the 'they'.

. . . and the wind still whispers, Jimi.

III

Flotation Is Groovy, Even a Jellyfish Will Tell You That

8
Facing Up to the Realities

JASSEN CALLENDER

On May 5th 1970, a man who as a child carried a broom to emulate a guitar, a man once named Johnny Allen Hendrix and later called "Buster" and "Jimmy James," draped in a blue dragonfly psychedelic camouflage, stepped to the Berkeley Community Theater microphone to introduce his next song, "Machine Gun."

"I'd like to dedicate this song to soldiers fighting in Berkeley— you know what soldiers I'm talking about—and oh yeah, the soldiers fighting in Vietnam too," Jimi Hendrix began casually, as if making the most mundane of comparisons. He slowly strummed the opening notes. "And dedicate it to other people that might be fighting wars too, but within themselves, not facing up to the realities." This latter phrase reveals the lie in Hendrix's seeming casualness. And it reveals much about the man.

I didn't hear this performance in person. I was far too young. It came to me through the ubiquitous cassette tapes of my post-vinyl teenage years. Today it is YouTube-able in dozens of variations. Still, this particular introduction and the version of the song that followed reached me, grabbed me, shook me to awareness that something important was being conveyed. Repeated rewindings eventually distorted the tape to wah-wah pedal proportions. But why did it have such an effect?

The answer, at least in part, lies in the phrase "the realities." Not "reality." He said, "the realities."

If this phrase doesn't immediately suggest why this intro, the song "Machine Gun," and the performer himself are important, ask yourself what kind of person thinks and uses language that way. Who talks about reality in the plural? Who implicitly asks questions like: What is it to face up to reality? Why do people fail to do so? And, if we make the effort, with what do we find ourselves face-to-face?

These are big, essential inquiries about authenticity and what it means to live an honest and, perhaps, virtuous life. These are themes we associate with philosophers and theologians, not rock stars. While James Marshall "Jimi" Hendrix sometimes comes across as a sweet, goofy kid in interviews, on the one hand, and is variously described as a guitar virtuoso, a rock vocalist, a psychedelic song writer, and so on, on the other, he is arguably a philosopher in his late lyrics. He was a thinker working through the medium of music rather than manuscripts, communicating through words sung, not printed.

The Kind of Philosopher Jimi Was

Most philosophers write. Most write a lot. And all of them touch on the nature of "reality" and what it means to know or experience it. Even the deepest division in philosophy, separating its Eastern and Western adherents, is rooted in these issues. In broadest strokes, Eastern philosophy assumes humans to be subordinate to the reality of a cosmic order, while Western philosophy asserts the primacy of free individuals in forging reality. Some philosophers, East and West, take the problems of facing reality as the focus of their work; others assume a definition of reality and develop its implications along tangents difficult for non-specialists to follow (in the unlikely event any are so inclined) and not readily discernable as addressing reality.

All that to say, philosophy is not a narrow or unified field. Even among those who take facing reality as their primary concern, there are numerous branches or sub-disciplines and even subsets within those sub-disciplines. And only some of these subsets think this line of inquiry leads to useful or ultimately positive ends.

The sub-discipline of Western philosophy mostly commonly associated with problems of what it means to face reality is Existentialism. It focuses on humans and their relationships with, and responsibilities to, each other and *Being*, or existence, in general. Heady, big-picture stuff indeed.

Of the many leaders of the many subsets of existentialism, Jean-Paul Sartre is arguably the most widely known. He is one of those philosophers who wrote, a lot. Author of treatises, such as *Being and Nothingness,* novels, such as *Nausea,* short stories, *The Wall,* and plays, *No Exit,* Sartre was prolific in both type and sheer volume of literary output. Despite this range and volume, however, Sartre always focused on the relationship between individuals and other instances of reality, including other people. "Hell is other people," a line from *No Exit,* is probably his most famous aphorism.

The core tenet of *Being and Nothingness* might be summed up as follows: we are not what we are; we are what we are not. Existentialism in general and Sartre's version of it in particular, however, are neither as pessimistic nor as self-contradictory or paradoxical as these lines at first suggest. Both phrases address the fundamental issue of the human condition: the battle between freedom and identity.

We are not what we are is shorthand for saying that our identity does not reside with any one, or even a summation, of the multitudinous roles and characters we play in our day-to-day lives. Joseph Campbell called them masks. Our existence precedes these roles.

We are what we are not addresses individual freedom. Human authenticity, according to Sartre, is not a simple "I think" or "I am". It arises in our ability to differentiate, to question, to negate. Unlike the *Being* of tables and chairs, our *Being* is unique in that it allows us to cast doubt—even on our own identity. This struggle between our desire for a comforting and stable identity, on the one hand, and the fact of our absolute freedom, on the other, creates us. If we choose the former we tend to betray the latter. The closer we cling to our freedom, the more authentically we live.

The most obvious evidence for categorizing Hendrix as an existentialist is the words to his early recording "Stone Free" and his posthumously released "Freedom." But this is also a bit superficial. I mean, "Stone free to do what I please" and "Freedom, give it to me, that's what I want now" are arguably little more than selfish cries to escape all forms of responsibility.

These and similar lyrics treat freedom in the way you would expect from a very young man raised first by a sometimes abusive, and at times simply neglectful, father and later adopted by overbearing fans who demanded his identity conform to their wants and needs. This is less freedom than fleeing.

The lyrics to "Machine Gun" are different. Radically so. It does not use words casually, despite how the words read when printed. Quite the contrary. "Machine Gun" explores the two sides of the human condition, the struggle between authentic freedom and its false other, bad faith, with all the seriousness of a philosopher. It is Hendrix's existentialist manifesto.

Bad Faith

Not facing up to reality, whether the latter is understood as singular or plural, is a habit existentialists call "bad faith." It is a lie you tell yourself to avoid responsibility for your actions, or lack of action. Sartre believed that we take this avoidance as far as calling our own identity into question in order to lift the weighty burden of freedom from our shoulders.

Psychologically, the way this works is straightforward: if we see ourselves as other than we are, we can't be expected to live up to the obligations specific to our real selves and individual talents; if we see ourselves as less than we are, we can't be expected to meet high ethical standards. In existential parlance, bad faith can seem to be heady stuff. But everyday instances of this are numerous. Each time we see someone in need—be it a person struggling with depression or domestic violence or simply broken down on the side of the road—and respond with "Yeah, I'd like to help but I am just a ——," we are trafficking in bad faith.

Instances of bad faith are so numerous that it is tempting to dismiss it as an automatic animal response. A Freudian might call it a defense mechanism. And yet, Sartre is insistent that bad faith is a project. Or, more accurately, bad faith is a choice founded upon the freedom that makes it possible to understand each person's life as a project. This is why existentialists' studies of bad faith matter. Attempts to justify or dismiss it as a natural trait are also acts of bad faith, and often invoked because these are easier than owning up to earlier lies. It's very easy, in fact, to find ourselves in a "reality" so composed of acts of bad faith that it is difficult to distinguish what's real from comforting lies. And therein lie bad faith's damaging consequences.

How did Hendrix expose this tendency? While he changed the lyrics to "Machine Gun" with each performance, there are core phrases that exist in every version even if they change slightly in wording or intonation. Most of these phrases are aimed at the bad faith inherent in all forms of conflicts—those of protest, of war or within the individual psyche. From the second May 5th show at Berkeley, there is this: "Evil man make me kill ya, baby, evil man make you kill me / Evil man make me kill you, even though we're only families apart / (such a shame)."

Notice there is no "free to do what I please" attitude here. No freedom is implied at all. The lyrics, in fact, suggest the opposite: conflict is rooted in an acquiescence of control on both sides. Evil man *makes me* . . . ; evil man *makes you* . . . These lyrics expose the most common form of bad faith, namely the belief that Providence, fate, or other hidden powers control our actions. As mere pawns of evil men who don't take an active role in the fight, the combatants in "Machine Gun" share no responsibility—they are, in fact, only families apart. Even Hendrix's under-his-breath rejoinder, "such a shame," calls to mind the phrase that so often follows those words in everyday life, ". . . but what can you do?"

Helplessness is both the most common and perhaps most crippling form of bad faith. But Hendrix knows that this is only one of its forms. He moves on from feigned helplessness to action that, at first, suggests breaking from bad faith and taking responsibility for your actions. "Well I pick up my ax and fight like a farmer / (I said I pick up my ax and fight like a farmer)."

In the very next line, however, Hendrix exposes action-doomed-to-failure as another form of bad faith almost as damaging to our identity as helplessness. This is the bad faith of blame. "But your bullets still knock me down to the ground / . . . / The same way you shoot me down baby / You'll be going just the same / Three times the pain / And your own self to blame / Hey-ey machine gun."

There's an immediacy and power in these lines that Sartre seldom achieved. In these lyrics, the source of our failure is located *out there* in another person, who should blame him- or herself, or in an inanimate object, such as a machine gun. Picking up an ax to fight a soldier armed with a machine gun is only ostensibly to take responsibility for one's life. Hendrix the philosopher reveals fighting like a farmer to be just another false identity worn to avoid the consequences and eventual pain of fighting wars with others and, more importantly, within ourselves and failing to face reality.

Authenticity

Facing up to reality, living at peace with the world and yourself, is an aspiration existentialists call "authenticity." For Sartre, authenticity is the equal and opposite other of bad faith. It is the use of our freedom to bring our spiritual or conceptual selves into balance with our bodily or material existence. Authenticity is facing the world without the misdirection of blame or helplessness. Hendrix begins "Machine Gun" by invoking the body, material objects, and the horrific effect of the latter on the former. "Machine gun, tearing my body [buddies?] all apart."

There is some debate whether Hendrix says 'body' or 'buddies' in the second Berkeley performance. It doesn't matter. Either way, these opening lines describe the metaphorical situation in which we fight our battles. Forces tear us apart—me, you, our buddies. The diversions of bad faith take place within this setting and in response to its horror. Hendrix shows how we transition from facing the reality of machine guns and bodies [or buddies] being torn apart to the helplessness of submission to evil but absent men to blaming better armed opponents before returning to reality in words that echo those of bad faith: "Let your bullets fly like rain, let'em fly / 'cause I know all the time you're wrong baby / And you'll be goin' just the same / Three times the pain / And your own self to blame / Lord, machine gun."

At first blush, most of these words are identical to those Hendrix uses to expose our desire to hide behind blame. Yet the tone of the reprise is utterly different. In part, the tone is shifted musically. These lyrics are sung in a musical calm between a dissonant guitar solo that calls to mind a battlefield and staccato playing that sounds like the eruption of machine gun fire. In other words, these repeated lyrics are framed by reminders of reality. But that doesn't explain the shift in tone sufficiently.

The first two lines of the reprise are crucial. "Let your bullets fly like rain" and "I know all the time you're wrong" are new and they change the meaning of the words that follow. The former is a statement of acceptance. Bullets and the other implements of injury are mere facts of the world in which we live. The latter is a judgment and assertion of freedom within that world.

"I know . . . you're wrong" is arguably the most confident and authentic phrase anyone can muster against the brutalities we battle from one day to the next. But from where does this knowledge, "I know," and this judgment, "you're wrong," get its force? To answer this question, we have to turn to the philosopher Hendrix himself and his notion of reality.

The Realities

So, what is reality? Is it multiple? And if it's multiple, what does it mean to face it authentically? As hinted at in the opening paragraphs, Jimi Hendrix is not an obvious example of a man who lived authentically or faced reality, whatever we may mean by those terms. He certainly did not live in a reality that most of us would recognize by that name. In fact, as a man of multiple legal names, nicknames, and stage names; a man who carried a broom to emulate a guitar; who draped himself in all sorts of psychedelic camouflage and consumed all sorts of reality-bending narcotics; it is difficult not to see Hendrix's legacy as one of denying reality with all the strength any human could muster. But such judgments miss the philosophical roots of his notion of reality or the ends toward which he aimed.

The crucial tenet of existentialism is this: existence precedes essence. Raw being comes first; then we make meaning of it. According to Sartre, "Man being condemned to be free carries the weight of the whole world on his shoulders (*Being and Nothingness,* p. 553)." Reality is therefore the essence or character that forms in response to mere existence.

When we accept responsibility for this process of becoming, we live authentically. And if we are honest, it is impossible to avoid the conclusion that each of us lives in numerous realities over time and in different circumstances. Thus, when Hendrix claims that our battles result from "not facing up to the realities," he is not being casual. It is a profound diagnosis.

As I've said, I didn't hear this performance in person. Very few who will read this did (and these numbers will decline each year). It is known to most of us through vinyl or cassette tapes or compact discs or, increasingly as time goes by, the Internet. This growing distance between the original performance and the present prompts two final questions: first, how real are these increasingly intangible recordings? And, second, how does the song continue to have an effect despite the passage of time? The first question is beyond the scope of this chapter, except to say that, if the purpose of philosophy is to learn to question reality, then listening to Hendrix via the Internet is at least as worthwhile as reading Sartre on a Kindle.

The second question—How does the song continue to have an effect despite the passage of time?—is the more pressing. And rewarding. At one point in the Berkeley performance, Hendrix seems to say the following: "I finally hit the ground, fight like a farmer baby / but you still shoot me down baby, back in the ground, back in the ground."

I don't know if those are the actual words or merely what I wish to hear. The recording is not as clear as we might hope. At first glance, it's a depressing coda. And yet, it's rewarding as a kind of eternal return: we have struggled, we struggle, and we will continue to struggle to live authentically; we will find ground, lose ground, and get back up.

Hendrix's "Machine Gun" and its introduction are addressed to more than his May 5th, 1970, Berkeley Community Theater audience, or even the "soldiers fighting in Berkeley . . . and oh yeah, the soldiers fighting in Vietnam too." He is specific; though his meaning was not necessarily grasped at the time. "Machine Gun" is dedicated "to other people that might be fighting wars too, but within themselves, not facing up to the realities."

For an existentialist, this struggle is the only thing that really matters.

9
Are You Experienced?

CHARLES TALIAFERRO

Have you ever had experiences that are so extraordinarily real, that it is shocking?

I don't mean only experiences you have in a crisis (though Winston Churchill once observed that "nothing in life is so exhilarating as to be shot at without result"); the experiences might be quite ordinary, but they feel so enormously, undeniably real to you that they seem uncanny and more real than your life in the past or future.

Maybe such experiences stand out as so profoundly different from the experiences we have when we're daydreaming, playing video games, watching movies, engaged in tired, mindless repetitious activity or any of the other ways we distract ourselves from the present moment.

That feeling of the poignancy of experience in the present became vivid to me as a boy when I encountered Jimi Hendrix's 1967 LP release *Are You Experienced*, an epic work of hard rock, drawing on rhythm and blues, free jazz, and maybe even soul music. I think I came to embrace a philosophy of *experientialism* inspired by Hendrix's dreamy, free-form, funk, and quasi-psychedelic work.

Experientialism is the view that our subjective, conscious experience is a fundamental reality, not a mere appearance or something speculative and theoretical. Believe it or not, some philosophers, often called *eliminativists* (after the term *eliminate*), argue that conscious experiences are in fact illusions created by evolution. These eliminativists claim that the world revealed in the natural sciences, especially physics, is fundamentally real, while conscious experiences are not real.

Such a view is radically mistaken: we can't have physics or any science at all without scientists who have experiences. Moreover, eliminativists have an embarrassing case of explaining how you and I can have illusions unless we are conscious beings and experience the illusions. It's not that experiences are more real than the natural world; we are in a *both/and situation* (experiences exist and so does the natural world); I am simply in the resistance when it comes to people who urge us to make an *either/or choice* and eliminate experience or fail to take it seriously.

In this chapter, rather than seek to argue for the reality of experience, I assume that experiences do exist and go on to draw some lessons about experience from Jimi Hendrix's heavy-metal album. If we're able to make progress in learning about experience from the band, The Jimi Hendrix Experience, we should be all the more confident that we are dealing with a subject of massive, central importance in our lives.

The Interpersonal, Interactive Nature of Experience

The title song, "Are You Experienced," starts with an alluring, romantic request, even an urgent beseeching, of another person; I will assume the person is female, though we need not know who in particular is being courted (perhaps his girlfriend at the time, Kathy Etchingham) and it seems to me there is nothing in the lyrics that would prevent a singer directing the focus to a same-sex or transgendered person.

The singer calls this person to leave a world which is little, compared to the higher, more expansive realm of the singer. In her world she is treated as a precious metal, gold, but gold is not living. Moreover, while the (potential) beloved is treated as gold, she is generally possessed and not able to move or be exchanged.

Martin Buber, a mid-twentieth-century philosopher who gave central place to the importance of experience, described relationships with other persons whom we treat as mere things as "I-It" relationships: "I know, I know, you'll probably scream 'n' cry / that your little world won't let go! / But who in your measly little world are trying to prove that / You're made out of gold and-a can't be sold."

The singer, instead, is calling to her from a higher plateau where their names are known: "Trumpets and violins I can hear in the distance / I think they're calling our names. / Maybe now you can't hear them, but you will / If you just take hold of my hand."

Experience, then, in the title song, is interactive or interpersonal, a matter of what Buber called "I-You" relationships. It is through intentional physical, non-coercive, reciprocal exchange (holding hands) that they can be free of the small world and find identity (their names are known).

In the absence of interpersonal, reciprocal experience, there seems to be a void or even a death-like state of mind, as in "I Don't Live Today": "Will I live tomorrow? / Well, I just can't say. / Will I live tomorrow? / Well, I just can't say ' / I know for sure I don't live today / Ain't no life nowhere."

Experienced

The absence of interpersonal, I-You relations seems the root of the lamentation, "The Wind Cries Mary." In that song, if there is an interpersonal relationship it is between the wind and the devastation the wind observes with increasing grief. The refrains gain in intensity. It begins with "And the wind whispers Mary," and then moves to "the wind cries Mary," which then escalates to "the wind screams Mary."

The Stability and Coherence of Experience Is Undermined by Vice and Distrust

In "Third Stone from the Sun," the singer exalts in our Earth's seas, mountains, and grass. The phrase "strange beauty" is used twice, "majestic" is used three times, "mysterious Mountains" twice. This makes the last stanza shocking, as the (presumably) powerful alien visitor resolves to put an end to the people of Earth because of their (presumably) senseless (perhaps unjust or wicked) ways: "Although your world wonders me / With your majestic superior cackling hen / Your people I do not understand / So to you I wish to put an end / And you'll never hear surf music again."

Notice that the alien does not set out to destroy the mountains, sea, grass, the animals and plants, just the people. The last line suggests (to me) some humor. I would mind very much being annihilated, whereas I would only be irritated if I had to live without surf music. Still, it's interesting that what marks death in the song is the cessation of experience.

I also interpret the song "Hey Joe" as implying that vice, in the form of a revenge killing out of jealousy, leaves a person without habitation, as Joe becomes a fugitive who must leave everyone ("Goodbye everybody. Ow!").

In significant songs on the album, the lack of reciprocal, trust-worthy love is painful. "Purple Haze" begins with the singer lamenting his disorientation. "Don't know if I'm coming up or down." He lacks an anchor or reference point largely—or so it seems—because "that girl put a spell on me." The song appears to be addressed to that girl, for the singer calls "Help me" three times and requests "tell me" twice. Not knowing she loves him the singer is in a disabling purple haze. "Purple haze all in my eye / Don't know if it's day or night. / You've got me blowin', blowin' my mind / Is it tomorrow or just the end of time?"

"Manic Depression" similarly presents us with a singer who suffers from the unavailability of a trusting, reciprocal love: "Woman so willing the sweet cause in vain, / you make love, you break love, / it's-a all the same when it's . . . when it's over."

The singer also does not find coherence and resolution in "Love or Confusion": "Oh my mind is so messed up / Goin' round and round / Must there be all these colors / Without names, without sound, baby? / My heart burns with feeling, but, / My mind, it's cold and reeling / Is this love baby, / Or is it confusion?"

As with many of the songs, the singer is addressing the desired, beloved person. "You tell me baby, is this love or confusion?" The singer is reaching out for the desired, reciprocal, "I-You" relationship that is valorized in *Are You Experienced*.

Reciprocal Love and Desire Are Liberating

While we've seen that a significant number of songs are lamentations and express unfulfilled desire, there are songs that celebrate desire. Some philosophies treat desire with great cautions, as we find in Stoicism in Ancient Greece and early Buddhist texts.

"Foxy Lady" is not a Stoic or Buddhist song, nor is "Fire." Both songs are erotic, joyful, playful, energized invitations.

"May This Be Love" explicitly lays down testimony that there is great strength and freedom in a loving, reciprocal relationship: "So let them laugh at me, / So long as I have you / To see me through, / I have nothing to lose long as I have you."

Having explored three dimensions of experience in *Are You Experienced*, why might some experiences seem more real to us than others?

Degrees of Reality as Degrees of What Matters to Us

Philosophers in the broad tradition that comes down from Plato hold that we live in a world where there is an order of love. It is good that we should love some things more or less than others. Presumably, we should love justice more than we love hearing a good joke.

We might have tough choices when it comes to ranking what we should love, but our understanding of the meaning of our lives is very much a matter of coming to terms with what we love, how much we love it, and why. If you really love cruelty, you are a cruel person, whereas if you really love caring for others, chances are you are a compassionate person.

As we've seen in this chapter, much of *Are You Experienced* addresses the anguish of unreciprocated love or uncertain, confused love, and a tribute to reciprocal, loving desire. It is at moments in our lives when these values and disvalues come to the fore that our experiences have a vivacity of increased intensity, which is why those experiences can stand out for us as having greater reality than others.

In an important romantic relationship in your life, do you remember the first time you reached out—or accepting the reaching out—of your partner's hand? Or the first kiss? If so, I bet that your memory of that experience is of almost timeless significance. On the other hand, the ending of a relationship can have a searing intensity. In an instant the meaning of your property, your photographs, and all, can have a sudden change of meaning. When one's spouse announces they want a divorce, suddenly your wedding album is on its way to being the album of your ex-spouse or your first marriage.

At the beginning of this chapter I said that we can sometimes have a sense of the increased or intensified reality of everyday, normal experiences. I believe that is true because each moment we are alive and experiencing the world we are experiencing an awesome value: *the fundamental value of simply being alive as an experiencing subject in relation to other persons (the I-You relations) as opposed to being in an impersonal world (the I-It relations).*

This is reinforced by the joyful, playful, mesmerizing beauty of the music itself with its upbeat use of feedback distortions in which cacophony—even noise—is seduced by the melody of Jimi's voice and commanding guitar. The consolation of the bare goodness of experience may be hinted at in "Manic Depression" when Hendrix mixes in with his lament of unreliable love an accolade of the consolation of music: "Music sweet music / I wish I could caress, caress, caress / Manic Depression's a frustrating mess . . . / Music sweet music, / I wish I could caress, and-a-kiss . . ."

It's the melody, the stunning artwork of the rhythm that assures us, or can assure us, of the goodness of experiencing ourselves in an interpersonal life in which we just find satisfaction.

It will occur to you, dear reader, that this thesis of experientialism will seem less than compelling under conditions of great suffering or depression or during times of great crises. Experientialists would concede this point. Just because something is of fundamental value (the bare reality of being a conscious, experiencing being) does not mean that, in the order of love, it may not be better to pursue some other value (the cessation of mind-numbing pain from an incurable disease) rather than a fundamental value. But experientialists urge us to settle such matters, not as a matter of abstract philosophizing but in the context of yours and my actual experiences. Who knows, but, in the midst of great suffering, someone might reach out to you and sing: "Trumpets and violins like up here in the distance, / I think they're calling our names. / Maybe now you can't hear them, but you will / If you just, take hold of my hand."

Maybe you might reply with a "No thanks." But I hope that whatever your stress, you might find in this world life-enhancing "I-You" relationships that make life worth living. Alternatively, you might hold out that "on the other side" of life there is something more, not necessarily a Christian heaven, but a site in which there is a goodness that goes beyond what we currently experience; kissing the sky, after all, is not a normal, natural event. "Purple haze, all in my brain / Lately things they don't seem the same / Actin' funny, but I don't know why. / Excuse me while I kiss the sky."

As I finished this chapter on the fiftieth anniversary of the release of *Are You Experienced*, I sought to kiss the sky. I am pretty sure it did not kiss me back, but you can kiss lots of things that do not kiss back.

It felt good, and as I recommend repeated listening to *Are Your Experienced*, the philosophy of experientialism, I also recommend (every once in a while) at least metaphorically, trying to kiss the sky.[1]

---

[1] Thank you, Ted Ammon. who invited me to visit his philosophy class one spring day in which he enthralled (and perhaps shocked) his students in recounting how Jimi Hendrix's music was life-changing. This chapter is dedicated to Lisa Nankivil and Ardy Magnuson for riotous dialogue on experientialism. Thanks to Dr. Todd Shea for helping me to continue to experience life with his expert surgery.

10
Hendrix Out of the Cave

Francis Métivier

Rock music has its own prejudices: it would not exist without its three muses—sex, alcohol, and drugs. And believe it or not, without philosophy, rock music wouldn't even exist.

Philosophy is Rock's fourth muse, conveying philosophy's questions to Rock, and sometimes philosophy shakes rock music. In the case of Jimi Hendrix, what could we find beyond the shadows of sex, alcohol, and drugs? A philosophical interpretation of the sense of life hides behind Rock music. And a shadow—the shadow of Plato—hovers above the Stratocaster.

In the Allegory of the Cave that Plato develops at the beginning of Book Seven of *Republic*, we're told that men have lived since their birth at the bottom of a cave, chained, facing the bottom wall of the cave. The exit opens behind them, up above, to the outside world.

The cave is the place of natural ignorance, of sense experience, in which prejudices and opinions are formed. These are formed by passing shadows that the prisoners watch on the walls. They live in a world of appearances that they mistake for reality. The prisoner ignores that he is trapped: the ignorant ignores that he ignores.

At the exit, there is a ground-level wall, on which you can see, as if they were puppets, replicas of objects of the external world. It's the shadows of these objects that the prisoners think are real, and that the fire projects. The shadow is a false knowledge, the darkness of intellectual comfort. Turning their heads toward the exit? The motion would be too painful and frightening for a neck numbed with opinions.

"Stone free!" The raw stone must be polished in order to become free, it must come out of its ignorance. It is both an initiation and an experience: to see the true light, the light of the sun, of the Form of the Good. But the prisoners themselves don't have any idea of how to do it.

So, what happens if someone from the outside comes to free one of these prisoners of the cave? To free him, you would have to first be violent with him, drag him, hoist him, hold him and expose his mental slavery, on the natural slope of laziness and cowardliness. Then, once reaching the exit, you would need to be more gentle, for otherwise, the prisoner would die from the transition. Measured brutality and caring are needed for the prisoner who has always lived with illusions, and who must now be shown the reality of the world outside the cave.

Let's imagine Jimi Hendrix having left the cave for a long time, and going back down into it. . . . The music of "Are You Experienced?" is just as allegorical as its lyrics. It is charged, complex: it's the moment when the prisoners find themselves for the first time in the sunlight. But they don't see, they don't understand. The evidence of reality offers itself to them, but they close their eyes, their hands cover eyelids, but the sounds and vibrations from the music continue to penetrate, from ears to chest. If rock music is amplified and surrounds us, it's for us to hear it, even if we cover our ears. In the cave, we were hearing echoes of real speech, those of the chatter of the men passing by on the path above. Outside the cave it's an immense reverberation assaulting the released prisoners in spite of themselves.

The allegorical and acoustic effect of the song is the result of the backward guitar. The wrong side is the right, the beginning the end: from the cave to the outside world, the relationships are reversed. Mitch Mitchell's cymbals also go along with this reverse effect. Hendrix adds some dead notes—strings struck without vibrating—and rubs the edge of his hand on the strings, a perverted use of the instrument, one breath away from scratching rap.

The prisoners do not yet fully believe in the virtues of exiting to the outside world, a backwards long rise punctuated by the impulse to crawl back down to their former habits. The Fender's buzz and the snare drum's roll give a heavy and repetitive temper to this forced walk towards an uncomfortable knowledge. Bend up, bend down: Hendrix strikes his strings, pulls up the moaning prisoner, abused and frightened. Walking towards the truth is always clumsy.

Everything is unstructured. The guitar parts are rather badly defined, melodies of unexpected pulses, of backward riffs and solos. Where do we go when we leave the cave? And still those damned rubs, behind the tempo, as chained slave feet drag bleeding on the ground. The changeovers from verse to chorus are marked by tonality shifts: at the exit of the cave, a new world appears, but it's not a game or a shadowplay. It's a matter of leaving the virtual behind to experience the reality. The sun, the Form of the Good, burns truly and the colors assault us.

The Stratocaster's backward effect reaches its peak in Jimi's solo as if, almost half way, we'd hit rock bottom and needed to start rising again. The allegory is psychedelic: Hendrix opens the doors of consciousness. It is painful, then satisfying. The truth is always satisfying. At the end of the song, the intensity lowers. The prisoner is tired and resigned. Fade out and back to a last signal, a final look down. The prisoners see their comrades. They look so small . . .

Let's rewind and pick up the same movement, this time with lyrics. The prisoner's head is chained, and watches, and as in a movie theater, the shadows come and go. Hendrix comes to grab it, this time with his voice. While the ignorant were hearing only their neighbors' chatter and echoes of voices coming from far behind, here a deep voice sings in his ears.

The prisoner is startled. "Come on across to me." Why? The prisoner was comfortably numb in the cotton of his perceptions. Someone comes from elsewhere. The prisoner discovers mobility, the possibility to move, to not be a fixed plant or a mushroom anymore. "If you can just get your mind together." The spirit can always wander about. But at what cost? The voice says: "We'll hold hands." The prisoner needs to be taken and brought elsewhere. Kind and steady hand, iron hand in a velvet glove.

"We'll all watch the sun rise from the bottom of the sea." The initiated does not intend, once outside, to put the prisoner in a new stranglehold, with instruments spreading his eyes open as in *A Clockwork Orange*. Knowledge isn't slaughter. The prisoner is used to reflections: the sunrise will be seen through a softened image, a reflection at the bottom of the water, so that the supreme Form, the Good, is approached by the Ocean of the Beautiful. He learns color.

And when the time comes to leave the world of grey shades, in that instant when the prisoner begins to understand, in that instant when, in his mind, the conversion was just completed despite the pain, Hendrix, philosophical master of ceremonies as he is, asks a ritual question: "But first. Are you experienced? Have you ever been experienced?"

"Are you experienced?" Hendrix asks his prisoner. "But first, are you experienced?" Have you had that initiation experience: the exit from ignorance? It almost seems like a question of secret words, of which the answer to the mystic question would be rather in spirit than in language. However, if he first has to be initiated before he can see the sun at the bottom of the ocean, the prisoner cannot prevent himself from wondering whether he will come back to prison.

"You'll probably scream and cry." His body cries but his soul is happy. He is ready, ready not to be a prisoner. "Cry baby" is the name of Hendrix' wah-wah pedal, which goes from a moan of grief to a moan of deliverance. The initiator knows this pain for he too, as all people, came from the cave. Exiting the cave is a political gesture, an emancipation from conformity and social pressure: "Your little world won't let you go". To vulgar people, imagination is void, thought is narrow and petty: "measly little world". The prisoners want to widen their consciousness and move towards the light.

"Have you ever been experienced? Well, I have". Hendrix is initiated, and so does the prisoner become. Philosophy and rock music effect transformations. Hendrix has lived this experience and now he is a master coming back to the cave to help others. He knows the light that shows us all that exists. His soul is lit up. The essential part of the initiation is to feel possession of your soul. The prisoners had souls, naturally, but they weren't aware of it: they must climb the hill and confront the light for the intellectual transformation to take place, for the being to untie, that psychedelic approach which derives, etymologically, from making the soul—*psyché*—visible—*déloun*.

They also need to bathe in the ocean of reality. "Ah let me prove it to you": the best proof is to go see it, to go do it. The clues are enticing: "Trumpets and violins, I can hear in the distance." The prisoner hears real sounds in the vast, beautiful sounds, not copies of distorted sounds anymore, not a suffocating, acoustic magma anymore. He does not yet understand the sense of these sounds. It's probably still too early but he feels the desire to stay. "Not necessarily stoned, but beautiful." Beautiful? Not stoned? What? The soul? Yes, it is now bathing in the ocean of the beautiful, where we have to swim to get to the ideas. Another level to overcome?

"Are You Experienced?" is a psychedelia free of hallucinations. It opens up consciousness without the use of LSD, just through an exercise of liberation from the prevailing opinion. The experience means abandoning prefabricated prejudices. While Hendrix burns his Stratocaster and fuels the flames with his mesmerizing fingers, he has ignoted Plato's fire, the fire that stands at the exit of the cave, the fire that certainly creates the shadows but that also forms a necessary step towards the outside.

Hendrix is an initiator, a guide. To what? A philosophic light that shows fire, reality, and ideas, as Harry Shapiro and Caesar Glebbeek suggest in *Jimi Hendrix: Electric Gypsy*:

> Sexual ecstasy? Altered states of consciousness? Or just finding yourself, taking time out to view what you're doing from the outside, 'from the bottom of the sea', letting go of the daily grind of the 'measly world'. It is all there for the taking. The secret is being at peace with yourself—'not necessarily stoned, but beautiful'. (p. 180)

Let's stop for a moment at that artificial zone, with that wall, the people passing by on the path, and the fire of the mystic immolation, the Stratocaster. Is it not a factory? The men are the manufacturers of both illusion and signals assuming the hypothesis of a world outside that of the cave.

The initiated, when rising towards the outside, pass by this sort of theater of puppets and projectionist. That is where the spirit perceives the colors. Beginning with . . . purple. The psychedelic effect can be produced, not necessarily by drugs, but by philosophy. Leaving the cave is philosophical. The psychedelia can refer to Hendrix's music, as he is inspired by the use of the hallucinogenic drugs that aggravate the strange and already vivid colors. But in fact, philosophically, the sounds are not strange and the colors not vivid. We just see it that way.

The passing through the machinery translates into a wonder before the discovery of the purple haze, probably produced by an inside mister. If "Are You Experienced?" is an initiatory song, "Purple Haze" is an experimental song. That experience is, above all, musical, the one of the power trio of which the sounds interlock around Hendrix famous guitar chord E7#9, special harmony, open and amplified just like Plato's spirit.

But there again, the complex evidence of the outside world assaults the prisoner, between the Larsen effects, wah-wah, mixes of hard rock and jazz, of heavy and light sounds. Wah reminds of the *"wow"* of amazement: stress of the vowell of the amazement and the extension of the spirit's resonance. Fear and enjoyment. That place is an event: it produces a new fact. A first rock gig where the difference is no longer between the guitar's rhythmic play and the solo play. The difference between solo and riff fades as well. It's an absolute sound where the voice chips in, mixing articulated chant, spoken words, yells, bushmen rattle, interjections—ooh—sighs—Aaaah . . . —affirmation of pleasure—hmmm—and pleading moans—Oh, no no . . .

The "Purple Haze" guitar intro is like a three-stage plane takeoff—positioning on the track, full gas speeding, and takeoff—or even a horseback riding episode: gait . . . trot . . . gallop . . . The song begins with two octave tones evoking the offset between two levels of reality, cave and outside world, or yet again, sensed world and intelligible world. In the Woodstock version, the two octave tones remind us of a donkey braying. We resolutely don't understand anything anymore, except the ambiguity itself of the sound, expressing a mix of pleasant and unpleasant.

A purple haze invades at the same time the prisoner's subjectivity—"Purple haze all in my brain"— and the outside world—"all around". The relationship between the subject and the world is perception: "Purple haze all in my eyes". What is this purple haze? From its author's confession, the song has a biographical origin: Hendrix dreams that he walks at the bottom of the oceans. The same self projection as in "Are You Experienced?" We no longer contemplate the sun's reflection in the bottom of the ocean, we dive into it to go reach and touch the major fire.

With "Where Is My Mind?" from the Pixies, the seabeds form the metaphor of a trial, one of the invaded, possessed soul, merging within the nature, the sea, mother nature, merger with the whole-everything. I am lava: am I the one releasing that smoke? Either way, the haze places Hendrix and his prisoners in a transformed reality: "Lately things just don't seem the same." The action in this new place is perceived as normal: "Actin' funny, but I don't know why." The spirit, fascinated by this purple haze, has itself become a purple haze, freeing itself from all ordinary sociability. The old me is dislocated.

There can exist another interpretation, rather classic, of the symbolism of the purple haze: the one that has blown his mind. She is an evil girl: "Whatever it is, that girl put a spell on me." But we thus place ourselves in an allegorical abyss: could the girl herself symbolize the drugs, a double meaning for "heroine"?

"'Scuse me while I kiss the sky." Why apologize? The prisoners probably think of their old comrades from whom they're escaping. He apologizes to them but he prefers that irresistible attraction to the skies, the blue, the gods, Plato's forms. "Sorry fellas, my new life is calling me up . . ." The physical and psychological senses of one's self are troubled. The prisoner has lost the shapes of his corporal pattern and, unexperienced, mixes the directions in space: "Don't know if I'm comin' up or down." The temporal references fade away as well—"is it tomorrow or just the end of time?"—in the confusion between obscurity and light: "Don't know if it's day or night". In the end, the prisoners are not able anymore to distinguish their own state of mind: "Am I happy or in misery?" Quite normal: in the cave, he only had one state of mind. "Kiss the sky" is the key moment of the in-between, between the cave and the outside world, tension, technologic and stupefying conciliation, unstable equilibrium between unconscious enslavement and call for freedom.

Hendrix's Platonic experience ends in the prisoner's delirium, a cry made to his master: "Help me help me Oh no no . . . no . . . no . . ." Yes or no? A choice must be made: to exit completely or to return down there. But the former prisoner, still detoxed of his *doxa*, cannot remain there, backstage, within the artist's secret. He must create his own path in the great plain of ideas. He must end up freeing himself of the presence of Plato and Hendrix, think for himself, find his own play. Otherwise, he will be nothing but a pale copy, a stooge, of those who raise objects on the path and create prejudices.

IV

Music Sweet Music

11
Vibrations and Echoes Long Ago

DENNIS LOUGHREY

It's tempting to forget the underlying technology upon which Hendrix's music was based—tempting because there is so much about Hendrix himself to consider. Just think of his nonchalance, his short life span, his toothy nuttiness, his looking as if he didn't eat his greens. Think too of how bold and different his musical imagination was, somewhere between Link Wray and the Man Who Fell to Earth. It is hardly surprising that our culture remains lit-up by a romantic image of Hendrix, as well as by a romantic interpretation of the music as the work of a genius.

Yet there is also a different story—the story of the recording technology that became available in the 1960s. This story involves cutting-edge innovations in music making, including feedback, changes of speed, and backwards reel-to-reel playing. This was the sound engineering that transformed Jimi Hendrix. It also transforms us, changing our perceptions, enabling us see the world in new ways.

The Isle Is Full of Noises

His name was Jimi Hendrix, and he recorded in England. This was the English Hendrix. Yet even with Hendrix's talent, the music industry in 1960s England must have seemed an unlikely place to achieve something new. With the benefit of hindsight, though, that impression changes.

Olympic Studios was new and it possessed a functional control room. Sound engineers such as Eddie Kramer exploited the capacity of their equipment with a package of novel techniques. Kramer's approach was experimental. He was a most excellent experimenter and assembler of sounds.

There was a tradition in England of such experimental sound making. The center of gravity of this experimentation lay in the BBC Radiophonic Workshop, which operated from the 1950s onwards. Some very talented music makers including George Martin worked there. The Workshop created the special sound effects for the early BBC science-fiction favorite, *Quatermass and the Pit.* Later, in 1963, Delia Derbyshire created the original *Doctor Who* theme. Derbyshire's musical interests advanced during her astonishingly creative years with the Workshop.

The word "workshop" suggests a place in which ordinary things are made. What Derbyshire and her colleagues served to make, though, was the eeriest, most disembodied sound effects for broadcasting ever heard. Their work left a generation of children with a love of TV and radio science fiction. When watching the pictures on TV or listening to the words on the radio, the children could hear the strange other-worldly sounds cut in, increase in volume, and fade. Pictures, words, and sounds merged. The sounds enhanced the children's media experiences.

And the output of the Radiophonic Workshop did something else. It nurtured these children, affecting their perceptions, offering them the possibility of seeing, or rather hearing, something of the vastness and unpredictability of space and time, and of sensing that they were part of that vastness and unpredictability. The children were guided beyond the average everyday way of experiencing things, the kind in which you stand apart from the world, and tell yourself you're not really part of it. Their experience was enriched to the extent that they could perceive other worlds, and other times, and in an immersive and playful way.

If anyone ever needed a reason to believe in the value of publicly-funded broadcasting, then the exemplary BBC Radiophonic Workshop provided it. And this story does not end with children. The Workshop did more to inspire early Pink Floyd and Jimi Hendrix than strong drugs ever did. Media theorist Friedrich Kittler has remarked that romantic poetry was the LSD of the nineteenth-century romantic era. Let me add to that, this: the Radiophonic sound was the LSD of the LSD era.

The business of the Radiophonic Workshop was producing new and innovative sound assemblies. Such innovations drove other innovations. Most famously, there was the music making of George Martin and the later Beatles, who breathed new directions into the innovations. Made in Abbey Road Studios, the *Revolver* album performed loops and backwards playing effects. *Sgt. Pepper's*, another Abbey Road product, stretched to an even wider array of effects. Later, the *Magical Mystery Tour* EP came out. On it, the exceptional song, "I Am the Walrus," dreamy and English and barmy, consisted of a layering of sound in which a radio tuner is used as input, resulting in recorded snatches of radio broadcasts, including an excerpt from *King Lear*. This happy music-making tradition continued as the *Sgt. Pepper's* and *Mystery Tour*–obsessed King Crimson took to the way of prog.

The Jimi Hendrix albums majored in different sound processes. Yet these albums also revised and deepened the new sound techniques of the day. Working on the Hendrix sound were some very clever innovators. These were Kramer himself, the staunch Chas Chandler, and others as well, including, pretty obviously, Hendrix. Together they developed the components of a furious and dense sound texture that was characteristic of the Hendrix recordings. What Abbey Road did, Olympic Studios did too, only in a twitchy, driven way. They produced the sound of tomorrow, today—yesterday.

In the Beginning Was the Sound

What was it about Olympic? It was not exactly a magic toyshop. So what then? Well, as in the case of Abbey Road, so too at Olympic, we need to bear in mind that nothing less than a set of logical processes was set up. The outline of this was simple enough. The studio—like a person, and like a computer—had a memory. This was the tape. Olympic used four-track machines rather than eight-track. Despite this limitation, the tape provided storage for the sound material that was to be worked on. During sessions, the engineers used the output of various sound effects—from instruments, amplifiers and the memory itself—as inputs by storing them in the memory. As a result of the changed states of the memory, the process of recording functioned as a performing instrument. The result was a sensational, yet logical, distortion of sound.

The technological innovations on display in the sound recordings of Hendrix fascinated other musicians. Mitch Mitchell of the Jimi Hendrix Experience has observed that *Sgt. Pepper's* marked the point at which everybody in the music industry started to listen closely to everybody else's recordings, attempting to determine how the new sound effects were produced, all this with an eye to reproducing them, and to extending them. Although Mitchell was being a little modest, since the Hendrix album *Are You Experienced* preceded *Sgt. Pepper's*, it is a good point. When new sounds arrive, artists actively want to learn from them, and what Mitchell describes is the way that new technological knowledge is circulated and amplified.

This is a powerful idea about musicians' learning from the work of other musicians. As a practice of close listening sprung up on the part of musicians, the listening process was modified by the effects of the listening. There was a fascinating feedback effect as other artists listened to, and emulated, the new music. It is hard to convey the extent of the influence.

And it was not only musicians who were attracted. Ordinary listeners—although "ordinary" hardly seems to be the word when we are talking about the music of Jimi Hendrix, for this is not music for everyone, and certainly not background listening—met the challenges of these new studio albums. These listeners became more open to the new ways of hearing the world, thus also creating a kind of feedback. The experience of listening produced a demand for more such new music, which inspired further innovations in music, a demand which the music industry worked to fulfill.

Silver Sound from a Time So Strange

The relationship between sound technology and the listener is a fascinating one. Few have explored the relationship farther than the aforementioned Friedrich Kittler. In his book *Gramophone, Film, Typewriter*, Kittler gives an account of Pink Floyd's post-Syd Barrett song "Fat Old Sun" from their *Atom Heart Mother* album. The recording of this song has a singer-narrator who seems to be playing a recording. The sound of this recording within a recording is described as "silver." Kittler wonders about the source of the silver sound. Is it the singer-narrator on the recording (Dave Gilmour), or the voice on the recording within the recording, or a voice from inside the listener's head? Such distinctions break down in this piece of music. There is, as Kittler puts it, an "unimaginable closeness of sound technology and self-awareness."

The heart of Kittler's view is that technology—whether computing or sound recording technology—is not a tool that we use, but rather that such "media determine our situation." This sounds really interesting. But what does it mean? Well, Kittler was particularly influenced by a claim made by Nietzsche. Upon becoming an early adopter of the typewriter, Nietzsche remarked that such machines were "working on our thoughts." Nietzsche did come out with interesting things. And so did Kittler, which is my way of saying that I find something really likeable here, and that is Kittler 's writing about the relationship between technology and us—and music, we mustn't forget the music. You don't find much music in philosophy.

But I am not going to pretend that I am not confused about some of this writing. I don't mind a bit of obscurity, but Kittler's way of formulating an argument seems to me puzzling. Fortunately, Geoffrey Winthrop-Young does a beneficial job in his book *Kittler and the Media* in presenting Kittler in a favorable light. In fact, Winthrop-Young does such a good job that he quite possibly makes Kittler's arguments sound more plausible than they really are. But be that as it may, there is something interesting in Kittler's insights about music technology and us, and his view should be part of a larger, improved view.

An equally audacious, though surely clearer, analysis of the nature of the relationship between us and technology is provided by two philosophers, Andy Clark and David Chalmers. They have worked together and independently.

Together, they have come up with what they call the extended mind thesis. This thesis states that our minds are not confined to our heads. Rather, our minds extend outside our heads, and include iPhones and other such devices, and also low-tech extensions, such as a blind person's walking stick. In a video, Chalmers cites the example of Hendrix's mind extending to his electric guitar. Like Kittler, Clark and Chalmers see a blurred line between our minds and our technology. Kittler's view seems to be that we are technology's extension. Unlike Kittler, Clark and Chalmers see our technology as an extension of our minds.

Individually, Clark and Chalmers have thought about augmented reality. Augmented reality contrasts with virtual reality. Augmented reality is not as immersive as virtual reality. The gist of augmented reality is that it is part real world, part digital reality. It's a mixed kind of reality, in which virtual objects are superimposed on reality. In a podcast, Chalmers discusses a famous example—the game of *Pokémon Go*. When playing *Pokémon Go*, virtual characters—computer-generated images—are mixed with the user's own view, through the camera of their phone, of the real world.

The sounds of Jimi Hendrix recording can usefully be discussed in this connection. Of course, the Hendrix recordings are not digital in the sense that *Pokémon Go* is. There is, though, something very similar about the Hendrix recording and the game. Just as *Pokémon Go* makes possible our interaction with the processes of our phone, so too does a Jimi Hendrix recording make possible our interaction with the processes that made that recording. These processes have their origin in Olympic Studios. Through the medium of the recording, studio-generated sounds mix with our vision of the world, changing it, augmenting it.

Of course, there is one clear difference between the game and the recording. The game is *digital*. By playing the game, you can therefore enjoy the responsiveness, the personalisation, the networkability, and the fastness of digital technology. Even if you listen to Hendrix by way of a digital recording, the recording processes at Olympic Studios were analog. They were from a different age, one before the microprocessor. So we can't apply the authoritative-sounding name, augmented reality, to a Hendrix recording. But is this what matters?

Consider the music recording industry. Digital recording processes mimic to a large extent the analog processes. For example, digital processes can mimic some of the backwards-playing, looping and feedback effects that we have discussed in connection with the experimental Hendrix processes. Digital recording can do this quickly and efficiently. But no matter how fast and efficient, it is merely a mimicking of the processes that we have from the Hendrix studio sessions. We don't gain anything that we don't already possess.

Besides, sound recordings are the reverse of children in Victorian times: heard, but not seen. *Pokémon Go* and other forms of augmented reality are powerful because they add new images to our view of the world. But what we have in the recordings of Hendrix are not images that can be superimposed on our view of the world, but *sounds* that can be superimposed on our view of the world. And these sounds are mixed with our view of the world, augmenting it.

Like an augmented reality game, the recordings can change our perceptions and help us to perceive new objects in the world—a new composite world. It can augment our reality. In fact, it could be argued that of the two, the Hendrix recordings are the more immersive. *Pokémon Go* is a game that people, both individually and collectively, have tended to lose interest in after a while. It's hard to imagine this happening with Hendrix. *Pokémon Go* is more Engelbert Humperdinck than rock'n'roll. The Hendrix recordings not only change our view of the world, and are significantly immersive, but they also continue to produce their effect.

Is It Tomorrow or Just the End of Time?

It's time to provide a fuller account of the change of perceptions that are produced in the Hendrix listener. I shall do this by considering some examples from the Hendrix studio recordings. So extraordinary, though, is the sound world to be examined, I do not progress beyond the first of the studio recordings, and in fact I only get as far as the two songs that bookend that album.

Consider first the masterpiece "Purple Haze" from *Are You Experienced*. Jimi Hendrix once claimed that "Purple Haze" is a love song. This is not a love song. Hendrix, I believe, was being unassuming about the nature of the song. It *is* true that Hendrix's songs often involve the lyrics of love. But such lyrics function to provide our bearings within the songs. It is in this way that I have used quotations from songs as some of the subheadings in this chapter. By contrast, the processes of the recording provide the immersive order of the sounds themselves.

It is there, hiding in plain sight, in "Purple Haze." The song's music-making processes—the feedback, the changes in speed, and the backwards playing—deliver us to the dynamic world of the sound. No song better exemplifies the extent of Kramer's sound creations. Kramer took a simple Chandler recording, optimized it in the mixing stage, and assembled the final product. The song comprises layer upon layer of recorded sound. These are strange operations: studio echoes and a kind of spasmodic sound produced by the recording and playback of Hendrix's guitar, disrupting the listener's sense of time.

Like writing, time is linear. It follows continuously from beginning to end. It does not stop. Or does it? Consider two quite different writers on time.

For the first, turn to the results of research about currency traders, as described by Katherine N. Hayles. These traders, who are employed by international banks, are in direct competition with other traders. They sit at their computer terminals for long shifts, and their inputs consist of their phones and their screens. The latter dominate their workspace. The foreign exchange conducts business around the clock. The market is "everything all the time." Yet the traders manage to create a space for themselves within passing time—"temporality becomes a place to inhabit." The fast-changing unfolding of the market on their screens changes the traders' perceptions to such an extent that they are able to experience time as a place in which they can dwell.

For the second view of time, consider Tom McCarthy's inventive novel *Remainder*, in which the serviceable villain Samuels provides a philosophy of armed robbery. Samuels explains that, when a robbery in in progress, the situation is a contest between bank robbers and bank staff. The robber's aim is "to carve out enough time for yourself." You do this by firing your gun in the air, creating "a suspension in which you can operate. A little enclave, a defile." Meanwhile, the bank staff's thoughts rush headlong, caused by fear.

On both these views, continuous time is presented as something that you can hack. There is a kind of secret passage, and the technology will help you find it. Samuels is old-school. For him, a "frightener" is sufficient to do the trick. By contrast, the currency traders are very up-to-date, and they create their passage in time by making use of more high-tech devices. Hayles points out that the traders are mostly men, and that their culture is one of fierce competition. (Hayles looks at an interesting implication of this observation, that there are factors other than the media that, as Kittler would say, "determine our situation.") The same could be said about Samuels on armed bank robbery. Those involved are mainly men, and very competitive, as well. Both traders and robbers interpret their situations from a capitalist view of the world.

The listeners of Jimi Hendrix have quite different world views. I remarked earlier that there is nothing "ordinary" about such listeners. They are people who are open to the new ways of experiencing the world. The song "Purple Haze" is perfect for such listeners. The song seems to come from elsewhere. It conveys no sense of identity. Nor does it provide comfort for listeners who already view themselves in a fixed kind of way. It is *alien*. It is for people who want to get away from all of that.

There is time in the song, and it is continuous time, but there is no secret passage to be carved out from it. Listening to this music, we see that the existence of such a passage is either self-deception or wishful thinking, the product of the sort of fantasies that are part of the capitalistic, competitive, everyday world. The music of Jimi Hendrix invites no such responses. On the contrary, the processes originating in Olympic studio, made available to us through the medium of a recording, return us to a pure sound world. Our perception of time is altered, but in quite a different and rather uncosy way. Our sense of time is disoriented. We find ourselves lost in time.

Unlike Samuels, we cannot carve a place out of time's continuity. Yet why should we think that carving out such a defile is a good thing? The idea belongs to the childhood stories of Enid Blyton, with its hidden treasures and its secret passages. But this is the music of Jimi Hendrix. We are not robbing a bank, or trading on the foreign exchange. We are sitting in a room, listening to music. We can afford to enjoy the sense of being lost in time, and approach it with a spirit of play. It is interesting. We can kill a bit of time.

There is another studio variation encoded in "Purple Haze." This is a powerful panorama effect. As you listen to the song, you become very aware of a moving of space—back and forth—before you. Left and right change places, and there is no place for the senses to settle. While this happens, the uncanny Purple Haze chorus occupies the background, or is it the foreground? There is a kind of tilting effect.

We are in a strange and distant place, disoriented, wandering through a haze. As with our sense of time, our sense of space is disrupted. Everything moves, the landscape changes as in a dream. This situation is not something to dread, though. We are listening to a brilliant piece of music. Why should we assume that we need to reach a destination? We can enjoy our wanderings, our disorientation. Perhaps there is some good to be had in being lost. There is certainly something intense about it, wherever we are. There is playfulness. We seem to go nowhere, and yet we do not need to go anywhere.

This is no ordinary music. Forget the lyrics (Hendrix did, on occasion). This is music that makes us aware of the world, exactly as it is: vast, yet moving, a world without refuge. Listening, we perceive a world in which we are lost, disorientated. Yet the experience is not terrifying. It is like the experience of listening to the science-fiction sounds of the Radiophonic Workshop. The sounds extend our perceptions beyond the ordinary way of seeing or hearing. We perceive a world that was created in the Olympic Studios for us. We gain access to the Hendrix ear.

Just Get Your Mind Together

Turn now to my second example, "Are You Experienced?," the last track on the album of the same name. This is not a love song either. In fact, it is more subtle than a love song, at least as we know love songs. It is an assemblage of parts, a masterpiece of deep overdubbing. And like a child's playing, this song affects the perceptions.

It does so by way of the practice of recording passages containing the guitar solo, the base and the drums, and then flipping the tape, playing the sounds backwards, everything in sync. The sound leaps, and it travels in opposite directions. As in "Purple Haze," we launch into a recast sense of the world, but on this occasion it is not in perceiving passing time or moving space in a disoriented way.

Rather we open ourselves to new perspectives of height and depth. This is disorienting in a new way. New perceptions are made available to us. We experience the world from "the bottom of the sea" as we watch the sun rise. To see the world from different points of view, to acquire distance, these are what we gain from listening to this song. Hearing the world differently: ways of hearing that are not the ways that other people hear, the people in "your measly little world". We hear how not to be part of such shared ways of hearing. We realize that the possibility of an escape from the go-ahead narrative of everyday life is open to us.

The song enables a kind of diving under and soaring above the surface of the everyday world. It is like the experience of playing *Pokémon Go*, only more immersive, and more disruptive. We are able to get our mind together, but not in the sense that we can find a place somewhere inside us that is still. Quite the opposite. We find that being disoriented can be interesting and fun. We can learn to like the disorientation, and to feel part of it. Experiencing changing states enables us to see and hear the world as it is, not as other people like to see and hear it. And we can do this thanks to the processes that were run in a music recording studio in England long ago.

Coda

Some might be surprised about the possibility of our interacting with processes executed in a recording studio back in time. Such people might think that listening to a Hendrix recording does not augment our reality.

Then try this thought experiment. Imagine the recorded music of Hendrix without the sort of music-making studio processes that I have described. What would remain? It would be a kind of Hendrix unplugged. It would comprise the song lines, Hendrix's voice, and the language of his guitar. It would be a faithful representation of Hendrix and his guitar. Imagine listening to it now. What would it sound like? Well, it would be fine, and perhaps enjoyable, to listen to.

Yet there would be something important missing. Lovely as the sound might be, there would be something of the object about the recording, because that's what representations are. Now imagine listening to an actual existing studio recording, with its artful effects, such as backwards playing, and changes of speed, encoded in the music. We would hear the dynamic, innovative music-making processes of the Olympic Studios, and they would become mixed in our world. We would interact with them, and experience a new way of hearing the world. Fellow listeners, we can experience it now.

12
The Broken Pieces of Yesterday's Life

ROBERT G. BOATRIGHT AND
MOLLY BRIGID FLYNN

The year one of us was twelve, his big Christmas gift from his parents was a stereo—the old compact kind, with all the components in one unit. Although it was 1982, his parents inexplicably gave him a machine with an eight-track player, which was almost thoroughly obsolete by that time. The only place he could find eight-tracks was in the discount bin at the local Woolworth's. It was there that he found the first Jimi Hendrix album he purchased, a 1971 compilation entitled *Jimi Hendrix Together with Lonnie Youngblood*.

It was terrible! Its sound quality was inferior to the average bootleg recording, the two performers had absolutely no chemistry, and the song selection was particularly uninspired. Rob's twelve-year-old self was bitterly disappointed—why did the older brothers of all of his friends worship Hendrix? It took some diligence for him to figure out what the "real" Hendrix recordings were.

This experience was surely not unusual for Gen-Xers like us, even though purchase of an eight-track tape was. There are only four official Hendrix albums released during his lifetime with his full co-operation—the three Experience albums and the live *Band of Gypsies* album. According to allmusicguide's listing, however, there are over 380 other Hendrix albums available—a list that includes compilations, outtakes, live recordings, picture discs, interviews, and a wide range of random collaborations. Eighty of these were released during the decade immediately after Hendrix's death—an extraordinary amount for the pre-compact disc era. Some of these are quite good, and some were released with some measure of support and involvement from Hendrix's former bandmates. Some are the type of relatively inoffensive repackagings that record labels tend to engage in to entice aging baby boomers to buy yet another CD of the greatest hits of their youth. But many have an undeniable "scraping the bottom of the barrel" quality. We have evidence that Hendrix himself was concerned during his lifetime about the release of subpar, unauthorized recordings, and a clear case can be made that Hendrix's legacy has been sullied by the flood of posthumous releases.

Hendrix was particularly unlucky in this regard. The posthumous discographies of other early decedents of that era are far shorter and far less shoddy. Similarly, many bands of that era that broke up (and more or less stayed broken up) also managed to exercise effective control over their posthumous releases, usually limiting themselves to a greatest hits compilation or two, a well-curated album of their best unreleased tracks, or a carefully mastered live album or two. Hendrix's post-death oeuvre has served as a warning to other rock stars of the consequences of dying without a musical will.

This may strike some readers as an antiquated concern. The primacy of the rock album, with the lyric sheet, the fancy gatefold sleeve, and the suitable-for-framing cover, has certainly passed. Music consumers download songs, not albums, and YouTube playlists make few distinctions between officially sanctioned releases and surreptitiously filmed concert footage. Similar paradigms exist outside the realm of rock music. As more of us get our information online, the primacy of the novel, the feature movie, or the elite journal of ideas or academic research is declining and access to everything, anytime, anywhere, has been democratized. Even apart from these contemporary developments, library archives abound with the unpublished materials of past writers, artists, politicians, and other figures. We might ask, incredulously, what right does anyone, including the creator of this work, have to restrict our freedom to access such material? When does the right to privacy or control over one's effects override the historical and aesthetic values of collectors?

Does Hendrix have a right to be judged based solely on the material that he intended to release? Can we separate the persona Hendrix sought to present to the world from that which emerged through the efforts of family, acquaintances, and record company executives to profit from his unreleased recordings after his death? Should we? Or, to put this on a more personal level, should Rob have been able to purchase that crummy eight-track, and should he have purchased it?

We contend here that there is no particular reason why the recording should have been available, but that the notion of "rights" in this circumstance is inapt. It's not clear that Hendrix has any sort of moral right not to be judged based on this recording, but it is equally unclear that we have any right to have access to such things. Ultimately, however, the responsibility is ours, not that of Hendrix or any of those associated with him—what we call our "prudential discernment" should lead us to discount the role such things play in shaping how we understand any artist, or human being.

Some Antecedents, Real and Imagined

There are a variety of comparisons we can make between Hendrix and other performers. Hendrix, who died on September 17th 1970, was one of three prominent rock stars to die of drug-related causes within the same year.

Janis Joplin died on October 4th 1970, and Jim Morrison, of the Doors, died on July 3rd 1971. Joplin did not leave behind a large body of work; *Pearl*, a studio album that had been largely competed before her death, was released in 1971, and a greatest hits album and a live album were released by her record label over the subsequent two years. Various compilations and live recordings have been released since, but they have been more or less the same material, only reorganized and repackaged for the CD era. There was no vault of material—or if there was, it has been closely guarded.

In Morrison's case, his bandmates vigilantly maintained the band's reputation. After the release of one unsuccessful album without Morrison, the band allowed the release of a greatest hits album in 1973 and a soundtrack to a movie about the group in 1978. A few other, less legitimate releases trickled out, but the Doors' handful of official posthumous releases made a much larger splash than did the flood of Hendrix releases. The Doors' decisions to manage their legacy this way was probably in their business interest.

We can, however, find cases where the profit motive was not the sole reason for posthumous frugality. The Beatles, who conveniently owned their own record label, released a pair of greatest hits double albums in the decade following their breakup, but they never sought to put together a collection of oddities, B-sides, or other such recordings. They definitely had some high quality songs in the vault—we know this because of the existence of the *Get Back!* Bootleg, and they certainly could have made a tidy profit. Maybe they simply didn't need the money or couldn't resolve their own personal disputes enough to agree on these. Led Zeppelin, whose career ended abruptly in 1980 with the death of drummer John Bonham, released one carefully curated album of oddities (*Coda*), included a few more as a bonus disc in a CD boxed set, and, in 2003 the band released a live recording of what had always been rumored to be one of its best shows. A handful of less-legitimate releases trickled out, but the band was said to have exercised tight control of its recordings. The Velvet Underground had a similar posthumous career; the band did not became very popular until long after its breakup, and the band was able to assemble a boxed set and two rarities compilations (*VU* and *Another VU*) in the mid-1980s, capitalizing on the popularity that had eluded it during its career. And then there are artists like Nick Drake, who was largely unknown while he was alive but became famous after his death and after the careful repackaging of his recorded work.

The demise of all of these artists was unexpected (except, perhaps, for the Beatles). It has served as a warning, however, to others. A single firm—Jampol Artist Management—manages the posthumous careers of most of the more prominent deceased rock stars (including Morrison and Joplin, as well as Michael Jackson, Tupac Shakur, and the Ramones), with a goal of balancing long-term profitability and artistic integrity. (See the Jampol website and the articles by Stefanie Cohen and Jonathan Edwards.) Since 2003 Jampol has overseen album rereleases, movies, Broadway musicals, commercial licensing, and other means of keeping dead artists in the public eye and burnishing their legacy. As some of the performers of Hendrix's generation have approached more predictable deaths, they have sought to play a more personal role in managing their legacy. During 2016, for instance, David Bowie and Leonard Cohen both released albums that seem like valedictory statements and that included lyrics that discussed their imminent deaths.

Hendrix's experience is also not just about his death; he lost control of some of his recordings while he was still alive, and according to David Moskowitz one of the most popular Hendrix recordings, the *Smash Hits* compilation, was released without sanction from Hendrix or his bandmates. Given that rock stardom often strikes people who are too young or inexperienced to negotiate their recording contracts wisely, some subsequent bands have been onlookers as their careers unfolded without their involvement. The Sex Pistols, who released only one "official" album, are a prime example of this—the band allegedly reformed in the 2000s in part to reclaim the ability to profit from its own recordings. This sort of chaos has, however, influenced other punk-inspired bands to thumb their noses at the distinction between the official "oeuvre" and less polished recordings. Guided by Voices, for instance, have deliberately released albums at a dizzying pace, mixing polished songs with slapdash experiments and studio out-takes. The band's entire ethos has involved a decision to abandon the sort of pretensions that are supposed to characterize the rock musician as "recording artist."

If rock music strikes the reader as trivial—if it's hard to imagine benefit or harm stemming from the availability of *Jimi Hendrix Together with Lonnie Youngblood* at that long-gone Woolworth's—it is instructive to consider examples from philosophy and literature. Scholars have no qualms whatsoever about mining archived collections of great writers' personal papers as grist for their dissertations. And there are many examples of such work entering the public sphere. Charles de Secondat, Baron de Montesquieu, author of *The Spirit of the Laws* and *The Persian Letters*, left behind notebooks published as *Pensées* (translated in English as *My Thoughts*). This was a common practice among French intellectuals of the era. The *Pensées* include much that is trivial, yet usually delightful to read, such as Montesquieu's reflections on birds that he had observed. Yet the book also contains many vital technical details on Montesquieu's works—the rationale for the order of chapters in *The Spirit of the Laws*, for instance, and Montesquieu's thoughts on the accuracy of reviewers' commentary on and criticism of the book. These sections aid scholars in understanding what Montesquieu sought to do and how his work influenced seventeenth-century French society.

We can usefully contrast Montesquieu with Adam Smith. Smith published only two major works in his lifetime, although he intended to do much more. According to Montgomery and Chirot's recounting of his life, Smith left behind no journal, collection of letters, or other personal documentation of his thoughts. Smith wrote two books (*The Theory of Moral Sentiments* and *The Wealth of Nations*) and there is some speculation that he had much grander writing plans in mind. His decision to destroy his documents, however, has likely deprived the scholarly world of the opportunity to see how Smith believed these books fit together or where he was headed in his intellectual odyssey. We have a few other fragments from his life—students' notes, his reviews of others' work, and some other miscellaneous papers that his executors collected—but if we really wish to discuss Smith's thought, we are limited to those two books.

The case of Friedrich Nietzsche presents a more troubling story of what can happen to a writer after his death. There has been a longstanding academic debate about potential manipulation of Nietzsche's later writings by his sister, Elisabeth Förster-Nietzsche. Nietzsche had a mental breakdown in 1889 and died in 1890. His sister edited his last few works, and some scholars (such as Christian Niemeyer and Robert Holub) have alleged that a number of anti-Semitic statements in those works were inserted by her. We do know that Förster-Nietzsche held anti-Semitic views, and we do know that Nietzsche, at least in his earlier works, did not share them. Our ability to sort out claims about Förster-Nietzsche's role is complicated, however, by the fact that Nietzsche was not mentally stable during this time and that interpreting his writings has always been complicated. Yet the manipulation claims, and the use by Nazis of Nietzsche's work to justify their own policies, shows the perils that can befall a writer if his posthumous work does fall into the hands of questionable custodians.

British philosopher Michael Oakeshott's posthumous career has proceeded in a more orderly fashion—as perhaps befits the thought of this British conservative. Oakeshott bequeathed his papers to his Cambridge colleague Shirley Letwin. Letwin worked with American political theorist Timothy Fuller to edit and publish a series of volumes of Oakeshott's works. The knowledge of and sympathy for Oakeshott's views has ensured that the posthumous publications are presented to the reader in the context of Oakeshott's other published works. Most, for instance, have lengthy editor's introductions explaining when the papers were written, why he chose not to publish them while he was alive, and what sorts of judgment calls the editors made in publishing them. One would assume from reading them that Oakeshott chose his executor well.

It would be easy to look at these examples from philosophy and evaluate them simply according to usefulness or harm to the public, either to the scholarly world or in the political realm. If it helps us to understand somebody's thoughts—and if those thoughts will be important to us after that person's death—then sure, we might say, let's give everyone access to everything. Given the continuing relevance of Adam Smith to economic debates today, it would arguably be useful for us to know more about what he meant. We could also say that it's important to get it right; Nietzsche's sister certainly did bad stuff, and a better or more honest trustee of his materials would have helped not only Nietzsche, but would have done a service to philosophers, historians, and even to Germany and the world. But it's hard to know whether this has been done when we don't have access to everything.

Maybe, however, we should not get hung up on this standard about doing good for the world. Consider some examples from literature. Franz Kafka published little during his lifetime and was largely unrecognized. Kafka directed his friend Max Brod to destroy most of his written work upon his death, and he died in 1924 at the age of forty. Brod refused to follow Kafka's direction, and it's due to Brod's work promoting Kafka (and Brod's escape in 1939 from the Nazis) that we now know Kafka's work. Brod guarded Kafka's work closely, however, releasing only the work he deemed appropriate for publication. Brod ultimately passed the remainder down to his secretary Esther Hoffe upon his death. When Hoffe died in 2007, the National Library of Israel challenged her will, and Kafka's remaining writings were finally made available, against his wishes, eighty-three years after his death. Had it not been for Brod's recognition of the importance of Kafka's work, we would likely never have known very much about him.

This is not to say, however, that all such decisions are wise. Vladimir Nabokov also sought unsuccessfully to destroy his unpublished papers upon his death. Perhaps he was wise to want this; the posthumous works of Nabokov have generally been panned by critics. A similar, albeit more challenging, case is presented by *Go Set a Watchman*, an early novel by Harper Lee, which was published in 2015. Lee published the classic novel *To Kill a Mockingbird* in 1960, and declared not long after that that she would never write another book. *Watchman* has variously been said to be an early draft of *Mockingbird* or a sequel to it. Lee was eighty-nine and in failing health by 2015, and it's unclear whether she agreed to the publication of *Watchman* and whether she was of sufficiently sound mind to agree to it. HarperCollins, the book's publisher, made an enormous profit from it but was also roundly criticized for it. Many reviewers also noted that Lee comes across in *Watchman* as more racially prejudiced than one might have inferred from *Mockingbird*.

Would the world have been harmed had Kafka's wishes been honored? Maybe, but any such claims about "harm" must be more speculative and more removed from the nitty-gritty of human economic or political wellbeing than such claims about someone like Adam Smith. Was the world harmed by the release of *Go Set Watchman*? If the verdict of history is, indeed, that it is bad, or that Lee was, to be blunt, more of a racist than we had thought, then perhaps it is too bad that the book was published. Yet much of the media coverage of *Watchman*'s publication had to do with the personal ethics of it all: was it fair to Lee for the book to be published? Was she taken advantage of by her agent or publisher?

It seems reasonable to allow the wishes of some citizens to prevail in these circumstances. In a September 17th 2017 installation of the *New York Times* "Ethicist" column, a reader wrote in to ask what to do with her recently deceased husband's journals. She was his second wife; he had written some harsh things about his first wife in journal entries written at about the time of their divorce. The letter writer asserted that she thought her husband's children (from the first marriage) might benefit from a fuller understanding of their parents' divorce, but that her husband would have preferred the journals be destroyed. The ethicist here (philosopher Kwame Anthony

Appiah) argued that the husband's wishes should be respected and that the children would not be harmed because they would not even know that such writings existed. Should we treat Kafka or Lee any differently? Are even the private papers of persons who happen, also, to be public figures, public property?

We should, finally, think a bit about the motives of the author who chooses to reveal or hide some of his thoughts from the world after death. Imagining Adam Smith, on his deathbed, consigning his personal papers to the flames strikes the modern reader as the stuff of tragedy; imagining Montesquieu organizing his random ideas so they can live beyond him seems profound. Yet most of us are not made of such stuff. To imagine that people will care one way or the other about our thoughts when we die is perhaps a conceit. Or perhaps we have something to hide?

This is the premise of Milan Kundera's story "Lost Letters," contained in *The Book of Laughter and Forgetting*. Kundera's character Mirek, an aging intellectual, frantically tries to track down his letters so that he can burn them. The reason? As a younger man, he carried on a love affair with an ugly woman. Mirek clearly wishes to control the way in which he is remembered, to create a selective version of himself that will outlive him. He comes across as somewhat self-important—we see little evidence in the book that anyone other than Mirek will care to remember Mirek's dalliances. No one has ever accused Kundera of being a feminist, but the humor of Mirek's story is also quite gendered; this is the sort of thing, it seems, that only men would care about. Kundera's story suggests that we should perhaps be skeptical of any attempt to curate a person's life: whether we have access to everything, to some things, or to nothing, we are not necessarily seeing the person as he was, but the person as he, or others around him, wishes us to remember. Kundera writes:

> Mirek is as much a rewriter of history as the Communist Party, all political parties, all nations, all men. People are always shouting that they want to create a better future. It's not true. The future is an apathetic void of no interest to anyone. The past is full of life, eager to irritate us, provoke and insult us, tempt us to destroy or repaint it. The only reason people want to be masters of the future is to change the past. (p. 22)

Yet if people wish to massage or even rewrite the past in order, as Kundera suggests, to better master its threat to irritate the present, it seems just as plausible to think that some wish to do so because they are irritated by and wish to master the way their imaginings fill the void of the future.

The Posthumous Career and the Creation of "Self"

There are many historical accounts that note the tremendous complications of Hendrix's estate and the many people who felt they had some sort of insight into what Hendrix would have wanted, how best to manage his legacy, or how to make a buck. There are also some relatively straightforward accounts from people close to Hendrix of the difficulty involved in doing the right thing by Hendrix and those close to him. Music writer John Platt, in his role as co-author with Experience drummer Mitch Mitchell, aptly summarized many of the competing perspectives:

> If work is issued very quickly after an artist's death, then the public, justifiably or not, will cry that their beloved hero's memory is being cruelly exploited for commercial ends. If the powers-that-be leave it too long, then they run the risk of the public "forgetting" the artist. Equally they may feel, probably quite rightly, that they have a duty with regard to the artist's "legacy" and the respecting of his "wishes" with regard to material that would have been issued and way only prevented from being so by his death. There is also the duty to the family of the deceased to ensure that the artist continues to act as a "breadwinner" even after his death, a concept in which there is nothing inherently immoral. Lastly, of course, there is the thorny area of the public's right of access to the artist's material. At what point does one say "No, the artist did not record this or that piece for public consumption"? (*Hendrix: Inside the Experience*, p. 162)

These are all legitimate reasons why we should give some thought to the ethics of Hendrix's posthumous catalog. Yet it seems to us that there is something deeper—all of Platt's claims presuppose that the identities of the people involved are fixed—that we are concerned with balancing the competing interests of the public, of Hendrix's family and associates, or of Hendrix himself. There are debts involved, perhaps. One concern, however, is with the way in which these recordings actually create the public personage himself. Our understanding of who Jimi Hendrix is, or was, is altered depending on whether we're permitted to think of him as the iconic performer of his greatest albums or the guitar noodle on that long-lost eight-track tape. Which is the "true" version? The distinction between the willfully presented "self" and the more complete body of work an artist leaves behind raises ethical questions about what we owe the dead, but it also shows the extent to which any public persona is an artificial creation.

Not a Matter of Rights

It's tempting to assume that everyone has "rights" here—the artist has a right to determine how he is remembered, or the consumer, collector, or student of that art has a right to a full understanding of the artist's work. But this is not the appropriate way to think about these issues.

We naturally feel that there is a conflict between, on the one hand, the right of the person to determine which private aspects of himself to make public, and on the other hand, the right of his family, his acquaintances, his scholars and archivists, or his public to know. As long as these are assumed to be moral rights, we seem to be caught in a conflict of duties—duties to the dead and duties to the living (present and future). This conflict, however, is produced by illusion that these are moral rights. There simply is no absolute right to privacy or to create your identity and no pure right to know anything about someone else.

A person has no right to create a public self and put into that public self only what he allows. We have no such right primarily because this is impossible, and based on a false idea of what a person is.

According to the Cartesian view of the self, it is a substance, asserted to exist metaphysically in radical distinction from the public world and the body, which it controls. The general idea is that this self, ego, or "I" is hidden from others and constitutes what each of us knows ourselves truly to be—and would still be, even were all incidental features (like our public identities and our bodies) removed.

But what if this view of the self is wrong? A different view of the self would follow the argument of Ludwig Wittgenstein.

In a famous thought experiment, Wittgenstein writes "Suppose that everyone had a box with something in it that we call a 'beetle.' No one can ever look into anyone else's box, and everyone says he knows what a beetle is only by looking at *his* beetle" (*Philosophical Investigations* p. 100). He suggests that people may have different things in their boxes, and some nothing at all, and it would make no difference: "one can 'divide through' by the thing in the box; it cancels out, whatever it is." While he is speaking of sensation here, the point applies generally to anything, like a self, that people may claim is permanently, essentially hidden from others. Rather, these things must either being able to show up publically, or they cancel out. Wittgenstein here is not so much interested in denying the existence, in some sense, of a self or soul (or of sensation), but in correcting a misconception about them, and thus about ourselves, about what we are. "The human body is the best picture of the human soul" (p. 178). We understand our and others' selves through their public manifestations, and we should reject any view that asks us to understand these as occult entities.

In favor of a more Wittgensteinian view, then, let's note that we all begin in public, expressing bodily what we see and hear. Babies make many faces we do not know how to interpret, but no baby has a poker face.

Still, even if we start with such a Wittgensteinian view, we should not wish to deny that there is something motivating the Cartesian impulse. Not only do persons experience private inner lives, there seems more to the person than what shows publicly, something we catch sight of even in baby faces. The spiritual dimension of the person may not be a Cartesian thing or substance, essentially hidden and existing in radical distinction from the body and its public displays, but it is more metaphysically weighty than the shadow of public performances. And this 'more' not only calls for respect but also allows the unfurling of an inner expanse, a place of much we choose not to show others and which we, not without reason, feel to be closer to us even than our bodies are.

So, yes, babies make many faces in naive expression of every feeling. But human beings develop an inner, private self as we learn not to make such faces, not to reflexively express all we feel and see. Likewise, speech is only secondarily an expression of private thought; rather, first, thought is, echoing Plato's

phrase, a dialogue made inner and silent, or as Molly's ten-year
-old son put it—"thinking is just a way of talking without both-
ering anyone else." The person carves out, within himself, an
unexpressed self, by learning not to express everything. We
learn to hide our filth but also our treasure, and the virtue of
intimacy requires the discernment of when rightly to disclose
what to whom.

This inversion of the Cartesian way of thinking about the
self allows us to appreciate that we are not masters of our identities. We are always much more than we have decided to be or
even want to be. Maturing, of course, involves the development
of a poker face, the conscious control of one's expressions and
actions, and a concern for one's public appearance—and we
should do all this not only to craft a public appearance, but
more importantly out of a decent respect for the opinions of
mankind. Nevertheless, maturing also involves facing as fact
the limitations of our power not only over our self and our identity, but also over how others might perceive, or misperceive,
us. It is this maturity that Kundera's character Mirek seems to
lack. Thus, there is no moral right to control what about oneself is known publicly, for the language of moral rights suggest
an absoluteness that is absurd in this case. The question,
rather, becomes a prudential one: to what extent does respect
for another person—in that person's public and private
aspects—call for allowing him or her more or less say over
what is publicized?

Likewise, there is no simple right to know. Even if we are
not primarily private selves with a moral right to be and to
show only what we choose, part of human maturation involves
the cultivation of a private realm, which is not everybody's
business. And even if we lack complete, masterly power over
ourselves and our identities, a forced transparency would be an
attack on the mature person, and undermines the maturation
of developing persons. After all, the person, even if not primarily a secret self, essentially involves the development of the
unexpressed, of the secret and hidden. And it is in the interplay
between these two essential aspects of the self—the expressed
and the expressible unexpressed—that makes it that human
persons are, by nature, capable of intimacy. There are, indeed,
human goods that are protected by honoring, to a great degree,
a person's wishes to keep some things private. Not only does

doing so respect the person, as a being capable of intimacy, but it frees all of us from the fear that every mistake might be recorded, and that we might be permanently hung on our below average—perhaps our worst—moments.

Some facts about us are more publicly relevant than others, and some people—those with large public identities—enjoy (and suffer from) having more things about them that are publicly relevant. Hendrix's mediocre recordings, scattered promiscuously in 1970s eight-tracks, are to some degree publicly relevant—for his public identity is a musical one; yet at the same time, any expert could tell you they are not actually all that relevant, even to his musical achievement. It is too much to call Hendrix's musically mediocre moments filth; yet we might remember, at the philosophical level, that is a good thing that a person be permitted to hide his filth, and there is something obscene in publicizing it. What is called for in such cases is not an assertion of a right to control our public image, but the prudential discernment of a decent human being who can judge relevance and how best to respect the artist as a person, even in death.

So What's the Answer?

It's tempting to search for some sort of formula here that would enable us to distinguish, with certainty, between what is legitimate use of a dead person's legacy and what is not. There are so many things, however, that make this impossible. Many people have legitimate interests here, but the assignment of rights is complicated. There are, in addition, a number of judgment calls. For every questionable bootleg recording, there is a lost masterpiece. For every artist whose reputation was sullied, there is another who acquired fame that eluded him (or her) during life.

In the absence of clear principles, then, the burden is largely on us. We don't have a legal obligation, or even an ethical one, to consider any artist only in the way he wished to be imagined. But as human beings seeking to understand each other and live together well, we have a less formal (but no less real) duty to think about how others would have wanted to be remembered, and to think about how we would like others to think about us after our own demises. This is not always easy to do; indeed, rock stardom tends to make it hard for us to see the actual people who recorded the music we listen to. And we certainly do not get started in consuming music because we want to take on what turns out to be a morally complex human relationship.

So what should our twelve-year-old protagonist have done with regard to that eight-track tape? Ultimately, we think the answer is that he should have done more or less what he did— think about it a little bit, go out and find a nice vinyl copy of *Axis: Bold as Love* (with that nice gatefold sleeve), and not worry too much when that eight-track tape met the obsolescence that all other eight-tracks met at about that time.

13
Did Jimi Play Rock?

SAM BRUTON

$\mathbf{W}$hat kind of question is that: Did Jimi play rock? You're probably thinking, "Of course! Jimi was the greatest rock guitar player who ever lived." Or perhaps you're thinking it's just a silly question. But the question is more interesting than it might seem.

Why is the question interesting? In an academic article from a few years back, Joel Rudinow asks: "Can White People Sing the Blues?" (This is not to be confused with the much funnier question once posed by the Bonzo Dog Band: "Can Blue Men Sing the Whites?") Rudinow considers whether whites (in our society) can have the life experiences needed to "sing the blues," whether they can express the kind of authentic sorrow needed for the blues to be at its mournful, bluesy best. Rudinow's answer is a qualified "Yes." (This is not far from the answer given by former Rolling Stones bassist Bill Wyman, who replied: "If they try really hard.")

What's interesting about Rudinow's essay lies more with his question than his answer. The question reveals that really "singing the blues" is not merely a matter of singing certain kinds of notes. It is not just a matter of singing plaintive lyrics to melodies in which the thirds of the chords are often bent flat and set over a standard 12-bar blues chord progression. The question also reveals that being white or black is more than the color of your skin.

The question I want to ask about Jimi is in some ways the flip side of Rudinow's. The question is not whether a white person can do something typically done (and typically done best) by blacks, but whether a black man (indeed, a *very* black man) can play a style of music that by the late 1960s had become the unmistakable domain of whites. Playing *rock*, as was recognized even in Jimi's heyday, is not merely about playing certain kinds of notes. Rock is in part also, for want of a better term, a matter of ideology. It involves certain attitudes, values, and beliefs.

An ideology, in this broad sense, is a kind of perspective or stance. Similarly, the question being asked here requires thinking of being "black" (or "white," or any other ethnicity) not merely in terms of biology. The problem of Jimi and rock is the problem, as Jack Hamilton puts it, of an artist whose "blackness rendered his music as inauthentically 'rock' at the same that his music rendered his person as inauthentically black" (*Just Around Midnight*, p. 15).

Kinds of Music

Think about the curious notion of a musical category or genre—a musical *kind*. Some categories that are part of our experience of the world have relatively clear-cut criteria. Whether someone's blood is, say, Type A or Type O is well-defined and readily testable. Likewise, what makes a car a Ford or a Chevy is uncontroversial, as is whether someone is a citizen of this country or that. And so too for a wide range of other examples.

But whether some bit of music is classical or jazz, bluegrass or country, or gospel or soul, is often trickier. The problem is not simply that borderline cases are plentiful, but that the criteria stem from several different aspects of the ways we experience music and find it meaningful and emotionally resonant. Granted, there are examples of most musical styles we can point to as definitive. Johnny Cash did country, Aerosmith plays rock, and Duke Ellington played jazz. Nonetheless, the categories defy simple characterizations and definitive tests. When Miles plays his classic cut, "All Blues," there is a clear sense in which he is playing both jazz and the blues at the same time, and transforming both in the process.

Think about the complex idea of "classical" music in the Western tradition. The prime examples of the kind are the works of Mozart and Beethoven. Various characteristic features set classical apart from other kinds of music. For example, it is typically created and performed "for its own sake" in some sense; it is meant to convey a seriousness not typical of music generated for sing-alongs, or dances, or for light diversion. For this reason, for a long time, Bach's music was not considered classical, since he was a working church musician who cranked out most of what he wrote for the upcoming Sunday worship services.

Furthermore, classical music is performed on certain kinds of instruments. Characteristically, these instruments are those of the standard symphony orchestra—violins, cellos, several woodwinds and brass instruments—but they also include honorary symphony instruments like acoustic pianos, timpanis, glockenspiels, and harps. Trap drum sets are party crashers in a symphony, but snare drums alone—a standard ingredient in any Nashville session drummer's trap kit—are part of many a symphonic score. (In the late 1960s, Wendy Carlos created a stir in classical circles when her *Switched-On Bach* record featured works of the great baroque composer performed on a Moog synthesizer.) Classical music is also set apart by its focus on composers rather than performers as the primary locus of aesthetic value. Performers in the tradition are expected to stick to the notes the composer wrote, distinguishing themselves from each other mostly through their technical skill and interpretations of the notes. Compare this with rock. Many rock fans are blissfully unaware of who wrote the songs they love—their attention is on the performers, and especially the singers. Rock artists are often musical illiterates, unable to read notes on the printed page.

Musical genres can be distinguished in other ways as well. While classical music yields "works," rock music produces commodity products: recordings sold as vinyl records, compact disks, and now electronic song files. Classical music, along with country, bluegrass, and other white musical styles, is typified by square-ish, even, rhythms. Black music—such as is exemplified by gospel, blues, soul and most of all jazz—*swings*. (In part, music "swings" when the notes are not evenly segregated, temporarily speaking, and the subordinate "upbeats" are played closer in time to the "downbeats." There is more to it than this, however.)

Harmonically, the three chord progressions that are the hallmark of pop or folk are much simpler than the dense chromaticism of jazz or the shape-shifting harmonic structures that result from Bach's contrapuntal melodies. And we can distinguish musical styles sociologically and politically. The blues is the music of rural Southern blacks, while bluegrass is the music of Appalachian whites. Reggae music is inseparable from the political anguish of oppressed, black Jamaicans (Can white people play reggae?), and white American folk music of the 1960s is enmeshed in progressive struggles of the day, such as the Civil Rights movement and opposition to the Vietnam War.

As a result, musical categories do not lend themselves to the Platonic ideal of concepts that can be articulated by means of logically necessary and sufficient conditions. Rather, they are good examples of what Ludwig Wittgenstein understood in terms of "family resemblances." That is, musical genres are not defined by a single essential feature, shared by all and only instances of that type. Rather, they are grasped by a series of overlapping similarities which all examples of the kind have to varying degrees.

So what then to say about the complex category of "rock-'n'roll," which by Jimi's time was referred to more frequently simply as "rock"? Ethnographically and historically, rock'n'roll was originally the product of American blacks. The style originated in the blues-infused "rocking and reeling" music of "Sanctified" or "Holiness" churches, where, as famed rock critic Robert Palmer describes, "guitars, drums, and horns were as acceptable as the piano or the organ, and more easily afforded" ("Rock Begins," p. 4).

The style was introduced to American pop consciousness by the likes of Chuck Berry and Fats Domino, although it took Elvis Presley, a white Mississippian, to give rock its first mass breakthrough commercial success. Through the mid-Sixties, rock was made by both blacks and whites. In 1965, *Time* magazine featured a piece titled, "Rock'n'Roll: Everybody's Turned On," with the all-black female group The Supremes on the cover. But by the end of the decade, the archetypal rock act was the British bad boys The Rolling Stones. By their own admission, the Stones were relentless and enthusiastic imitators of American black music. Nonetheless, their whiteness was as undeniable as their flaunted sexuality and their churlish rebelliousness.

How did this change take place? How did rock change from black to white? The change was not purely musicological, although there was some of that. The guitar-dominated driven rhythms that typified the Stones, matched with bluesy chord progressions and simple melodies, were not that different from the musical elements pioneered by American blues greats like Muddy Waters and Howlin' Wolf that the Stones emulated. Instead, the change was as much social and political as aesthetic.

There were several crucial developments in these years. Bob Dylan, a Jewish boy from Minneapolis, made acoustic guitar-driven folk into some of the most incisive social criticism of the decade and was transformative. Dylan had a message, and he made popular music a vehicle for conveying seriousness, authenticity, and individualism in a way it had never been before. The significance of the Beatles-led "British Invasion" is also hard to overstate.

Within a few short years, the Beatles moved pop music's thematic center of gravity from the schoolgirl naivity of "I Want to Hold Your Hand" to the seriousness and self-indulgence of the concept album, *Sgt. Pepper's Lonely Hearts Club Band.* The band that started out imitating early Motown and its appeal to mass sensibilities ended up singing about "Lucy in the Sky with Diamonds," a not-so-sly countercultural reference to the psychedelic drug LSD.

The effect was to move their music far from that of the young Aretha Franklin, daughter of a black preacher, and another star of the late 1960s music scene. Rock became exemplified by white bands like the Beatles and Stones; what Aretha did, by contrast, was labeled "soul". Her music was played on R&B (rhythm and blues) stations and charted by *Billboard* magazine as R&B; it seemed quite different from what the white boys of the time were doing.

Though correct are far as it goes, this quick sketch ignores social and political trends that were just as significant. While nowadays, white Americans think of the Sixties with self-congratulatory nostalgia, as a period of positive improvement in Civil Rights and race relations generally, the "facts on the ground" were more like the fog of a cultural war. Malcolm X and the black nationalist movement had become increasingly vocal, and race-related riots in Detroit and Los Angeles put

many whites on edge. At the same time, a rising feminist movement, led by white women like Betty Friedan and Gloria
Steinham, had men on the defensive. The fight against com-
munism, America's great international cause of the previous
generation, was turning into a bloodbath in Southeast Asia
soaked with humiliation and futility.

In such a social context, it's not surprising that whites, and
young white males in particular, sought a means of positive
social identity and a way of shaping how they were perceived
by others. Rock music became a way for young white males to
tell the story of themselves they wanted told and wanted to
believe. It was the story of people captivated by a sense of their
own rebelliousness, anger, originality, masculinity, and whiteness. As writers like Simon Frith and Franco Fabbri have
argued, categories of popular music are streamlined ideologi-
cal, sociological, and even political arguments, indicating how
communities of people see themselves and wish to be seen by
the outside world. Rock, for a particular group of people at a
particular point in history, became the possession of people
seeking just such a self-concept.

The change was swift, although once having been made, it
has been remarkably stable. When in the 1970s, Wild Cherry
sang "Play that Funky Music White Boy," the result was not
funk, and neither was it intended to be, although the sexual
aspirations of the band's name came through clearly. Even in
their day, the names of 1980s rock bands like Great White and
White Snake seemed not so much clever or humorous as ways
of belaboring their obvious narcissism. So-called "death metal"
is not an alternative to rock; it is selected aspects of rock taken
single-mindedly to an extreme.

To this day, the incidence of music by females or blacks on
"classic rock" stations is small, and it remains the favored
music of many white men who were in their teens and twenties
in the late 1960s and the 1970s. The genre has stopped pro-
gressing not because it has exhausted the aesthetic resources
available to it, but because it has become the victim of rigid
expectations about what it should say and for whom. Much the
same can be said of classical and jazz music too. The more
definitive the boundaries, the more that exemplary items of a
given aesthetic type seem like museum pieces.

The Jimi Problem

So what does all of this say about whether Jimi played rock? Given the multidimensional nature of musical categories, and the complexity of Hendrix and his music, the question can be approached in various ways: historically, musicologically, and socio-politically. From most perspectives, the question defies quick or simple answers.

This was true even in his day. He was regularly shunned by radio stations, too hard-edged for stations programmed for blacks, and too radical and black for those courting a white audience. White outsiders could never quite get past Hendrix's race. As one critic said in an epitaph, Hendrix was "a black man in the alien world of rock." For his part, Jimi steadfastly resisted efforts to pigeonhole him. As he told one reporter, "What I don't like is this business of trying to classify people. Leave us alone." He continued:

> It's like shooting a flying saucer as it tries to land without giving the occupants a chance to identify themselves. You don't need labels, man. (Ritchie York, *Los Angeles Times*)

We can see such individualism as a move toward the world of rock and an attempt to steer away from traditional forms of black music like gospel, which historically have been rooted in attempts to create community and mutual support. Jimi often talked about doing "his own thing." But in the late 1960s "doing your own thing" was not an entirely individualistic thing. It was a way of creating community with a younger generation disenchanted with conventional forms of life.

Exhibit A in any argument that Jimi played rock is the fact that he was, is, and always will be, a virtual *god* of the electric guitar, hands down the definitive instrument of choice for rock musicians. His virtuosity is such that even the best guitarists of his day instantly recognized him as head and shoulders above them. Consider the reaction of Michael Bloomfield, widely hailed as one of the best blues guitarists of the 1960s, upon first encountering Hendrix playing in Greenwich Village in 1966, "Hendrix knew who I was, and that day, in front of my eyes, he burned me to death." Bloomfield adds, "How he did this, I wish I understood. He just got right up in my face with that axe, and I didn't even want to pick up a guitar for the next year" ("Michael Bloomfield Reminisces").

One of the most innovative aspects of Jimi's playing is that more than any guitar player before him and most since, Jimi made the amp and electric gadgets part of one big instrument. The amp and effect boxes were as integral to his sound as his Strat itself. And he played them loudly, much louder than he ever dreamed of or could have gotten away with while touring the so-called "chitlin' circuit" as a side man in the early 1960s. Jimi's innovations extended beyond electronics, and included the nihilistic dive bombing effects he created effortlessly with his whammy bar, his artistic use of feedback, and the earthy funkiness his foot coaxed from a wah-wah pedal.

This electrified funkiness spawned many imitators and became a signature urban sound in the 1970's in the theme from *Shaft* and other recordings. His music was made "rockier" and whiter by the white British musicians he worked with for much of his solo career, Noel Redding and Mitch Mitchell. While white musicians backing up black artists were integral to the way Stax Records of Memphis and Motown cranked out soul and R&B hits, Jimi brought his white musicians on stage with him. This increased the countercultural impression created by the trio and gave Jimi's blackness an even greater visual prominence. Jimi credited blues great Muddy Waters as the one who opened his eyes to the possibility of the electric guitar, but Jimi made the guitar something it had never been before.

There's much to be said also for thinking of Jimi's music as blues, jazz, and even black gospel. All the way to the ending psychedelic, strung-out haziness, Jimi's music shows unmistakable signs of the various musical influences upon him. Jazz was the music of his childhood home; it was the music of his dad and beloved mother. It has always been heavily improvisational, and Jimi's music was always more improvisational than most rock or soul. Other guitar players take solos, but Jimi's solos always seemed fresh and spontaneous, as though he was playing things he'd never played before. And they are often very long. In these respects, he's closer to a free jazzer like Ornette Coleman than a rock guitarist like the Stone's Keith Richards or The Who's Pete Townshend. The famous guitar solo that ends Lynyrd Skynyrd's "Free Bird" is long but hardly improvised. Jimi's song "Machine Gun," a dark piece from late in Jimi's career, harkens to the jazz tradition in a different way. Its one-chord D Dorian tonality is closer to the modal approach of Miles Davis's "So What" than anything from rock.

Also like jazzers, Jimi tended to rework both his own material and traditional songs, often utterly changing them both in terms of their musical character and their emotional content and meaning. A good example is his re-working of Dylan's "All Along the Watchtower." Hendrix's version is lush and airy and emotionally engaging, while Dylan's treatment is sparse and detached. But the most iconic instance of this kind of dramatic re-interpretation, of course, is Hendrix's breathtaking revision of "The Star-Spangled Banner." His best-known performance of it is the Woodstock version, which contrasts notably with an earlier performance at the Los Angeles Forum. At the Forum, Hendrix's spoken interjections give an aura of adolescent anger. The later treatment has much more political potency. Hendrix biographer Charles Shaar Murray singles out the Woodstock rendition as "the most complex and powerful work of American art to deal with the Vietnam war and its corrupting, distorting effect on the American psyche" (*Crosstown Traffic*, p. 24).

The rootedness of Jimi's music in older, blacker forms of music like gospel, ring shouts, and work songs is much deeper than his quirky descriptions of his music as "electric church music" or "space church" music suggest. Bloomfield once described him as the "blackest" guitar player he'd ever heard, one whose music was rooted in the oldest forms of black music. And Jimi's self-identification as the "Voodoo Chile" explicitly points towards even older African spiritual traditions. Much of this influence was filtered to him through his early career stints with black stars like Otis Redding, Little Richard, the Isley Brothers, and lesser lights like "Gorgeous" George Odell. Echoes of the emotive guitar playing of soul greats like Curtis Mayfield and Bobby Womack come out in "The Wind Cries Mary" and other pretty Hendrix tunes. Lessons he learned imitating thick studio arrangements as a side man shaped his later trio playing as a front man. But more than anything else, the influence of the soul tradition on Hendrix's career is rhythmic. Especially late in his career, after Billy Cox and Buddy Miles have replaced Redding's square grooves and Mitchell's looseness, these roots can be heard in the groovy funk of tracks like "Who Knows."

Arguably the best match, genre-wise, is the link between Hendrix and great Delta blues artists like Muddy Waters and John Lee Hooker. Jimi studied the stylings of many of these blues greats, and once made a kind of pilgrimage to Waters, traveling to one of the master's recording sessions where he spoke with him at length. Even his physical performance tricks, such as the phallic antics of his breakthrough appearance at the Monterey Pop Festival and on many other occasions, and his facility at playing with his teeth and behind his back, are traceable to black blues forbearers like T-Bone Walker and Buddy Guy. Many of Jimi's greatest songs are basically blues tunes. "Red House," which he played often, is a slow blues. Tunes like "Manic Depression" (from *Are You Experienced*), while overlaid with edgier, rock textures, have a repeating blues structure rather than the verse-chorus structure characteristic of most rock and pop. Not long before his death, he spoke of wanting to "get back to the blues." Still, bluesy as he was, the great Delta guitarist B.B. King demurred from categorizing him as a blues musician. When asked if Hendrix was a "bluesman," King replied, with pity at the ignorance revealed by the question, "I consider him to be a *musician*, a great, *great* musician" (*Crosstown Traffic*, p. 2).

While the musicological aspects of Jimi's music are complicated, the broader social and cultural meaning of his work is perhaps even more elusive. More than any other musical form, rock is typified by its emphasis on authenticity and self-expressions of individual identity. Given that Hendrix's musical genius is like no one else's, his authenticity credentials would seem beyond dispute. Yet aspects of Jimi's persona and performance style point in a different direction. His flamboyant modes of dress took him in the direction of Motown showmanship; most white rockers of the time favored clothing that was more insolent and working class. His use of over-the-top sexual gestures on-stage also was frequently thought to be inauthentic. One rock critic, Robert Christgau, reacted to Hendrix's Monterey debut by labelling him "a psychedelic Uncle Tom," and Eric Clapton, though humbled by Hendrix's overabundant musical talents, suspected him of cheaply pandering to white audiences' expectations.

Another side of Hendrix on stage is his flirtation with violence. Though often soft-spoken and withdrawn, Hendrix's flame-throwing demolition of his guitar at Monterey is forever seared in popular memory. Such exhibitions can be interpreted either as displays of sincere emotion or mere spectacles. None of this, though, has voided Hendrix's reception as an "honorary white," and neither has it erased his standing as the lone great black musician in rock's short list of immortals. In no small part because of Hendrix, violence and male sexuality remain central parts of rock ideology.

His musical inventiveness also lends ambiguity. Jimi's originality fit with rock's self-image as a realm of individualism, but his inventiveness was of a different kind than that of the great white musicians of rock. Gifted singers and instrumentalists though they may have been (Ringo Starr aside), the core of the Beatles' greatness was in their songs. Yet Hendrix's strength was not song-writing, and like blues and jazz players, he was mostly content to stick close to songs and song structures written by others. His vocal imprecision put him closer to Jagger's swagger than McCartney's accuracy and Motown's smooth slickness. But Jimi was not a great singer, important as his rough-hewn vocal style may be to the overall impression of his music. And while he was an underappreciated lyricist, he has never approached Dylan in giving authoritative voice to political aspirations.

A deep and racist myth about black musicianship attributes their greatness to natural musical gifts, and Jimi is as gifted a musician as rock music has ever known. But the countless hours of practice and study, and the untold miles of paying his dues playing as just another underpaid, anonymous backup musician, are hidden to most rock fans. They come away from encountering Jimi with the impression of effortless mastery. The result is that Jimi's greatest musical skill—his guitar virtuosity—often conveys the sort of natural talent stereotypically associated with musical blackness.

His Own Thing

Perhaps it always will be difficult to appreciate Hendrix's art without seeing it through race-colored lenses. One risk is that classifying his music as rock enables him to be used as the exception that proves a dubious rule, a self-congratulatory counter-instance used by white rockers and fans to argue that their preferred music is more race-neutral than it in fact is. A different risk is to reduce Hendrix's intent to social power struggles between blacks and whites. Consider remarks Pete Townshend made long after Hendrix's death. Commenting on Jimi's early appearance on the London music scene, Townshend reports thinking that Hendrix's message to them was:

> You've taken this, Eric Clapton, and Mr. Townshend, you think you're a showman. This is how we do it. This is how we can do it when we take back what you've borrowed, if not stolen. (*Just Around Midnight*, p. 226)

Townshend's 'we' and 'them,' of course, imagined through Hendrix, is the dichotomy of black and white. One wonders if Townshend's interpretation merely projects his own insecurity onto Jimi's ambitions; Townshend was palpably humiliated by Hendrix. Ultimately it seems fairer to Hendrix to follow his lead and consider him simply as having done "his own thing." While our fondness for musical labels may be unavoidable, Jimi's legacy is a cautionary tale against using them unreflectively.

14
Hendrix from the Bottom Up

Eric Griffin

This is a world of lead guitar players, but the most essential thing to learn is the time, the rhythm.

—Jimi Hendrix to Mike Bloomfield

On January 1st 1970 the most electrifying performer in pop music, Jimi Hendrix, stunned his Fillmore East audience by "performing stock still" and "shunning nearly all of his patented stage gymnastics" (McDermott and Kramer, p. 247).

Accompanying rock's greatest guitarist that day were two chitlin' circuit veterans: to his far left, on bass, stood Hendrix's longtime friend Billy Cox; at center stage loomed powerhouse drummer Buddy Miles, formerly of Mike Bloomfield's Electric Flag, whose own band, the Buddy Miles Express, Hendrix had recently been producing. Together, the three were billed as "A Band of Gypsys."

Although the album they recorded that evening sold well upon its April 1970 release, responses to Hendrix's altered lineup immediately divided both critics and fans, a substantial number of whom still feel that the live performances captured at the Fillmore East don't measure up to the breakthrough recordings cut by the Jimi Hendrix Experience. But musicians, especially black musicians, have revered *Band of Gypsys*. This is the Hendrix that inspired Miles Davis, George Clinton and P-funk, Bootsy Collins, Nile Rogers, Vernon Reid and Living Color, Lenny Kravitz, and, among many other major musical figures, Prince.

But *Band of Gypsys* didn't come out of nowhere. A careful listening to Hendrix's third American album, *Electric Ladyland*, reveals the guitarist already moving in the Rhythm and Blues direction the later project would take. In the midst of the sessions that became the double album Hendrix remarked, "A couple of years ago, all I wanted was to be heard. 'Let me in!' was the thing. Now, I'm trying to figure out the wisest way to be heard" (*Hendrix: Setting the Record Straight*, p. 117). What I hear when I listen to particular moments of *Electric Ladyland* (1968) and *Band of Gypsys* (1970) is an artist shaking up the rhythmic foundations upon which his earlier records had been based in search of the "wisest way" deliver his expansive musical vision. In his rhythmic reshuffling, I hear a master musician drawing new inspiration from the blues, R&B, and jazz traditions he had studied coming up, even as he is opening these traditions toward the rapidly advancing technologies and changing social conditions that characterized that cultural moment. In these sonic explorations I hear Hendrix attaining, albeit fleetingly, an increasing sublime mastery of musical time and musical space. I want you to hear it too.

All You Need Is Ears

"All you need is ears," George Martin once wrote, tweaking the title of the generational anthem he had produced for his most famous clients. Of course, all ears don't hear alike any more than all philosophers think alike. Intuition, inclination, training, and experience (not to mention anatomy and physiology) all play a part in the many ways individuals listen. I must confess that as a result of the way these factors combine in me, I hear things differently. While almost everyone I know hears pop music from the vocal or solo instruments down, I'm among the happy few who have been destined to go through life hearing tunes *ass-backwards*—or as I prefer, from the bottom up.

Confession number two. What I do for a living now has not always been my main line of work. While I teach literature by day, I am still a drummer by night. Although these days my drumming life mostly involves accepting an occasional weekend gig or tinkering in the home studio I've cobbled together, during my rather prolonged first attempt at a making a career

I spent enough time in and around the recording studios of Southern California to learn how records are made. Rather, I learned how they *used to be made* back in the age that gave us the so-called "classic rock" that remains the soundtrack of so much popular culture.

In that long-ago era of magnetic tape, white grease pencils, and razorblades, before the advent of drum machines, sequencers, sampling, click-tracks, plug-ins and Pro Tools, records were built from the bottom up. Sure, it became much easier to overdub as the number of available tracks kept increasing: from four (can you believe that such sophisticated productions as *Pet Sounds* and *Sgt. Pepper*'s were recorded on four tracks?) to eight (the *White Album* and *Abbey Road*), and then from twelve (the short-lived format on which Hendrix and Eddie Kramer cut *Electric Ladyland* at the Record Plant) to the sixteen track machines that first arrived in late-1968 and were widely available by the early 1970s (*Exile on Main Street* and *Ziggy Stardust*).

Until the advent of the first workable drum machines and samplers in the early 1980s, a record didn't go forward unless a rhythm track was got right. Once captured on tape, it could be enhanced in various ways, say, by adding echo, layering percussion parts, altering playback speed, making tape loops, or even by running tracks backwards (like Martin did with Ringo's kit on "Rain"). In extreme circumstances, they could be altered by actually cutting and pasting on the master reel (yes, with an X-Acto knife, an editing block, and a roll of adhesive tape).

But while all of the other instruments could be fixed later on in the process, the drums couldn't be faked: if the bottom weren't solid right out of the gate, there was no way the end-result was going to get traction. At its worst, this approach to recording produced numberless sides of disposable pop; at its best, it gave us the three-minute masterpieces that still inhabit our cultural imagination. Such was the world of analog recording that Hendrix knew.

The Grooves Don't Lie

A truism of recording in the 1960s and 1970s was "The grooves don't lie." It was an axiom that referred to both the literal grooves in the acetate test-pressings that used to circulate through the various stages of record production *and* to the aural spell an accomplished rhythm section could cast over a performance. Although the few elites who became the most eminent members of the trade could knock out record-worthy tracks in the three hours the Musicians Union allotted for a "session," for the many self-contained groups seeking record deals in that era the quest for the magic take could be almost endless.

Even The Beatles, whose group chemistry was without peer, might run through twenty or thirty takes to get a basic track. Having been trained in the listening dynamics of that age, an era in which the bottom was the only thing that could not be "fixed in the mix," I now find it very difficult to listen for much else. It's a limitation my top-down friends labor to live with.

And I do mean limitation. For although this way of conceiving musical time and space requires the development of a certain skillset, what I was learning was the kind of "mercenary art" Immanuel Kant associated with "craft." Although the craft of playing on tape was among the facets of the musician's trade that Hendrix was in the process of mastering, his was not an art easily contained within the constraints of the medium. Jimi's spirit, like the spirits of the blues and jazz masters he emulated, was of a far greater proportion than was typical of the highly competent musical "jobber," a term session ace Leon Russell often used to describe the role he had played during the golden age of record making.

Unlike Leon and the LA studio cats I was emulating, Jimi's art was "stone free" of the constraints demanded by the medium that, by the 1960s, had become the primary delivery system of the art form that the era valued above all others. It was no simple task to capture the magnitude of Jimi's gifts within the three minutes allotted by commercial radio, or even on the fifteen-minute vinyl sides that were beginning to rule the FM dial. Record production presented Jimi Hendrix with challenges he was still working through when his career was cut short on September 18th, 1970.

Twinning Traditions in *Electric Ladyland*

After opening *Electric Ladyland* with the experimental re-creation myth, "And the Gods Made Love," Hendrix's title track,

"Have You Ever Been (to Electric Ladyland)," dawns like a gentle Curtis Mayfield ballad. Always quick to acknowledge his admiration for the gospel-inflected stylings of the singer-songwriter guitarist, Hendrix's double note fills, reminiscent of those he had previously woven into the fabric of "The Wind Cries Mary," "Castles Made of Sand," and "Little Wing," are complemented in "Have Your Ever Been" by falsetto harmonies in call-and-response. Clearly, these vocal gestures were designed to leave the "Impression" (pun intended) that the Experience was coming down from the skies in tribute to their leader's R&B roots.

The mood these opening tracks conjured left young fans anticipating the aggressive distortion of "Purple Haze," "Foxey Lady," and "Spanish Castle Magic," wondering when the guitar hero they idolized was going to deliver. Many a late-Sixties air-guitarist (my younger self included) was inspired to drop a tone arm at track three for the expected Experience-fueled fireworks, which finally arrived with "Crosstown Traffic." But even this track incorporated R&B-style backup vocals not typical of Hendrix's earlier recordings. And yet, with several listenings, even the amped-up teenager I was then could begin to intuit what seems so obvious now, that the album's sequencing had been arranged with an educational purpose.

Jimi sings, "(I wanna show you), the different emotions/ (I wanna run to) the sounds and motions," and this is exactly what the record proceeds to do. Hendrix and his expanded cast of collaborators *show* us "different emotions" than we are used to hearing from him as the four sides of *Electric Ladyland* "run to" (and through) a kaleidoscopic collection of "sounds and motions."

But it was when "Crosstown Traffic," a tried-and-true, but nonetheless sexy application of the Hendrix-Redding-Mitchell formula, gave way to the opening strains of "Voodoo Chile" that our schooling in how deeply Hendrix's identification with blues tradition commenced. Although his live performances had typically featured at least one slow blues number like "Red House," "Catfish Blues," or "Hear My Train a-Comin'," with "Voodoo Chile" came the revelation of both Hendrix's profound devotion to and his utter mastery of the form. Retaining the Experience's Mitch Mitchell on drums, but complemented by Jack Casady, probably the most highly accomplished bassist to have then emerged from the San Francisco scene (and whose association with the Jefferson Airplane belied his East Coast R&B roots), Hendrix repaid his debts to the first generation of electrified Delta bluesman, particularly Muddy Waters, Howlin' Wolf, and Hubert Sumlin.

While "Voodoo Chile" delivers a veritable how-to clinic in the electric blues, tellingly, from the track's opening moments onward it is Steve Winwood's Hammond organ that holds the performance together by leaning insistently backwards on the Muddy Waters–style figure at the heart of the tune. With Casady fingering his hollow-body Guild Starfire, which made for a far deeper and more contrapuntally varied accompaniment than the mid-rangy honk Redding tended to produce with a pick on his Fender Jazz, Mitchell's intricate riffing leans forward, rising and swelling to fill any available sonic spaces. The constant tension in Mitchell's time-feel pushes the ensemble from Delta blues toward jazz. Following brilliant solos from both Hendrix and Winwood, the take dissolves (my young ears felt marvelously so) into the sort of dexterously adept feature that, as I would learn upon seeing the band play live in October 1968, his drummer was often given in the Experience's live shows. As Mitchell rolls his solo to a close, Hendrix masterfully reasserts the number's blues head to call forth a final verse and out chorus at his opening tempo.

Standing back to look at the whole, "Voodoo Chile" demonstrates how closely related the related traditions blues, jazz, and rock were in Hendrix's mind. So strongly did the guitarist want to declare his allegiances to these roots in *Electric Ladyland* that he famously closed the album with its famous coda, the ferociously rocked-up "Voodoo Child (Slight Return)." Taken together, as well as in the R&B light cast by "Have You Seen," Hendrix's two versions of his original blues "standard" demonstrate both how well he had mastered, and how far he could project, the traditions from whence he had come into new sonic territory.

Hendrix's uniquely different renditions of "Voodoo Chile" don't comprise the only pairing through which he twins tradition on *Electric Ladyland*. The opening tracks of sides three and four also reveal Hendrix reclaiming traditional roots in order to move forward, even as they predict the rhythmic reorientation his music would undergo with the Gypsys. But if

"Voodoo Child" had delivered a blues primer, "Rainy Day, Dream Away" instructs from a differently orchestrated angle.

Gradually emerging from a loungey, organ, saxophone, and conga vamp, the tune settles into a spaciously laid back R&B groove. Whereas in "Voodoo Chile" Winwood's organ had provided a tonal and rhythmic center against which Hendrix's and Mitchell's improvisations tugged, "Rainy Day" is driven by a palpably solid Buddy Miles shuffle. This apparently "simpler," and yet more exacting approach to tempo opens sonic space in ways that allow Hendrix to utilize tonal colorations previously unheard in his oeuvre. As organist Mike Finnegan's pulsating bass pedals "lock in," the way Miles feels time nails the beat to the studio floor. Together, the two provide a foundation that frees Hendrix from having simultaneously to mark the number's sustaining rhythm *and* venture solo improvisation.

The unburdening inspires a qualitative difference in Hendrix's sound. By entrusting the time to Miles, Hendrix, as though emerging from a rhythmic fog, is able to expand dramatically his guitar vocabulary. And I do literally mean vocabulary. For in the two "Rainy Day" tracks Hendrix's playing attains a clarity and vocal-like quality beyond anything audible in previous recordings, extending the electric guitar's experimental adaptability beyond what had been demonstrated by another of his masters, the seminal jazz guitarist and inventor, Les Paul, with whom Hendrix had in fact been consulting.

Forgoing Marshall stack distortion in order to deliver the cleaner sound associated with the blues explorations of important jazz guitarists such as Wes Montgomery and Joe Pass in "Rainy Day, Dream Away," Hendrix puts on full display his brilliant command of the mellower aspects of the twin idioms. As Finnegan recalls the session, "Jimi said, 'You be like Jimmy Smith and I'll be Kenny Burrell . . . that's what I'm looking for" (*Electric Ladyland*, 1993 liner notes, p. 16). After two full minutes of understated comping with sax man Freddie Smith, weaving Albert King licks into his Burrell vibe over Larry Faucett's swinging conga pattern, Hendrix's vocal introduces the tune's melodic core. Leading the ensemble through a verse and bridge, Hendrix inserts a syncopated R&B figure after which he lays on a Wah-wah infused overdub that culminates in one of the most inventive solos ever recorded. In this quasi-alchemical moment, Hendrix comes remarkably close to wringing from his Fender Stratocaster a human voice.

Obviously, Hendrix and engineer Eddie Kramer realized that they had conjured a sonic breakthrough, for Side Four of *Electric Ladyland* begins where "Rainy Day" had left off. Via Kramer's cut and splice, Hendrix's Wah-wah vocalization calls in a nearly four and half minute reprise of the very jam that had produced the track on Side Three. In the ensuing continuation and coda, Hendrix trades licks with Finnegan in much the manner that he had jousted with Winwood in "Voodoo Chile." A key difference is that in "Still Raining," rather than playing off of the Burrell-King connection as in part one, Hendrix elevates a solo into the blues-rock stratosphere that constitutes his own extension of tradition.

Bloomfield once recalled that "Hendrix was extremely interested in form—in a few seconds of playing he'd let you know about the song's entire structure" (Shadwick, p. 130). This is precisely what we hear in "Still Raining, Still Dreaming's" brilliantly orchestrated out-section, in which Hendrix can be heard cueing the band into multiple accents reminiscent of the show-stopping syncopations he had played with acts like the Isleys, the Squires, and King Curtis's Kingpins. Hendrix may as well have been saying to his listeners, "I've done my homework. Here's what I take from Kenny Burrell and Jimmy Smith; this is what I borrow from Albert King; and these are accents I learned playing R&B; put them all together and 'hear my train a-comin'.'"

Together, the two "Rainy Day" tracks demonstrate how grooves that were far different in feel from those listeners were accustomed to hearing Hendrix play with the Experience, could be matched with traditional structures in ways that provide support of a very different character than Redding and Mitchell could ever deliver. With this different accompaniment, we hear Hendrix extending his engagement with the traditions from whence he had come by exploring time in musical modes simply unavailable to his original trio. Against the paradoxically tighter, and yet more rhythmically spacious backdrop, Hendrix's licks are released from the crowded confines of the still viable, and yet increasingly constraining formula of the Jimi Hendrix Experience, who are, as a group, featured on fewer than half of *Electric Ladyland*'s sixteen tracks.

Making Time

Kant treated the aesthetics of music only incidentally. And although he could not have imagined how the effects of mechanical reproduction would one day alter musical reception, some of the vocabulary the philosopher employed in his attempt to articulate what he called the "Transcendental Aesthetic" can help us to gauge some of the differences we hear in Hendrix's playing as he developed musical collaborations that stepped outside the Experience formula.

For when musical performances are projected into the special realm of electronic reproduction, the relationship between listener and sound source get changed significantly. In person, an imperfectly voiced note or a dropped beat may slide by an audience member caught up in the temporal flow of a unique musical occurrence. But when a performance becomes available to repeated listenings, the mind's efforts to discern form in a musical event heightens our awareness of its fleeting idiosyncrasies, rendering it far more available to positive or negative judgment. If its eccentricities do not overtly distract us from a performance's form (and like many thinkers who have examined the principles of aesthetic judgment, Kant believed the human mind is wired to seek out pleasing forms) such features may be perceived as contributing positive defining character. In the most fortuitous instances, these idiosyncrasies add an ineffably "human" quality to the electronically captured musical representation; in not-so-fortunate cases we perceive in a take's eccentricities the stench of "clams"—moments unfit for aural consumption.

In other words, absent the presence of the performers, unable to feel the ambience and energy of the room, idiosyncrasies of time and tuning become ever more apparent. And in the temporally magnified recorded representation, a moment of musical silence may become as powerfully felt as the loquacious "flash" (if I can recall a word we often applied to the lead guitarists of Hendrix's day) that so impresses in live performance. Record making thus tends to require an evenness of delivery, a control of tuning and tempo we might characterize as "impassioned constraint." At their best, this is what the studio cats delivered; it's what eared Leon his late-Sixties reputation as the "Master of Space and Time." As Hendrix continued his transition from live performer to studio musician, and subsequently from artist to producer, he was doubtless learning these crucial distinctions. What makes listening to the Band of Gypsys performances captured on January 1st 1970 so exhilarating is that we hear in them the most visually demonstrative of guitarists, inspired by the Fillmore crowd but not playing to them, channeling his talents in full awareness of the different requirements of the recorded medium.

A Band of Gypsys

As was revealed by the relatively complete Band of Gypsys collection, *Live at the Fillmore East* (1999), the group's four December 31st 1969–January 1st 1970 performances delivered occasional rough patches amidst flashes of brilliance to match anything in the Hendrix canon. Left out of that compilation was the opening set of their two-night run, recently released in its entirety as *Machine Gun* (2016). Now that we have all of the material from these shows, it is possible to hear both the promise and the uneven application of Jimi's second great trio.

Marred by opening night jitters and technical issues, it's easy to see why these takes remained unreleased. The Band of Gypsys' first set demonstrates how paradoxically dependent exciting pop records often are on the relaxed delivery, sonic control, and intent focus—the impassioned constraint that tends to characterize a good studio performance.

To my ears, it is the bravura renditions of "Stone Free" and "Machine Gun" from January 1st that best showcase comprehensive character of Hendrix's musical imagination. In "Stone Free," their opening night's over-aggressive pressing has abated and we hear a relaxed, assured, and yet still energetic band supporting their leader through a rendition of one of the Experience's first recorded tracks. Released more than three years earlier as the B-side of "Hey Joe," the tune expands from its original length of 3:36 to wander through fourteen minutes of errant improvisation. Mounting theme upon theme in a manner reminiscent of beboppers like Dizzy Gillespie or Dexter Gordon, or as Miles Davis himself posited, John Coltrane, we hear Hendrix at once in full flight and anchored by the Buddy Miles–Billy Cox rhythm section. Here, as in the "Rainy Day" jams, Hendrix is liberated from the necessity of both steering the rhythm section and playing lead. As a result, the clarity of Jimi's playing is astonishing, as is the adaptability of the apparently "simple" grooves Miles and Cox bring to the "freer" fusion of rock, blues, and R&B traditions through which the Gypsys wander.

While there is much we might say about the terrible beauty of the amply praised "Machine Gun," in the interest of space I want to point to a not-so-fleeting moment in the track issued as "Power to Love" on the 1970 *Band of Gypsys* (but named "Power of Soul" on subsequent releases). This take, I believe, reveals the potential of the band to attain a temporal sublimity quite unlike anything the Experience could deliver. But before we go there, I want to point out what I hear as the difference between "Power to Love" and "Power of Soul," as the same number from the December 31st early show is called on the *Machine Gun* release.

Hendrix clearly considered "Power of Soul" to be the new band's signature number, and the four Fillmore shows give us four very different takes to explore. In Take One, we hear a band understandably on edge and not quite able to settle into the sort of groove they will eventually hit. With their leader revealing that "even Hendrix" was subject to nerves, we hear the guitarist rushing slightly ahead of his drummer and bassist. A top-down listening might give the impression that Hendrix's R&B-oriented rhythm section is unable to keep up. Absent from the opening set performance is precisely what had been present in the "Rainy Day" jam: time felt so communally that the music breathes in and out with collective power, a power that is absolutely present in the canonical take, "Power To Love."

Doubtless accustomed to the sound of the Experience, an early *Rolling Stone* reviewer wrote of the 1970 *Band of Gypsys* release that with "lots of powerful, together guitar, able bass by Cox, and at times overbearing drums by Miles," Hendrix "overcomes on pure tension alone . . . as both 'Message To Love' and 'Who Knows' aptly demonstrate" (Von Tersch). My different ears hear a very different record. What the young critic did not pause to consider is that what his Experience-tuned ears perceived as "overbearing drums" was in fact the foundation upon which the "strength" he heard in the record's guitar-work was being raised. For the tension we sense in the most powerful moments of the Fillmore East performances is *ensemble* tension. There is no way that musical tension of this sort can be produced "alone," and together, in their fourth effort, the Gypsys get it right.

In "Power to Love," much as in opening the measures of "Rainy Day, Dream Away," Hendrix's intro begins with eight undistorted bars in the Albert King mode, followed by four bars that introduce the figure around which "Power of Love" is built. These twelve bars culminate in a one-measure rest. Well, the rest is something on the order of a measure. For in the slightly retarded moment leading up to the pause, and in the sustained chord that overhangs it, the Gypsys collectively feel rather more than the expected four beats. I urge you to get hold of the track and to try counting out this temporally pregnant moment. Do so and you'll see that their meter is not marked by metronomic perfection in the way the session cats might play the tune (or that Pro Tools would correct it). But, the way this moment is intuitively and communally felt opens a rift in time unheard in the Gypsys three previous takes of "Power," and it is in this temporal shift that we approach the rock'n'roll sublime.

It has been said that during the second night's performances especially, Hendrix was focused more on the record-in-the-making than on entertaining the Fillmore crowd. With apologies to those present who may have been disappointed by Jimi's uncharacteristically "stock-still" presence, in the relaxation (or enabling fatigue) of their January 1st performance we hear, in potential, the kind of groove alchemy the Band of Gypsys might have realized had the project been able to go forward. For when Miles's slightly delayed snare shots call them back in, the three Gypsys *as ensemble* crash into a groove *within* which Hendrix is able to deliver a solo as exhilarating as any ever heard on record. It is a moment of collectively realized space and time that, if not sublime in the "boundlessly" or "absolutely great" sense that Kant understood the word, is *felt* as exceptionally and undeniably *bad ass*.

Those of us who revere Hendrix's prodigious talent have often speculated about where his music might have taken us had he lived beyond September 1970. Maybe the much-anticipated collaboration with Miles Davis and Tony Williams, who had anchored Davis's second great quintet and is widely considered the most important jazz drummer to emerge in the era, would have seen Hendrix play an even more vital role than he did in the dawning jazz fusion movement. Or perhaps he would have turned increasingly from live performance to record production. What we do know, however, is that Jimi Hendrix, who had once counseled Mike Bloomfield, "This is a world of lead guitar players, but the most essential thing to learn is the time," said on New Year's Day 1970, even as he, Cox, and Miles were laying down grooves that would thereafter influence generations of players, "I want to bring it down to earth. I want to get back to the blues, because that's what I am" (*Machine Gun*, p. 9). It's clear that Hendrix was referring here to the musical tradition he valued above all others. But in voicing his desire to "bring it down to earth," he may also have been talking about the virtues of rock solid time, collectively felt.

15
You Can't Use My Name

RICHARD BILSKER

Jimi Hendrix changed music. His influence still reverberates fifty years after the release of *Are You Experienced.* As noted in interviews from 2010, with those around him in his last days, Jimi was still thinking about ways to shake things up. As David Fricke notes in "Jimi's Last Ride"

> In one of his final interviews . . . Hendrix told Britain's *Melody Maker* that he had nothing but the future on his mind. "I want a big band," he declared. "I don't mean three harps and fourteen violins. I want a big band full of competent musicians that I can conduct and write for. And with the music we will paint pictures of Earth and space, so that the listener can be taken somewhere." Hendrix also said he'd been "thinking that this era of music—sparked off by the Beatles—had come to an end. Something new has got to come, and Jimi Hendrix will be there."

He wasn't, though. His last months were filled with disputes with musicians, management, and the contractors working on his recording studio Electric Lady. When Jimi died in September 1970, he left no will. His estate passed to his father who controlled the legacy and in 1995 created Experience-Hendrix, LLC.

Jimi's story is well-known, his image is iconic, and the recordings still confound and inspire. What is less known by fans of his music is that Jimi Hendrix changed the nature of law. Twice.

ExperienceHendrix v. PPX Enterprises

In 2015, ExperienceHendrix, the entity that has the rights to the music of Jimi Hendrix, released an album with an unlikely title. *You Can't Use My Name: The RSVP/PPX Sessions* by Curtis Knight and the Squires collects recordings by singer Curtis Knight that included Jimi Hendrix.

It has often happened in the music industry, and especially in rock'n'roll, that artists would be signed to contracts that were either misunderstood by the artists or not fulfilled by management. David Kirby, in his book on Little Richard reproduces a 1987 conversation between Little Richard, Bo Diddley, and Chuck Berry regarding their early contracts, where they discussed earning a penny for every two records sold. Further, Chuck Berry was so used to not getting paid by venues he performed in, that he started demanding to be paid up front, in cash, before he would take the stage. Unfortunately, this had its own consequences as he was later charged with tax evasion for not reporting the cash. In more recent years, Prince had a dispute with Warner Brothers over his contract and changed his name to 🎜 from 1993 until 2000.

The story of Jimi Hendrix's affiliation with Curtis Knight is one in which there was a misunderstood and exploited contract. When Chas Chandler signed Jimi Hendrix and started the run of music that fascinates to this day, he thought all of Jimi's earlier ties were settled. Hendrix had performed and recorded with others before meeting up with Curtis Knight. These included Little Richard, The Isley Brothers, Don Covay, Joey Dee and the Starliters, and King Curtis.

Producer Ed Chalpin, who had recordings Jimi did with Curtis Knight in 1965–1966, became aware of Jimi's resurfacing with the Jimi Hendrix Experience and tried to enforce the 1965 contract. The ensuing legal entanglement hounded Jimi until his death, resulted in the *Band of Gypsys* album released on Capitol instead of Reprise in the US, and was not fully resolved until 2003. One thing that was in dispute was whether additional recordings that Jimi made with Curtis Knight in 1967, but not as part of Knight's band, could use Hendrix's name. Jimi always maintained that he told Chalpin that his name could not be used. Chalpin said that Jimi had never said that.

As the 2015 release indicates, with audio evidence, Jimi said repeatedly, "You can't use my name." Chalpin repeatedly reissued the recordings with more recent images of Hendrix, implying that these were recent recordings of Hendrix as frontman. The first resolution of the case in 1973 determined that the only recordings that Chalpin could market were the original 1965–1966 recordings. Chalpin and PPX did not honor this decree and licensed recordings a dozen times. In 2002, the English Courts upheld the original decree and US courts followed in 2003. In 2007, ExperienceHendrix won a $900,000 judgment against PPX and in 2014 struck a deal which gave total control of the recordings to Experience Hendrix once and for all. This resulted in the release of *You Can't Use My Name*. As John McDermott notes in his liner notes for the release, "The 1968 settlement with PPX would weigh heavily on Hendrix throughout 1969" and even though *Band of Gypsys* was delivered to Capitol in fulfillment of the US lawsuit, litigation in the UK was ongoing and Jimi died before the scheduled trial. Another compilation, "Curtis Knight (featuring Jimi Hendrix): Live at George's Club 20" was released in 2017 by ExperienceHendrix in conjunction with Sony, but available only on the ExperienceHendrix website. It contains live recordings from December 1965 and January 1966.

This saga helped change the law in confirming a new standard in breach-of contract cases. Typically, the remedies for breach of contract are either specific performance or damages. Damages is financial compensation for the loss generated by the breach. When courts order that the contract be fulfilled in some way, it is called specific performance. This is the less common result and is used when damages are not adequate. Damages are based on the claimant's loss.

A newer standard arose from a 1974 case, *Wrotham Park Estate Co. v. Parkside Homes Ltd.* In this case, damages were not based on loss, but rather on an anticipated profit. *Wrotham Park* was considered an exception to the rule. This standard was extended in 2000 by the High Court in the case *Attorney General v. Blake. Blake* was about an ex-spy who published a memoir in violation of English law. The government, though, could not claim that it suffered a financial loss, so the court awarded all the profits to the government.

In 2003, the Blake standard was used as precedent in *ExperienceHendrix* v. *PPX Enterprises*. ExperienceHendrix was awarded "such sum as might reasonably be demanded" if the contract had been relaxed. We have arrived at a situation where we have gone from loss (the usual standard), to profit (*Wrotham Park* and *Blake*), and now this new standard of profit that *would have* occurred if the ExperienceHendrix *had* allowed the breach (*ExperienceHendrix*).

Experience Hendrix L.L.C. v. Hendrixlicensing.com Ltd.

This second case involves whether or not Jimi Hendrix's brother Leon Hendrix and his business partners could use Jimi's image, name, and signature on products. The area of law here involves Right of Publicity. Right of Publicity refers to a person's right to control the commercial exploitation of their likeness. Some states recognize an extension of this called Postmortem Right of Publicity. In 1985, California enacted the Celebrities Rights Act which granted that rights of publicity survive the celebrity's death and pass to the heirs. Given the importance of celebrity in California, it is not surprising that this idea would start there. It was partly in response to a 1979 court ruling that Bela Lugosi's heirs did not inherit his right of publicity. Twelve other states have such laws. These laws have only applied, though, depending on the state where the celebrity maintained a residence (domicile) at time of death. Jimi Hendrix died in New York, which does not have such a law.

What is new in this case is that the state of Washington passed the Personality Rights Act (WPRA). This law from 2008 extends the right of publicity, regardless of the state of domicile at death. It essentially applies Washington property law to what would normally be governed by New York law. In light of this, ExperienceHendrix (which is based in Washington) prevailed against Hendrixlicensing.com Ltd. in 2014.

At first this seems like a victory for celebrity rights. As pointed out by Robert Rossi in a note in the *Harvard Law Review*, this case could be the beginning of a Constitutional problem. Rossi argues that the WRPA violates at least three sections of the United States Constitution: the Due Process Clause, the Full Faith and Credit Clause, and the Commerce Clause.

Due Process guarantees that states can't deprive you of life, liberty, or property without legal process. The Full Faith and Credit Clause guarantees that states must respect each other's laws. The Commerce Clause gives Congress the power to regulate interstate commerce and prevent states from interfering in Congress's regulatory power. If Washington's statute stands, it will produce confusion in interpreting the Constitution, a situation Rossi calls "Jurisdictional Haze."

Conflicting Philosophies of Law

Legal Realism (and its successor theories like Critical Legal Studies) implies that the law is whatever the courts say it is. This view opposes theories like Natural Law Theory and Legal Positivism. Natural Law Theory holds that what the law is, is determined by checking it either against some standard (like the word of God or the natural order) or against some process (how the law was made). On this view, it's possible that something looks like it is law, but is not *really*, because it falls short either in content or what procedures lead to its becoming law.

Legal Positivism is the view that the law is whatever is made by duly authorized legislated bodies (it is *posited*). According to the Positivists, whether a law is a good one or not, is a separate question from whether it is a law or not. The Realists, though, reject both Natural Law Theory and Legal Positivism as depending too much on written law. For the Realists, if a law is on the books, but not enforced, it may not be law. Law is what is actually enforced. For example, if one judicial district interprets the law one way and another district another way, what the law is, is different in those two locations.

Oliver Wendell Holmes, a Realist and Supreme Court Justice once said, the law is what the bad man thinks it is, because that is what guides his behavior. The Critical Legal Studies movement takes this one step further. The fact that you cannot predict entirely accurately what the courts will do, or even whether laws on the books will be declared constitutional, means that there's no such thing as a law.

If we accept a view like Realism, Jimi Hendrix, through ExperienceHendrix, changed the law in significant ways. It is not often that significant changes to contract law happen in common-law countries like England and the US. This new

standard is also philosophically interesting. The High Court
mentions in the ruling that the *Blake* standard is the exception, rather than the rule, but does not give any guidance as to
how and when it should be used. In *Blake*, this was said by
Lord Nicholls:

> No fixed rules can be prescribed. The courts will have regard to all the
> circumstances . . . A useful general guide, although not exhaustive, is
> whether the plaintiff had a legitimate interest in preventing the defen-
> dant's profit-making activity and, hence, in depriving him of his profit.

This amounts to saying: the court knows it when it sees it. In
the PPX case, this court does not further clarify how the standard is to be applied, but does say that any reasonable observer
of the situation would conclude that, as a matter of practical
justice, PPX should make (at the least) reasonable payment for
its use of the masters in breach of the settlement agreement.

The "reasonable person" standard has a long history in common law and is usually co-variant with the "jury of one's peers"
idea. The problem is, who gets to decide what's reasonable?
This new standard also changes the predictability of contract
law proceedings. How can you know in advance which standard
will the court use?

The implications of the WPRA case are more troubling. The
Full Faith and Credit Clause undergirds many important protections in the United States. It's what allows us to not have to
get a new driver's license for each state we drive through on
vacation or for a state to force a couple to get married again
when they move to a new state. In order for Due Process to still
apply, it has to be the case that one state's laws do not invali-
date another state's laws, and that a defendant would need to
know the laws, potentially, of all fifty states and not just the
state of domicile at the time of the celebrity's death.

Washington's law seems to grant postmortem publicity on
everyone, whether they ever lived in the state of Washington or
not. It will be interesting to see whether this law can withstand
challenge of its constitutionality. Either way, the law has
already affected publicity rights significantly. There was some
controversy in recent years regarding the US Supreme Court
case *Citizens United v. Federal Election Commission* 558 US
310 (2010) which granted free speech protection to corpora-

tions. This is because of the growing trend of treating corporations as legal persons. The WPRA case raises the specter of dead people as legal persons (undead persons?) and setting standards for who can speak for dead persons or use their images in advertisements, on products, or on holographic performances.

In Aesthetics, the Institutional Theory of Art has some parallels to Legal Realism. According to the Institutional Theory of Art, art is whatever the art world (critics, museums, buyers, and sellers) says it is. This view opposed the idea that anyone could provide an essential definition of art. An essential definition is one in which you specify all the characteristics needed to be included in the class of things you are defining.

Essential definitions are hard to produce, falling prey to being too broad or too narrow. Take the word "chair," for example. "Something you sit on" would be too broad, because that includes couches, the floor, benches, etc. "Something to sit on, designed for one person, with a seat and four legs" would be too narrow, because chairs can have three legs, one leg (like a barstool), or no legs (like chairs designed for gamers). One way around this is a cluster definition. A cluster definition is the idea that there may not be a list of necessary characteristics to make something fit the class you are defining, but there may be a list of characteristics that you might have a sufficient number of to meet your standard—a cluster of the larger list. The philosopher Ludwig Wittgenstein said that this would be a good way to define a game, given the variety of things we consider games.

A problem arises regarding how many characteristics we need to list. When it comes to particularly thorny concepts like art and religion it's very hard to specify how many are enough or whether all are equally important or whether some parts of the cluster are more important than others. For example, in defining religion is a belief in a higher power more important than specific devotional practices?

The Institutional Theory is prompted by the hopelessness of a satisfactory cluster definition, due to the nature of artists. As soon as you have a comprehensive list of characteristics, some artist would challenge the notion and produce something that would be considered art, but not meet the earlier standards. Instead, the Institutional Theory says that something is

considered art when it is deemed so. Whether or not it is art is
not determined by the qualities inherent the work, but rather
is socially constructed.

Is Hendrix's version of "The Star-Spangled Banner" art? At
the time of his performance in Woodstock, many considered his
version to be noise, as the melody of the song is interspersed
with feedback. As noted by Jennifer Liu, Hendrix

> began his solo with pronounced single notes from the melody, but
> when the guitar melody coincided with the lyrics "and the rockets' red
> glare, the bombs bursting in air" he introduced the electrical distor-
> tions and simulated war sounds before returning to the initial state of
> the melody.

In middle school band, my music teacher Mr. Moscoso defined
music as "organized sound." The implication was that disorganized sound was noise. How far from the melody can Hendrix
go before it moves from organized to disorganized? On the
other hand, if we reject essentialist definitions, the question is
different. Do the director of the movie, the record label, or other
performers at Woodstock consider it art? What of the movie and
music critics? From the perspective of the Institutional Theory
of Art, the views of the people just mentioned would be more
important than the assessment of the average Joe watching the
movie or the casual listener.

Jimi Hendrix changed the way people listened to and
thought about music and he revolutionized the way people
played guitar. Now, after death, he is altering legal reasoning
and the way the law operates. We shouldn't underestimate the
importance of his impact on the law.

V

What Any of It
Is Worth

16
Artistic Expression in the Land of the Free

David MacGregor Johnston

I remember the first time I heard Jimi Hendrix's performance of "The Star-Spangled Banner."

It was my sophomore year in college and my friend Jim was playing the soundtrack album from the movie *Woodstock*, probably on vinyl, given his amazing collection of LPs. A group of us were hanging out in his room, drinking beer, playing cards, and enjoying the tunes floating through the background.

Suddenly, what I heard then as nothing more than the harsh tones of electric distortion invaded my head. I recognized the notes of our national anthem, but my conservative upbringing had not prepared me to accept this rendition as anything other than a bastardization of a song that should never be so desecrated. I screamed inarticulately in distress as I pleaded for the noise to stop, but I found no sympathy from my friends, who were relishing what *New York Post* critic Al Aronowitz called "probably the single greatest moment of the Sixties."

Thanks to my friends' guidance, I would soon come to appreciate the counter-culture ethos and psychedelic sounds of the Woodstock era. Eventually I recognized Hendrix's guitar playing for the virtuosity that it was and understood it as the work of a genuine artistic genius.

Although Hendrix had performed the anthem live many times before, and even recorded a studio version, it's unlikely that any of these earlier renditions would have been heard by establishment ears averse to the psychedelic sounds of Hendrix's guitar, but this performance of "The Star-Spangled Banner" found attention from the publicity surrounding 1969's

Woodstock Music and Art Fair, and especially from the release the following year of the Academy Award-winning documentary of the festival and of the soundtrack album a few months later.

The press reaction to the Woodstock performance was minimal compared to coverage of José Feliciano's jazz-infused World Series performance of the anthem a year earlier, but conservative Americans again heard the song as an unpatriotic spectacle in the midst of Vietnam War protests. Hendrix publicly disavowed any suggestion that it was intended as a protest, and even if it were, such a performance is far from unpatriotic. Rather, Hendrix's version of "The Star-Spangled Banner" is an original expression of his unparalleled individuality. Such originality in the social and political realm is a focus of John Stuart Mill's *On Liberty*, and originality in artistic endeavors is a central concern of Leo Tolstoy's *What Is Art?* With this performance of the national anthem, Hendrix shows us how political freedom and artistic freedom are inextricably linked through the value of individual expression.

O Say Can You See?

In *On Liberty*, an essential work of classical liberalism, John Stuart Mill focuses specifically on issues of social conformity and governmental authority. Although the book was published 110 years before Woodstock, in the midst of England's Victorian era, it is fully in the spirit of the counter-culture of the 1960s.

Much like American mainstream square society of the 1950s and 1960s, the Victorians operated under a strict set of social values that emphasized hard work, thrift, and respectable behavior, and both eras are characterized by a burgeoning middle class that promoted high standards of personal morality, including sexual restraint, a low tolerance for crime, and an outward appearance of dignity. Mill understood the social institutions of his era as restricting the free expression of individuality, ultimately arguing that nonconformity should be nurtured and protected, a central tenet of Sixties counter-culture.

Mill begins his investigation of individual freedom by tracing the history of how governments have tyrannized their people. Rejecting the notion of an originating social contract, he describes the earliest societies as being under the rule of powerful individuals or ruling castes who claimed authority through sheer strength or family lineage. In societies ruled by masters and monarchs, absolute authority is a threat to individual freedom, as the rulers and the ruled find themselves in a necessarily antagonistic relationship. The pursuit of liberty in these societies is an effort to defend the people from tyrannical rulers. The subjects sought out protection by establishing specific political rights and through the development of constitutional checks on power.

As history progressed, humans came to regard their leaders as serving and reflecting the will of the people. As such, it was deemed that there was no need to limit the power of this sort of leader, since there was no fear of the people tyrannizing themselves. When "We the People" established a democratic republic, it became clear that the people really did not rule themselves.

First, the rulers generally were not the same sorts of people who were ruled, and they exercised power over those without it. Second, it is possible for a majority of the people purposefully to oppress a minority of the population. Such a "tyranny of the majority" is far worse than the traditional tyranny because its reach extends beyond the political arena into "the prevailing opinion and feeling" of society, which is the basis of cultural norms and against which there can be no legal safeguard.

Indeed, public opinion and social pressure often do more to restrain individuality and to suppress dissent than any law could accomplish. Furthermore, when a majority party attempts to impose a particular belief on the society as a whole, the focus is on what beliefs the society should prefer, not on the broader question of whether a society should impose prevailing beliefs on some faction that does not share them.

So, given that the only justification for preferring a particular belief is the individual's own preference for it, Mill concludes that, "the only purpose for which power can be rightfully exercised over any member of a civilized community, against his will, is to prevent harm to others. His own good, either physical or moral, is not a sufficient warrant" (*On Liberty*, p. 11).

In other words, if I were to blast "Purple Haze" through stereo headphones at the risk of later hearing loss or to go naked on Max Yasgur's farm one rainy August weekend, I would not be harming anyone else and accordingly should not be prevented from doing so. On the other hand, if I were to blast "Purple Haze" through stereo speakers on my porch in the middle of the night or to flash unsuspecting people on a city street corner on a sunny afternoon, then I would be causing harm to others and so may justly be prohibited from engaging in such acts.

Mill does add the caveat that this principle applies only to people in the "maturity of their faculties," so we are right to interfere in the free actions of children and members of a "society in which the race itself may be considered in its nonage" until such time as they are able to act rationally in their own self-interests. Of course, the latter group's inclusion betrays the prejudice of British imperialism that was synonymous with the Victorian era, and Mill claims that despotism is a legitimate form of governing such a society, provided that the overseers act toward the betterment of the populace.

The Land of the Free

Promoting the general welfare is fundamental to Mill's utilitarian perspective, which entails that a society is just when it maximizes happiness and minimizes harm. Certainly, preventing harm to others supports these ends, and interfering with an individual's liberty is a form of harm that can be justified only if that liberty causes harm to others. My freedom brings happiness to me and society's interfering with it brings me harm. Viewed collectively, maximizing individual freedom benefits the society as a whole.

Mill acknowledges that there are times when the greater good may require the individual to take some action, such as paying taxes or rescuing a drowning child, since not doing so would be a harm to others, but in general society has only an indirect interest in that part of my life that affects only myself. "The only freedom which deserves the name, is that of pursing our own good in our own way, so long as we do not attempt to deprive others of theirs, or impede their efforts to obtain it" (pp. 14–15). To that end, Mill enumerates three areas of individual liberty that must be protected if a society is to be considered free.

First, there is the liberty of thought and opinion, what he calls the "inward domain of consciousness," and of the free expression thereof. Second, we require what he calls the "liberty of tastes and pursuits," that is, doing as we like with our own lives even if mainstream society would consider it foolish or wrong, so long as we do not harm others. Third, we have what he calls the liberty of "combination of individuals," in other words the "freedom to unite" for peaceful purposes. The key point here is that allowing the greatest possible liberty of thought and action actually is good for society.

If we consider the consequences of suppressing unfavorable opinions, there is a greater potential for harm than for good. Acknowledging that any belief is either completely true, completely false, or most likely partly true and partly false, Mill shows that the expression of each sort of belief will support the common good. If the suppressed opinion is completely true, then we have deprived the society of the benefit of hearing it and thereby of correcting a false belief. If the suppressed opinion and the commonly held belief each are partly true and partly false, then we have deprived the society of improving itself through the clash of ideas, which allows us to build whole truths from the various true parts.

Even a wholly false belief benefits society by allowing us to develop vigorous arguments against it, which in turn allows us to support commonly held true beliefs on rational grounds and not purely out of prejudice. The danger here is that a dogmatically held true belief will become moribund if the masses who hold it do not fully understand it and cannot coherently defend it against attack. Clearly, there is more good in itself from holding completely true beliefs instead of partly true or wholly false ones, and since we have a duty to act on our beliefs, we must do all we can to ensure that our beliefs are correct, which means being open to criticism and debate.

Mill adapts these arguments for the liberty of thought to the liberty of action, since the expression of individuality is essential for personal and social progress. Conformity in tastes and pursuits is dangerous not only because it stifles creativity and diversity, but also because the nurturing of individuality is what produces fully developed human persons:

It is not by wearing down into uniformity all that is individual in themselves, but by cultivating it and calling it forth, within the limits imposed by the rights and interests of others, that human beings become a noble and beautiful object of contemplation . . . (*On Liberty*, pp. 64–65)

Furthermore, society benefits from "different experiments of living" as a way to attack the "despotism of custom," which Mill sees as the main obstacle to human advancement.

Simply accepting the society's customs without question is a reflection of poor moral character. Rather, we need to make free choices to exercise our full human faculties. Such liberty of action also serves society because society may learn something from nonconformists, and nonconformity allows genius to develop. Thus, we should value what originality brings to the world, since what each individual needs to flourish may be different from what others need. We learn about our own weaknesses by observing the weaknesses of others, and we can better ourselves by combining the best traits of others into our own expressions of originality.

Mill does not include a specific argument in support of the freedom to unite, but applying a similar king of argument we can say that such a combining of individuals maximizes happiness by allowing people to exchange ideas and to share ways of living. We cannot deny that the Sixties' counter-culture was a grand experiment in alternative lifestyles and nonconformist ideas, and by all accounts, the Woodstock Music and Art Fair was a peaceful combining of individuals. As the festival relates to mainstream America of that time, Mill's words are prescient:

> In this age the mere example of non-conformity, the mere refusal to bend the knee to custom, is itself a service. Precisely because the tyranny of opinion is such as to make eccentricity a reproach, it is desirable, in order to break through that tyranny, that people should be eccentric. (*On Liberty*, p. 69)

No one of the era was more eccentric than Jimi Hendrix. From his iconic fashions to his innovative guitar playing, Hendrix was the personification of nonconformity.

By the Dawn's Early Light

The Jimi Hendrix Experience had played its final gig less than two months earlier at the Denver Pop Festival. Hendrix arrived at Woodstock with a new, larger group that would perform only two more times, and when they finally took the stage for the closing set on the morning after the festival originally was scheduled to end, the crowd had diminished significantly, down to perhaps fewer than ten percent of an estimated peak of between 400,000 and 500,000 people earlier in the weekend.

The band started with a variety of fan favorites and unfamiliar songs. "The Star-Spangled Banner" wouldn't come until the last quarter of a more than two-hour continuous performance. Sandwiched in the middle of a medley that included "Voodoo Child (Slight Return)" and "Purple Haze," Hendrix's solo performance of the anthem seems to arise as a spontaneous improvisation that wowed fans both at the venue and after the release of the documentary and soundtrack album. In fact, he even tells the audience they can leave, since, "We're just jammin', that's all."

Although he had recorded close to thirty live performances of the anthem prior to this day, fans and critics agree that there was something special about this rendition. Perhaps it was the eerie, morning quiet of a relatively deserted venue, but most critics point to his exceptional use of distortion and feedback interspersed throughout the middle of the verse that evokes the chaos of war, including bombs bursting, jets screeching, and even people wailing in anguish.

To be sure, Hendrix's version of "The Star-Spangled Banner" is unconventional. Many mainstream detractors heard an anti-American protest, but Hendrix rejected this interpretation of his performance. Appearing on *The Dick Cavett Show* soon after the festival, he responded to a question about the controversy over the anthem by saying, "I don't know, man. All I did was play it. I'm American, so I played it. I used to sing it in school. They made me sing it in school, so it was a flashback."

Disagreeing with Cavett's characterization of the performance, Hendrix stated, "That's not unorthodox. I thought it was beautiful." Three months later, at a gathering of the Black Associated Press in Harlem, when asked why he played it, Hendrix replied:

> Oh, because we're all Americans . . . But nowadays when we play it, we don't play it to take away all this greatness that America's supposed to have. We play it the way the air is in America today. The air is slightly static, isn't it? (*Hendrix on Hendrix*, p. 217)

So, at the very least, Hendrix seems to admit that his version was intended as a commentary on the contemporary state of affairs. The inclusion of several bars of "Taps" after the warlike sounds and just before the last couplet of the verse suggests that it was at least a comment on the war in Vietnam, if not also on the establishment's response to domestic political protests, for example what had happened at the Democratic National Convention a year earlier in Chicago. As such, it is a musical expression of belief about then current affairs and should be supported on Mill's utilitarian grounds.

Irrespective of whatever opinion may or may not have been intended to be expressed by this performance, Mill would celebrate it solely as a demonstration of individual taste and originality. Certainly, it does not conform to the expectations demanded by the customs of traditional performance, but whether we like this psychedelic rendition of "The Star-Spangled Banner," his playing it causes no harm: If you don't like it, you don't have to listen to it, but maybe you should.

> Originality is the one thing which unoriginal minds cannot feel the use of . . . The first service which originality has to render them, is that of opening their eyes: which being once fully done, they would have a chance of being themselves original. (*On Liberty*, p. 67)

Hendrix's originality is a sign of his own artistic flourishing, and his genius as a guitarist has inspired other players. His free choice to perform the anthem in this way was an exercise of his full faculties that opens new possibilities for the rest of us.

So Gallantly Streaming

Precisely because of its expressiveness and originality, Hendrix's performance is a genuine work of art. In 1897, Leo Tolstoy completed *What Is Art?*, a work that also resonates well with the Woodstock era. Much like Mill, Tolstoy favors creativity and originality over customary approaches to art, but much of his analysis is influenced by a midlife spiritual awakening that led him to hold positions of pacifism and Christian anarchism, which rejects hierarchical structures and authoritarian rule.

Tolstoy's ideas on nonviolent resistance directly influenced Mahatma Gandhi and Martin Luther King, Jr., so Tolstoy is really the primogenitor of the American civil rights and anti-war movements. We can imagine that he would be delighted by the prospect of a festival that promised "Three Days of Peace and Music," and while his endorsement of chastity and sexual abstinence would have clashed with the free love aspects of the hippie lifestyle, his opposition to private property would have integrated well with the counter-culture ethos.

By the time Tolstoy was writing *What Is Art?*, the practices of making art and of art criticism had, in his view, degenerated from art's original "religious" focus and had succumbed to the "charm of obscurity." In Tolstoy's view, early Christian art was inspired by the unity of humankind with God and with each other, and promotes the Christian tenets that we are all children of God, that we are all equal under God, and that we all should strive for mutual love among humankind. More generally, religious art focuses on expressing universal truths about the meaning of life.

With Church patronage, art shifted its focus toward worshipping religious figures, and private patronage and Renaissance ideals led to pleasurable art that focused on the exultation of beauty. Beauty, however, is an illegitimate criterion for distinguishing genuine art from "counterfeit art," works that should not be considered truly artistic, because such a nebulous concept cannot provide an objective definition of art. Rather, beauty in whatever aesthetic philosophy equates simply to the pleasure received by the consumer of a particular, usually popular, artwork. Once beauty becomes the standard, artists must create works that fit the fashion of the day.

Furthermore, professional artists are not trained in a way that promotes genuine originality. Instead, art schools teach people to imitate the styles and methods of the great masters, and presumed originality comes from art's becoming "artificial and cerebral." Artists compose their works with technical acumen and fill them with cultural allusions, but in so doing the works become incomprehensible to the masses who have not been trained to solve the puzzles that the works present or who are unfamiliar with the aspects that align the works with a particular class, region, or style. The main indicators of this sort of illegitimate art are borrowing, which is recycling common elements from earlier works to mimic real art; imitation, which is characterized by highly detailed realism; effectfulness, which highlights the spectacle of the medium; and diversion, which adds intellectual interest through gratuitous content such as the melding of styles or the establishment of arbitrary parameters for the work.

Tolstoy claims that the development of art criticism as its own field is a symptom of the degeneration of art, since artworks now need to be explained in order to be appreciated, and such intellectual analysis alienates us from experiencing the art as art. Art criticism also adds to the problem by honoring the acknowledged masters, since new artists are cajoled into imitating great works instead of expressing their own feelings in truly original ways. In this respect, we see Tolstoy echoing Mill's ideas about the tyranny of the majority and the despotism of custom.

Indeed, it is this "manifestation of feeling in his own particular fashion" that marks the true artist for Tolstoy (*What Is Art?*, p. 98). The true artists do not create beautiful objects of contemplation that people of particular tastes find pleasurable. Rather, they create works that communicate "feelings of the simplest, most everyday sort, accessible to all people without exception, such as the feelings of merriment, tenderness, cheerfulness, peacefulness, and so on" (p. 130). Such universal art unites us with one another, because the work moves us as a consequence of its expressing a universal emotion that we then feel.

> Art is that human activity which consists in one man's consciously conveying to others, by certain external signs, the feelings he has experienced, and in others being infected by those feelings and also experiencing them. (*What Is Art?*, p 40)

What matters most, then, in valuing different artworks is the depth of feeling that is expressed, in other words the degree to which the artist "experiences the feeling he conveys," and the extent to which that feeling infects the consumer of that work of art.

Thus, the worth of an artwork is not determined by its content. Instead, Tolstoy identifies three criteria for valuing works of art: particularity, clarity, and sincerity. Particularity relates to the degree of specificity of the emotion expressed. A more particular emotion, for example the fear of a bad trip from dropping the brown acid, is more effectively imparted than a general feeling of fear.

Clarity relates to the purity of the feeling expressed. An emotion that is clouded by distractions, perhaps by mixed emotions, is less effectively transmitted from the artist to the consumer. Sincerity relates to how strongly and genuinely the artist feels the emotion to be communicated. Sincere artists are to some degree compelled to express strongly felt emotions and create art for their own satisfaction rather than "just in order to affect others."

Whether these conditions really are separate criteria or whether particularity and clarity are characteristics of sincerity, Tolstoy highlights sincerity as the most important measure of artistic merit. As consumers, we are drawn into, or infected by, sincerely expressed artworks, but we are resistant to, or even repelled by, works when it is clear that the artists do not feel what they're trying to express.

When artworks are created for reasons other than the artist's own satisfaction, we recognize a level of artificiality that, as it were, inoculates us from infection, no matter how particular or clear the emotion is or how proficient or innovative the artist is in technique. "Thus art is distinguished from non-art, and the worth of art as art is determined, regardless of its content, that is, independently of whether it conveys good or bad feelings" (p. 123). The more particular, clear, and especially sincere the performance, that is, the more intensely the artist experiences the individual emotion he or she unambiguously conveys, the greater the infection of that emotion in others, and thereby the greater the work of art.

The Home of the Brave

For Tolstoy, art conveys emotion from one person to another, just as language conveys thought. In fact, it is only through artistic talent that feelings get conveyed, which for him is the purpose of art. When he mentions "good or bad feelings," he is making a sort of moral claim. An artwork's being good or bad is a judgment about the moral worth of its content, not about the aesthetic merit of its infectiousness.

When Hendrix added his unique musical phrasings to the prescribed notes of "The Star-Spangled Banner," he was expressing bad feelings, but he was making great art, perhaps on a level approaching Pablo Picasso's famed *Guernica*, a highly infectious artwork that expresses moral outrage in a way that is anything but beautiful in the classical sense of that term. That painting was created in response to the 1937 bombing of the town of the same name by Nazi German and Fascist Italian warplanes at the request of the Spanish Nationalists during the Spanish Civil War.

Guernica was a significant communications center in the territory controlled by Republican forces, but the attack gained infamy because of the deliberate use of military forces to strike civilians. The bombing lasted almost two hours and was particularly devastating because it occurred on what would have been a market day, when farmers and other people from the surrounding area would have come to the city to conduct business. Contemporary reports put the number of casualties at close to 1,700 people, but now historians believe that it was somewhere between 170 and 300. In any case, the bombing of Guernica was a massacre.

Picasso had been commissioned by the Spanish Republican government to create a large mural for the Spanish display at the 1937 World's Fair in Paris, where he was living at the time. His original plan was to design something around the theme of the artist's studio, but an eyewitness account of the Guernica attack so moved Picasso that he abandoned his initial idea and was compelled to create what is now recognized as one of the most moving anti-war statements ever created. To be sure, the emotion expressed in *Guernica* is particular, clear, and sincere. It expresses not a general abhorrence of the ugliness of war, which might be particular enough, but the specific cruelty of this individual event. There are no distractions from the horrendous injustice, and there is no doubt about the intensity of Picasso's feelings regarding the bombing. It is a hard heart that is not fully infected with those same feelings upon seeing the painting, even reproduced in print or online. Hence, it is great art that expresses bad feelings, placing the immorality of that event fully on display.

Hendrix's version of "The Star-Spangled Banner" similarly expresses bad feelings about the immorality of a particular war, but there is no indication that Hendrix was responding to a specific incident in Vietnam, such as the My Lai Massacre which had happened prior to Woodstock, but received no American news coverage until September of 1969. Rather, he was addressing "the way the air is in America today." In other words, he was not expressing some general feeling of distress, but a particular angst in response to contemporary events.

That emotion comes through clearly, even though it is expressed through the feedback and distortion of his screaming guitar, and he is sincere: he is playing what he wants to play in precisely the way that he wants to play it. Furthermore, the listeners are fully infected by that emotion. Michael Wadleigh, director of the movie *Woodstock*, also served as a camera operator during Hendrix's set. He recalled the response to "The Star-Spangled Banner" from the people still at the festival:

> I looked out with one eye and I saw people grabbing their heads, so ecstatic, so stunned and moved, a lot of people holding their breath, including me. No one had ever heard that. It caught all of us by surprise. (Michael Ventre)

Even my own initial reaction of dismay could be considered a symptom of being intensely infected by his negative emotional expression. So, Hendrix created a genuine work of art on Tolstoy's account, and it is a great work because of the way that it infected and still infects listeners with the intense emotion he sincerely felt.

Other unorthodox renditions of our national anthem may or may not be genuine works of art, but they generally fall short of the greatness of Hendrix's performance. Consider two examples: José Feliciano and Roseanne Barr. Feliciano's performance before Game Five of the 1968 World Series was the first nontraditional version heard by masses of mainstream Americans. Coming only five weeks after the severe police reaction to protests at the Democratic National Convention, it's not surprising that it garnered disapproval from establishment stalwarts weary over anti-war protests, but there's no sense that Feliciano's interpretation was intended as a protest, or as an expression of any other opinion. The only issue was that he performed it in his trademark mellow style and included minor alterations to the traditional arrangement.

In other words, instead of a rousing anthem, he performed it as a sort of folk ballad, which should be respected from Mill's perspective supporting individual liberty, and which probably counts as art on Tolstoy's account. He is presenting the song in his own, original fashion, but it's not clear what particular emotion he intended to express. To that end, his performance seems a bit insincere, as if he's just doing the national anthem in a style that was expected of him and not because he was compelled by intense emotion to do it that way. So, it was a nice performance, but it was far from great art.

Roseanne Barr's infamous performance in July of 1990 at San Diego's Jack Murphy Stadium was anything but nice, and its reception was affected by coming only a week before Iraq's invasion of Kuwait. San Diego is the homeport of the Pacific Fleet, and US military forces in the Persian Gulf had already been put on high alert. So the public's response must be understood in the context of burgeoning patriotism at a time of impending war, which links Barr's performance more closely with Hendrix's and Feliciano's than might be thought at first glance.

The producer of Barr's hit sitcom *Roseanne* had taken ownership of the Padres only a few weeks earlier and wanted to raise interest in the team by inviting his top celebrity to sing the anthem. Barr is a comedian, but she had been including songs in her stand-up act at that time, and she claims to have planned to present a good version of the anthem. As has happened to more talented singers, she started too high and soon realized she'd just have to push through it. So, her unorthodox performance was merely a mistake from an unaccomplished singer rather than an intentionally original rendition. Moreover, her shrill performance was punctuated after the song by grabbing her crotch and spitting, which she claims was suggested by some Padres players as a funny way to mock baseball stereotypes. In the context of her botched singing, which already drew the crowd's ire, the public and the press did not take her gestures as a laughing matter. To be sure, the general perception was that the performance as a whole was intended to be the joke.

Although Tolstoy includes jokes as the sort of things that can count as art, Barr's performance, either as a whole or as only the gestures, fails as genuine art according to his criteria. First, there does not appear to be any emotion being expressed, much less a particular and clear one. Furthermore, her performance seems insincere, as if she's just playing up her TV personality in a sort of extreme buffoonery because that's what was expected of her. In any case, even if there were some emotion being expressed, baseball fans and other Americans who later heard the performance were far from infected with whatever feeling it might have been. Fans at the stadium heckled and threw large objects at her, and others later drove a steamroller over a boom box containing a cassette tape of her voice. Columnist George Will likened it to the Japanese sneak attack on Pearl Harbor. Then-President George H.W. Bush on national television called it "disgraceful." Whether it's reasonable to turn the national anthem into a joke, Mill would argue that she should have the liberty to do so, but Barr's performance met none of Tolstoy's conditions that would let it count as art.

So, we may reject Feliciano's version as being great art, and we may reject Barr's performance as being art at all, but the sincerity in Hendrix's rendition of the anthem communicates the deep emotion that he experienced in the midst of the Vietnam era. Part of Hendrix's artistic accomplishment may come from the unusual context of its performance during a rock concert as opposed to the familiar setting of the beginning of a sporting event, but as Dick Cavett later said in response to rewatching his interview with Hendrix, "I suppose I could have added that since we somehow acquired the most dismal, virtually unsingable dirge of a national anthem of any known nation, we should decorate Hendrix for turning it into music" (Michael Ventre).

Rather than an unpatriotic performance, Hendrix's unorthodox version of "The Star-Spangled Banner" sincerely expresses a clear frustration with the then-current state of affairs surrounding the Vietnam War and so counts, from Tolstoy's perspective, as great art, and should be celebrated, from Mill's perspective, for its free exercise of nonconformity.[1]

---

[1] I thank especially my valued colleague Kristi Castleberry for her thoughtful advice on earlier drafts of this chapter.

17
The Cry of Love

HANS UTTER

Jimi Hendrix's life and music are full of contradictions. His Adonis-like sexuality, virtuoso guitar playing, and onstage theatricality often overshadow the poetic and philosophical concerns of his life and music. The plight of loneliness and loss expressed in songs like "The Wind Cries Mary," "Burning of the Midnight Lamp," and "Belly Button Window" contradict the image of the all-powerful sex symbol and guitar god. The intensity of his acid-drenched psychedelic rock, coupled with his raw, on-stage display of sexual energy and bravado is in stark contrast to the many interviews highlighting his gentle nature and soft-spoken, shy personality.

For Hendrix, the message that he was trying to convey was dictated by the times in which he lived, the spirit of the age, the *Zeitgeist*. Philosophically speaking, Hendrix embraced *idealism*, seeking for both personal redemption through love and the collective evolution of humankind as a whole. Hendrix reveals himself to be a philosophical and romantic idealist in two ways.

First, he nurtured a view of women as semi-divine figures, and sought spiritual and sexual union with an idealized beloved. Secondly, the messianic conviction of "Are You Experienced" and "New Rising Sun" reflect his desire for transcendence and awakening, and his quest for a new vision of the world. Hendrix's artistic output was a battleground where his internal conflicts coalesced into a virtuosic, innovative force that propelled sonic experimentation into previously unrealized realms of self-expression. Hendrix's conviction that a concert hall could be transformed into an "electric church," reflects his determination to hasten the dawning of a new society.

Idealism

Although idealism is often defined in common parlance as "rose-colored glasses" and naivety ("youthful idealism"), it is an ancient underpinning of Western philosophy.

Plato (428–347 B.C.) sought to understand the nature of knowledge—how do we know, and what can we know? Plato came to the conclusion that authentic knowledge emanates from beyond the experience of our senses. In his famous Allegory of the Cave, he compares the prevailing human experience to an individual confined in a cave. Living in this cave, and knowing nothing else, he believes that the shadow play on the cave's wall is reality—even the process of illumination is occulted. In Hendrix's words, "You can't really believe everything you see and hear, can you?"

Yet, what if those individuals turn around, and realize the existence of real objects, and not merely their shadows? Plato contends that they would find the Ideal Forms (the eternal essences of the things we actually see), perennially existing outside of time and space, and discover true knowledge. For Plato, 'The One' was the source of all manifestations in the material world and the Ideal (or perfected) Forms. The question that manifests is: "How shall we find The One?" For Hendrix, love was the answer.

Plotinus and Divine Love

Plotinus (A.D. 205–270) adapted Plato's ideas into a new philosophical school, Neo-Platonism. His influence ranged from the austere theologian Saint Augustine, to the exuberantly romantic troubadours—the medieval minstrels. Plotinus brought Plato's conception of The One into a mystical and dynamic relationship with the real world. Instead of rejecting sensory experience, Plotinus believed that the Ideal Forms could be experienced in the material world. According to his philosophy, a unique beloved exists for everyone, but remains veiled. By discovering and uniting with their Beloved, an individual can directly experience The One.

The passion of love, *eros,* is a key for reaching the higher planes. Instead of renouncing the world, the "rainbow bridge"— between the momentary and the eternal—is found in the transitory experience of Beauty and Desire. Love is the essence of reality. The experience of Beauty can heal and uplift the soul. Nothing is more important in this world. In order to begin this journey, individuals must realize that they have been separated from The One. Without this understanding, they remain asleep in Plato's Cave, spectators to a parade of unreal images.

Roomful of Mirrors

"Room Full of Mirrors" is not what it first appears to be. The driving guitar riff, a variation on the classic train rhythm from "Killing Floor," is transformed into a weapon, capable of shattering the walls of Plato's Cave. Over a generic 2/4 country rhythm Hendrix invokes a primal ceremony of awakening: "I used to live in a room full of mirrors / All I could see was me."

Reality is hidden, veiled by personal projections and consensus reality. Even the typical blues riffs Hendrix employs are electrified by his vision, supporting Plotinus's contention that mundane phenomena can become transparent to Ideal Forms. Hendrix chooses freedom over comfort, "So I take my spirit and I crash my mirrors," turns away from the shadows towards The One, exclaiming "Now the whole world is here for me to see!"

Leaving the apparent world for the real one is not a comfortable process. The aftermath is dislocating: "Jangling breaking glass all in my brain / Cutting screaming crying in my head." Shattering his illusions even penetrates the barrier between waking and dreaming: "They [glass shards] used to fall in my dreams and cut me in my bed." His sexual relationships are revaluated, "I said making love was strange in my bed," setting the stage for the quest for his "true love to be." Suddenly, what was dark is illumined, "Nowhere to stumble / Nowhere to fall," and he sees "nothing but sunshine / all around." In the final verse his visionary experience of The One rends the fabric of the profane: "Love comes shining over the Mountains/ Love comes shining over the sea," finally revealing his hidden "other half," "Love will shine on my baby, then I'll know exactly who is for me."

Intimacy and introspection are evident in the diversity of extant recordings. In a 1969 Toronto concert, he announces the song thusly: "We'd like to talk about the rise of Atlantis, but that's history man. It's universal . . . Thank you very much, that's a fairy tale I dreamed one month ago. I grew up to play this song." In this rendition, he diverges from the lyrics to graphically depict several romantic relationships, concluding with the lines "I will realize I've been hypnotized / When I'm six feet underground."

And She Spread Her Wings High Over Me

The nurturing female, a divine mother, visits Hendrix in many of his works. Unlike the occasionally dark portrayals of his romantic liaisons, Hendrix always connected his angelic, nurturing females with freedom. His second album, *Axis: Bold as Love,* introduces "Little Wing," a free spirit "walking through the clouds," her mind free of any worries, "butterflies and zebra moonbeams and fairy tales, that's all she ever thinks of." She is free, flying through the world. Little Wing comforts Hendrix in his moments of despair, "when I'm sad she comes to me." Like a divine mother, she asks for nothing "With a thousand smiles she gives to me free," telling him that "It's all right, she says it's alright / Take anything you want from me." The song fades out on Jimi's invocation to "Fly On." In the words of Plotinus, "Then the soul, receiving into itself an outflow from thence, is moved and dances wildly and is all stung with longing and becomes love and is truly winged" (*Enneads*, VI.7.22).

In the song "One Rainy Wish," Hendrix describes a romantic encounter with either the spirit of music, a specific woman, or, an amalgamation of both. In this song Hendrix transports us to the transcendent realm of "Gold and Rose." This takes place in a dreamscape that merges color, sound, and scent. He meets with a woman under the "tree of song, sleeping so peacefully"; even though she is sleeping she is waiting for him: "In your hand a flower placed / Waiting there for me." Yet, in the waking world she is veiled. The song's chorus shifts from R&B ballad to hard rock, underscoring Hendrix's longing: "I have never, laid eyes on you / before this timeless day." The timeless day is the non-temporal realm of the Ideal Forms and The One, and he goes on to describe the "Eleven moons" that blaze "across the rainbows" above them.

In the song "Angel," Hendrix describes being visited by the semi-divine female presence, in this case clearly expressing the spiritual component of this love. The song opens with the words "Angel came down from heaven yesterday," and she offers him support: "and she stayed with me just long enough to rescue me."

Angel communicates the divine nature of love: "And she told me a story yesterday / About the sweet love between the moon and the deep blue sea." Plotinus's articulation of love as visible beauty, "therefore the productive power of all is the flower of beauty, a beauty which makes beauty" (VI.7.32), echoing the Ideal Forms inherent in The One. The temporal immediacy of the song is highlighted in the next verse, as Angel has returned to Hendrix as promised in the morning: "Sure enough this morning came unto me / Silver wings silhouetted against the child's sunrise."

Like a child, he sees the world anew, the sunrise also conveying the dawning of new experience of the world. The use of the words "unto me" reflect the grammar and word usage found in the King James Bible, and underscore the spiritual aspects of this encounter for Hendrix. "And my angel she said unto me / "Today is the day for you to rise / Take my hand, you're gonna be my man / You're gonna rise" / And then she took me high over yonder."

Hendrix is raised above the suffering and turmoil of the world through the potency of the divine feminine. The song fades out on the word "Fly on my sweet angel . . . forever I'll be by your side." The music mimics the sense of flying through continuously ascending guitar lines beneath a static bass line.

Bold as Love

Can we, as individuals, serve a greater purpose than our own personal happiness? Is there any method or meaning behind the chaotic and tumultuous events through recorded history? For Hendrix, the answer to both questions was a resounding Yes! Beyond his personal freedom and redemption, Hendrix thoroughly believed in the ability of music to transform society. For Hendrix, his music was an expression of his times, mirroring the intensity of social conditions, as well as foreshadowing

the collective evolution of humanity. Seen from this philosophical perspective, all consciousness is part of The One—ultimately there is only a single perceiver.

   The philosopher Georg Hegel (1770–1831) asserts that the
Zeitgeist (literally "time-spirit") of any given historical period—
the conflicts and resolutions between distinct cultural and social
forms reflect the evolutionary process of humanity towards The
One. For Hegel "Spirit is thus the self-supporting absolutely real
ultimate being" (*The Phenomenology of Mind*, p. 469) and the
experienced world can only be understood through its relationship to The One. Through every individual, The One is striving
towards a transcendent, self-contained, self-conscious, and completely free mode of existence. Each stage in world history is an
expression of The One's movement towards unity.

   Hendrix beckoned all to join in his visionary search for a
new world. His projected final album, *First Rays of the New
Rising Sun,* although never completed because of his death,
was intended for this purpose. Hendrix's belief that there is a
grand design for humanity, and that each individual could
experience a connection with The One, is found throughout his
entire body of work.

Come on Across to Me

The backwards guitar and drums that announce the title track
of *Are You Experienced* create an otherworldly feeling, as if
time was flowing in two directions at the same time. The
rhythm guitar abruptly enters, injecting suspended chords and
vaguely eastern melodies over the march-like drum patterns.
"If you could just get your . . . mind together / then come on
across to me"—sung in a soft, intimate timbre—invites and
challenges the listener to become "experienced." It is never
clearly explained what "experienced" refers to in the song. Is it
a plug for the band, homage to psychedelics or sex, or something entirely different?

   The song reflects a challenge as much as an invitation.
The listener (or whomever Hendrix was thinking of) becomes
the subject of the song, and offers a different perspective on
reality. But first we must let go of their "measly little world,"
where "you're made out of gold and can't be sold." This is the
world of limitation, defined by other's opinions, a world that

"won't let you go." These projections veil The One, but Hendrix calls us back towards another reality: "Trumpets and Violins off in the distance / I think they're calling our name," and he offers us aid, "Maybe now you can't hear them / but you will, if you just take hold of my hand." Celestial trumpets and violins ring in the distance, a distant dream of another life. To be "experienced" implies it is possible to wake up to The One within this world, requiring individual effort and courage, but allowing for unexpected possibilities: "We'll hold hands / and then we'll watch the sunrise, from the bottom of the sea."

As with Hegel, freedom is available to all, but requires conscious choice and action. In "Message to Love" Hendrix again offers a challenge: "If you wanna be free, come on along with me," acknowledging the resistance and difficulty of this endeavor "Don't you run away / look at your heart, baby / come on along with me today." As a messenger, Hendrix wants to share the new reality he has encountered, "Well I'm traveling at the speed / of a reborn man / I got a lot of love to give / No mirrors in my hand." By making this choice, the individual must first find themselves, and then their talent, and finally "work hard in your mind / so it can come alive."

In "Power to Love" Hendrix proclaims the "power of soul": "With the power of soul / anything is possible / with the power of you / anything you wanna do." Connecting with The One doesn't produce an army of zombies, but is the fulfillment of individuality. "Power of Love" critiques the drug culture of the Sixties, asking the audience to "shoot down some of those airplanes you've been riding" which can result in bad trips, or "floating so long and so slack" through life like a jellyfish. Inside of getting high, Hendrix invites us to "come on up to Earth," not escaping but reconnecting with our hidden potential, and connect with the "streaming rays of reality." Both of these compositions were slated to be part of *First Rays of the New Rising Sun*.

New Rising Sun

First Rays of the New Rising Sun was part of Hendrix's new direction, and he saw it as a vehicle for the process of social and individual evolution. The album's title track "New Rising Sun" merges both redemption through the divine female presence and the transformation of the world as a whole in a single lyric. The first iteration of the song was entitled "Gypsy Boy," and expressed an aching melancholy. The lyrics are in the form a dialogue: "Hey gypsy boy, where do you come from? / Said I come from the land of the New Rising Sun. / Hey gypsy boy, where are you trying to go to? / I'm going to spread a lot of love, and a lot of peace of mind too."

A self-described gypsy, Hendrix thought the song could be viewed as a dialogue with himself. In later versions of the song, Jimi introduced the words "Hey Baby," invoking a female presence. While retaining the basic chord progression, Hendrix opened the song with a highly complex instrumental piece that brought together elements of flamenco and Classical music. He is beckoned towards an ideal place, the "land of the new rising sun," and asks, plaintively, "May I come along?"

Hendrix believed that he was a messenger, which echoes Hegel's portrayal of an artist as a "spiritual workman":

> Spirit has raised the shape in which it is object for its own consciousness into the form of consciousness itself; and spirit produces such a shape for itself. . . . When the spirit has gained the shape of self-conscious activity, the artificer has become a spiritual workman. (p. 709)

Spirit (The One) exists in potential in the form of consciousness itself. Through the "shape" it assumes—the totality of the personality and activities undertaken—it can become self-aware, connecting the individual with The One. This echoes Hendrix's appeal to find your innermost essence, discover the unique talents and gifts that you can bring to world, and expand your consciousness ("work hard in your mind"). The "shape" of "self-conscious activity" implies that by awakening to your true potential, the artistic activity undertaken transcends superficial "artifice" and material production, and becomes, in fact, a spiritual process.

Jimi's Message for the Ages

For Hendrix, developing new sounds and refining his lyrics were parallel processes. At the same time, his individual yearning for love and presentation of new potentials for humanity were parallel processes. He was compelled by the suffering of others to share this message. In *The Lost Writings of Jimi Hendrix*, a collection of handwritten notes found after his death, he laments and identifies with individuals trapped in suffering:

> And I smell the scorch of the burnt out minds . . . who searched for the hurting truth of space and the dizziness they felt inside reflected off the spinning slave pebble earth as fragments of my life, some floating, some soaring in space.

For Hegel, free will requires a conscious choice for responsibility, and the awareness of the effects of our actions in the world. Hendrix saw himself both as free and as part of the enslaved masses of humanity.

He expresses his belief in The One in this fragment:

> We are not here alone, that there is God besides the temples they shall call bodies or vehicles, that each stone they touch, they shall learn more and more of the purpose of living and giving and receiving.

For Hegel, the evolution of the individual, through self-awareness, increased their connection with the "world-spirit" at the same time. As an individual expresses their unique talent more fully, they will also become more connected with all humanity.

Hendrix sees himself in this role, as a messenger serving a greater role in the conscious evolution of humanity:

> Forget of my name. Remember it only as a handshake . . . introduction to my belief which is God. Ride instead the Waves of my Interpreture. Music, Sound, Hypnotic if you choose. But truth and life regardless of your questionable timid compromises which I intend to erase . . . which I will erase without a hint of a reward as I am only a messenger and you are a Sheep in the process of evolution.

At the end of the day, we are left with his music, his image, and our own subjective experience as listeners.

Hendrix's idealism was a driving force in both his life and music. He never obscured his intentions behind superficiality, but expressed what he felt at that time. It requires great courage to step outside the walls of the cave, and look for the essence of reality. Did he find his divine, his beloved? Probably not, at least as far as recorded evidence tells us; yet, his belief that there was someone waiting for him, granted through visionary experience, still reverberates over the decades.

At least the integrity of his life's work, dedicated to higher ideals, although perhaps never fully realized, can serve as an inspiration to us all. Hendrix saw himself as a wanderer, a gypsy who traveled the world to share his music, without a home in any particular locale. Perhaps all of us share his sense of wandering, of traveling between birth and death, but how many of us have dedicated ourselves to a vision of Reality beyond the world we perceive with our senses?

Even though he never lived to see the release of *The First Rays of the New Rising Sun*, I believe that his intention is inspirational. If we aim for the stars and only get to the Mississippi Delta, grounding our goals in ideals that transcend our finite experience can only produce a richer and more deeply felt life experience.

18

Musical Order from Sonic Chaos

David Morgan

When you think of the defining characteristics of the guitar sound of Jimi Hendrix, you probably think of distortion, perhaps the wah-wah pedal, and almost certainly, feedback.

Hendrix was not the first guitarist to make use of the sound of guitar feedback in rock music. But he was the one who elevated its use from a "special effect" or sonic gimmick into a genuine source of new musical content and expression. And he was arguably the first to play the feedback itself in a way that fundamentally changed the vocabulary of the electric guitar.

Turn It Down! The Physics of Acoustic Feedback

We're all familiar with the sound of a microphone experiencing feedback. A person steps up to a podium in an auditorium or a conference hall and begins to speak. At first, their words are punctuated by a tiny whistle or hum, usually a high-pitched frequency, that falls away quickly as they speak. But at some point, this tiny whistle escalates rapidly into a piercingly loud squeal. People scramble to turn down speakers, angle and redirect microphones, adjust "EQs," and try various other remedies to try to make the annoying sound go away.

This type of audio feedback is caused when the microphone, which picks up sound and sends it to a speaker to be amplified, unintentionally picks up some of the sound coming *out of* the speaker. So the sound coming out of the speakers is literally "fed back" into the microphone to be amplified yet again. The resulting escalating cascade of sound is therefore called "feedback."

An electric guitar can produce feedback in much the same way. The vibrating strings produce a relatively quiet musical sound which is picked up by electronic components cleverly named "pickups". The resulting electrical signal is sent to an amplifier, which—you guessed it—amplifies the sound and makes it louder.

If this sound is loud enough, or if the guitar is very close to the amp's speaker, the vibration of the air can be intense enough to cause the guitar's strings to resonate and vibrate harder. More vibration in the strings leads to more sound to the speaker, and more sound from the speaker leads to more vibration of the strings. Feedback.

But at some point, instead of rushing to turn down the amp or move away from the speaker, rock guitarists learned to embrace the feedback—to manipulate it, and to bend it to their will. A new frontier of sonic possibilities was revealed, with Jimi Hendrix as one of its first explorers.

This type of musical feedback is a sonic innovation unique to electrically amplified instruments. An acoustic guitar or a violin can resonate, but they can't feed back. The strings of a grand piano may vibrate in sympathy with their neighbors to produce a rich chord full of harmonic complexity, but the volume of sound produced by a piano string always decays over time. A single piano string can't gather up the vibrational energy of a chord and increase its volume to emerge from the background notes louder than before.

What constitutes the musical instrument being played by Hendrix and his guitar-hero descendants when they employ a technique like feedback? When Hendrix bends feedback to his musical will, the "instrument" he is playing is not merely a Fender Stratocaster. It is a combination of the guitar, the amplifier, and the very air in the room.

The thing about feedback and electric guitars is, it's sometimes difficult to control or predict which note will actually be the one that resonates and feeds back. You can certainly help things along by fretting certain notes on certain strings while muting others, but coaxing the note you want out of the process of resonance and feedback isn't as simple a task as plucking a note with the pick.

You can hear this struggle in Jimi Hendrix's iconic performance of the "Star Spangled Banner" at Woodstock. At the start of the anthem, you can hear the feedback just starting to peek out over the notes at the end of each musical phrase. The notes are feeding back naturally, not always intentionally, and not always quite in tune. The incipient feedback is adding richness and sustain to each phrase, but it isn't quite rising to the level of new musical material on its own. But by the end of the performance—as we get to the "wave" in "Oh say, does that star-spangled banner yet wave . . ." and again at the "O'er the land of the free"—the feedback *is* the note. Hendrix is often not picking the notes with his left hand at all, he is just hammering away at the whammy bar while he works the strings with his right hand to simply pull those notes out of thin air.

When a pure musical tone emerges from the maelstrom of distorted guitar noise and electrical hums of an overdriven amplifier, we are witnessing an auditory example of what mathematicians and scientists sometimes call a "complex dynamical system", which is connected to a field of study more popularly known as "chaos theory".

Predictability, Randomness, and Something in Between

Feedback is more than just an acoustic phenomenon. Feedback loops arise in all sorts of physical systems—from our planet's climate to our body's metabolism.

If you start reading up on "chaos theory," you'll find that the scientific notion of chaos is somewhat difficult to define, and that no single definition satisfies researchers in every field. But if you take a step back and look at the broader implications of chaos theory, you'll discover that whatever definition you adopt, there are some philosophical implications that challenge our notions of the role of scientific laws and theories.

Take physics, for example. From the time of Isaac Newton until the mid-twentieth century, physicists assumed that nature was predictable, and that their job was to uncover the laws nature obeyed. Using these physical laws and the tools of mathematics, they could make predictions about how a physical system would behave. The assumption was that physical systems were "deterministic"—that the present state of any physical system uniquely determines its future state.

So if you knew the present state accurately enough, and applied the mathematical laws of nature, you could entirely predict the future of any physical system. For example—if you have a metal string of a certain length, and this density, under a certain tension, and pluck it with a particular force, it will vibrate at such-and-such frequency with a predictable volume. As long as you could measure all of the parameters, you could accurately predict what would happen.

This worldview of the predictability of nature led to an extreme sort of determinism among some scientists and philosophers. Pierre-Simon, Marquis de Laplace (1749–1827) wrote in his *Philosophical Essay on Probabilities*:

> We may regard the present state of the universe as the effect of its past and the cause of its future. An intellect which at a certain moment would know all forces that set nature in motion, and the respective positions of all items of which nature is composed, if this intellect were also vast enough to submit these data to analysis, it would embrace in a single formula the movements of the greatest bodies of the universe and those of the tiniest atom; for such an intellect nothing would be uncertain and the future just like the past would be present before its eyes.

In other words, a sufficiently perceptive and powerful intellect (whether God-like being or a massive supercomputer) should have the power to predict the future of the universe with unerring precision.

This worldview began to falter when it was recognized that many physical systems in nature (and the mathematical laws that describe them) are "non-linear". In a non-linear system or equation, a tiny change in the input to an equation can lead to a very large change in the resulting calculation. So in order to predict the behavior of a non-linear system, it would be necessary to know the current state of the system to infinite precision. No approximations are permitted, since even rounding off at the twentieth decimal place could result in a prediction that could be off by a factor of a hundred.

The inherent unpredictability of non-linear systems was summed up by American meteorologist Edward N. Lorenz

(1917–2008) when he mused in the title of an early presentation on the topic of non-linearity in atmospheric models, *"Does the flap of a butterfly's wings in Brazil set off a tornado in Texas?"*

If some physical systems have behavior that is inherently non-linear, then they are also inherently unpredictable. One of the mechanisms that can cause a system to behave in a non-linear fashion is feedback. Plenty of introductory physics textbooks have sample problems that ask questions about a vibrating string. None of them have questions about six vibrating strings, a stack of Marshall amps, a hundred decibels of distortion, and a reverberating arena. Such situations are much better explored via practical experimentation rather than theoretical analysis.

Feedback, Emergence, and Chaos

To say that a system is "chaotic" is not to say its behavior is random, only that it is sufficiently complex that an accurate prediction would be a practical impossibility, even for Laplace's imaginary being. In fact, chaotic systems often give rise to unique sorts of order.

Tornadoes are both wildly unpredictable and ruthlessly organized structures. When the single note of feedback that launches the song "Foxey Lady" slowly rises from Jimi's scraping of the strings against the fret, this is an example of organization stirring itself up out of chaos. (Watch the video of Jimi at Miami Pop in 1968 and you'll see how, with just the slightest turn towards the stacks of amplifiers behind him, he is able to pull that note out of the noise.) Two key terms that come up often in these contexts are "self-organization" and "emergence." Both terms refer to situations where order, structure, and new behaviors spontaneously emerge from a system under certain conditions.

A good example of self-organization can be found inside your own body. Your heart beats when millions of cells contract at once. These heart cells communicate only with their nearest neighbors. There is no "master signal" to the whole heart that tells the cells to beat at the same time. The timing of each beat is a result of the collective communication between cells. Flocking birds and schooling fish demonstrate this same sort of

decentralized collective behavior. The coherent, almost con-
scious-seeming behavior of a flock of birds is an emergent property of the individual reactions of each bird to its neighbors.
There is no "boss bird" tweeting *"Turn!"* when faced with an
obstacle. The flock is an emergent entity whose behavior arises
via self-organization.

Likewise, the sound of electric guitar feedback is an emergent phenomenon. The vibrating strings, the noise of the fuzz
pedal, the overdriven amplifier, and the vibrating air together
constitute a dynamical system. The system involves feedback
in the technical sense of the word when the output of the system becomes the input—that's when the sound from the amp,
which was caused by the vibrating strings, itself moves the air
and vibrates the strings some more. The vibration increases
non-linearly, and the sound of feedback emerges.

Feedback, complexity, self-organization, emergence, and
chaos are all closely interconnected and interdependent concepts. One of the hallmarks of chaotic dynamical systems is
their inherent instability. Small changes in the parameters of
the system can cause drastically different behavior. It was this
inherent unpredictability of complex feedback loops that fic-
tional chaos theorist Ian Malcolm warned about in *Jurassic
Park*. This is true of guitar feedback as well. The tiny difference
between the treble knob on an amp being set to 7 or 8 can make
the difference between a quiet hum and a note that screams
with feedback. When Hendrix learned to "play" the feedback, he
was learning to play chaos.

Order and Aesthetics

Interesting things happen at the border between order and
chaos. There are some philosophers who believe that the border
between order and chaos is the place where "musicality" and aesthetic experience arise. There is an entire branch of philosophy—
aesthetics—devoted to exploring beauty in nature and in art.

While there is no simple or universal answers to the question of what makes something beautiful, many philosophers
have framed the question of aesthetic beauty in terms of order.
Aristotle stressed the importance of qualities like "symmetry"
and "unity" in art. Eighteenth-century philosopher Francis
Hutcheson stated that beauty requires "uniformity in variety".

Nineteenth-century philosopher and psychologist Wilhelm Wundt even went so far as to attempt to quantify this relationship, producing a graph relating human interest and "arousal" to the complexity of a stimulus. If a stimulus is too simple, we're bored by it. Too complex and we can become overstimulated or anxious, by the increasingly complex. Somewhere in the middle, the arousal curve peaks, at the perceptive sweet-spot between simple and complex.

These philosophical and psychological analyses seem convincing to me when applied to our perception of music. Pure order is boring because it is predictably repetitious and lacking in surprise. On the other hand, complete chaos lacks interest because complete "noise" is utterly devoid of information or pattern. Our aesthetic appreciation of music demands something between the ticking of a metronome and the cacophony of a tuning orchestra. The tension between order and complexity, or between expectation and surprise, is important to the aesthetic experience of music.

There are artists who have tried to stretch the boundaries of order and chaos. Experimental "minimalist" composers such as Philip Glass and Steve Reich created music featuring extremely repetitive and static phrases and structures. At the absolute extreme of this practice, John Cage's 1952 composition *4 33* subjected the listener to four minutes and thirty-three seconds of silence—the ultimate order of nothingness. And at the other extreme, as rock music has become increasingly amplified and distorted, it challenges the listener to accept as "musical" sounds whose harmonic structure includes more and more noise—in the literal and mathematical sense of the term—riding along with each musical note.

Consider for example, the title track of Frank Zappa's *Weasels Ripped My Flesh*. We are all familiar with the lament of parents to their children—"That's not music! That's just *noise!*". There is no insult more frequently used to describe whatever music a particular listener doesn't find aesthetically pleasing. In a sense, this accusation probably often has merit. The ears and the attitudes of the listener have simply not adapted to the changing standard of how much chaos is admissible in a musical sound.

Extremes of musical experimentation and expression aside, there is clearly some sweet spot between order and disorder that corresponds to what most people would regard as "musical" sound. Friedrich Cramer, a German chemist and philosopher, wrote about the importance of imperfection and disorder in art. Speaking specifically about visual art, he wrote, "Art is not perfect harmony, nor perfection. Beauty is apparently most in evidence, most striking where it voluntarily puts its own order at risk." From the slight facial asymmetry of a Dürer self-portrait, to the subtle tempo changes of a concert pianist, to the nearly-unhinged explorations of a jazz improvisation—the things we consider aesthetically pleasing to our eyes and ears are often those things that flirt with the border between order and chaos. It is here that I think we can use the distortion and feedback that infuses the music of Jimi Hendrix as a metaphor for the creative act itself. For the act of wrestling a guitar note out of the noise and making it sing in tune above the din is the act of making something beautiful out of chaos. Which is arguably the definition of art itself.

19
Elemental Jimi

SCOTT CALEF

Shortly after meeting Chas Chandler and moving to London to kick-start his solo career, Jimi was referred to in the British music papers as "the Wild Man of Borneo." That can't have been very PC, even in 1966. The description was also used of Jimi by London scenester Ronnie Money, whose home was his first stop after arriving in England. More surprising is the fact that the "Wild Man from Borneo" moniker was later also applied to Hendrix by *Ebony* magazine.

This label reflected the perception that there was something primitive or primeval about Hendrix and his sound. Right at the beginning of the 2001 *Experience Jimi Hendrix* DVD Alexis Korner's thick English accent intones:

> Part of Jimi's success and part of Jimi's enormous pulling power is because there is a very primitivistic feel around at the moment and it's becoming more and more and more so. Everything is becoming primary at the moment—colors, attitudes, music. And Jimi Hendrix is a sort of number one primary in these things.

Korner goes on to relate this to the "violence" of a Hendrix concert, noting a time at the Saville Theatre when a frustrated Jimi attacked Noel and proceeded to drag and kick him around the stage. As Korner sees it, Jimi was a "catalyst" bound to work only with people who could "react" to his violence by "counter-attacking," as Mitch Mitchell did on the drums. Tom Robbins wrote about Hendrix in a similar vein: "To ignore his savage discourse is to leave ourselves at the mercy of some new

225

meaning that may lurk in ambush at the center of a primitive blaze" (quoted in *Room Full of Mirrors*, p. 213).

In Search of the Elements

This curious idea that Jimi's music is "primary" and "primitivistic" can be related to the earliest ("pre-Socratic") philosophers in the Western tradition, who sought to reduce all of reality to the four "primary" elements of earth, air, fire, water, or some combination of these.

In his excellent little book on *Electric Ladyland* John Perry observes that "When you examine Jimi's work as a whole, the elements of Fire and Water seem to feature far more than Earth or Air" (p. 93, n22). Now, since (as we shall see) none of the early Greek philosophers made earth the cornerstone of their theories, we'll focus on fire, air and water, the power-trio of primary elements.

The first philosophers were largely interested in two questions: What's the nature of reality? And how did the universe come into being? The first question was understood as a quest for the "first principle" (or *arche*) of things. The *arche* can be thought of as either the *original source* of all things, or as what all things *are*, in their innermost essence.

The earliest Greek philosophers embraced philosophical monism—the idea that reality is fundamentally *one*. Though later this supposition was largely abandoned, it seemed simpler originally to posit one primary source or kind of stuff rather than many different ones.

But this leads to the second question: since the universe as we "experience" it now clearly has many different kinds of things in it, how do we get a plurality of things—the rich diversity that we encounter in the world—from one simple, original, primary substance? This problem is sometimes referred to as the problem of the one and the many. If reality is one, how or why did it evolve into a multitude of things with many diverse qualities?

In a way, this second question has always invoked in me a similar wonder to that produced by music. The blues—the backbone of so much of Jimi's playing, and indeed of all rock music—centers around the pentatonic scale, a musical scale which in its pure form has only five notes. And yet, from these five notes, or twelve at most, if you reach beyond the pentatonic scale to every semitone from octave to octave, a player like Hendrix can coax a seemingly infinite variety of tunes, solos, and sounds. How can so few elements be combined to produce such wonderfully diverse phenomena? That, in a way, is the problem of the earliest, pre-Socratic philosophy.

Since the pre-Socratics were philosophers and not mythic poets, they largely sought naturalistic explanations, and in that sense were early scientists without much technology or what we now consider the scientific method. But they didn't just speculate; evidence and argument were important to them just as they are to us.

Water as First Principle

The first philosopher of the Western tradition was Thales of Miletus (around 600 B.C.), who argued that the *arche* of all things is water. We don't have a lot of evidence about why he thought this. Perhaps he was influenced by neighboring Near Eastern accounts. Genesis, the first book of the Bible, states that at creation, the spirit of God moved upon the surface of the waters, for example. Water features crucially in Babylonian and Egyptian creation accounts also.

But Thales was also very likely impressed by the relationship between water—or more precisely, the moist element—and life. (On *Axis*, the song "Bold as Love" refers to the "life giving waters.") The seed of the male is moist, and when a woman gives birth, her water breaks. Blood is associated with life and blood is wet. "The life is in the blood" (Leviticus 17:11). And in the relatively dry, eastern Mediterranean, where Miletus was located, fresh water was an especially precious commodity.

Around the time of Thales the harbor of Miletus was silting up, so the waters that flowed into it seemed capable of becoming earth. The reverse phenomenon could also be witnessed; as banks are eroded and the soil swept away, earth becomes water. ("Castles made of sand fall into the sea, eventually.") The Greeks were impressed to find fossils of marine life far inland or in the mountains, suggesting that the earth emerged from the sea. (Some such notion is alluded to in the song "Valleys of Neptune": "Look out east coast, you're goin' to have a neighbor / Rebirth land and home of the prayin' sand. / And we know there were three continents, so much older. / And they shall rise . . .") But beyond all this, water is changeable enough to rapidly assume different forms under different conditions—it can be liquid, a frozen solid, or an airy mist—and anything which could qualify as the absolute stuff of the universe must at least have that capacity.

While it may not be apparent to the senses that all things are water, neither is it apparent that ice is the same stuff as steam; nevertheless, we discover it to be so. Scientific conclusions are often alien to common sense or everyday observation. Heat is motion and your "solid" table is mostly empty space. So the surprising or counter-intuitive nature of Thales's hypothesis shouldn't by itself lead us—or, rather, his contemporaries—to reject it.

Escape to Atlantis

Jimi's music probably has as many references to water as to anything else (except, possibly, women and various sci-fi-related themes). This is especially true of the original second LP of *Electric Ladyland*, which abounds in watery images and descriptions of underwater worlds—"Rainy Day, Dream Away" (with the rather monistic sounding line "Everything's gonna be ev'rything"), "1983 . . . (A Merman I Should Turn to Be)," "Moon Turn the Tides . . . Gently, Gently Away" (with its reference to Atlantis, a mythic city described in antiquity by Plato), "Still Raining, Still Dreaming."

David Stubbs nicely describes the effect of the "1983" sequence: "As the suite bleeds into 'Moon, Turn the Tides . . . Gently, Gently Away', Kramer [Jimi's sound engineer] and Hendrix brilliantly evoke, by means of phrasing, backward taping and varispeed, a sense of amphibious descent, a darkening shade of submarine turquoise, of new forms of marine life zigzagging in the shoals, peeking curiously into the cabin windows, of purple starfish darting in and out of the coral, giant sea-horses and electric eels torpedoing through the depths" (*Jimi Hendrix*, p. 91).

The storyline of "1983," roughly, is that through war and ecological devastation, life on dry land will be extinguished, but Jimi and his lover have built a vessel to bear them underwater to Atlantis. They invite skeptical friends to join them, but are rebuffed for the impracticality ("It's impossible for a man to live and breathe underwater") and unnaturalness ("It would be beyond the will of God") of their scheme. The wonder craft does its duty, though, and under the sea, there is life: "Starfish and giant foams greet us with a smile." Jimi and his love Catherina will "be reborn . . . forever." The sea is eternal. Atlantis awaits, full of cheer.

Although there is something Jules Verne–like about the lyric, there is also something unmistakably primordial about returning to the sea from which all life evolved, and the Atlantis reference reinforces the ancient even as futuristic references to nuclear destruction ("Giant pencil and lipstick tube shaped things continue to rain and cause screaming pain") set the stage.

Similar themes are developed in "Valleys of Neptune", which also repeatedly references the ancient civilization of Atlantis. Jimi sings, "Mercury liquid, emerald shining / They're showing me where I came from, baby." Our source—"where I came from"—lies in Thales's *arche*, water. Lost, submerged, older continents "shall rise and tell us much more the truth of man . . . And this ain't good news, bad news, or any news. Lord, it's just the truth." Ancient, forgotten wisdom comes from the depths. "The life giving waters taken for granted / they quietly understand" ("Bold as Love").

Fire and Water

The pre-Socratic philosophers quickly noticed a problem with Thales's account: If everything either is water, or comes from water, and water is wet and cold, how could fire—that which is dry and hot—ever hope to exist or come to be? How can water give rise to its opposite? Water doesn't make fire; it puts it out! This worry reflects the Greek belief in a principle of like-to-like; effects resemble their causes and so unlike things cannot interact or cause each other.

To heat the water in the kettle, you must apply a source of heat. You wouldn't try to boil the water by putting the kettle in the refrigerator. If something is set in motion, it must be caused to move by something itself in motion. To move the cue ball, you hit it with the cue stick, which is itself already in motion. If you don't move the stick, the ball stays where it is. If you want your coffee to be sweet, you add sugar, which is already sweet. You wouldn't add something bitter to your coffee to sweeten it. And so on.

So, if like causes like, water can't cause fire. *But neither could fire cause water! Or earth air! Or air earth!* The problem that confronted Thales's decision to treat water as primary seemed applicable to any of the other elements too. None of them could serve as an adequate first principle since each of the four primary elements had "opposites."

The immediate successor to Thales, Anaximander, tried to avoid this problem by arguing that the first principle had *no* qualities; the *arche* was "unbounded" or undifferentiated. After all, if the original stuff that comprises the universe was neither hot nor cold, it wouldn't need to give rise to the opposite of hot or cold.

Although clever, this solution too was soon seen to fail. For the universe contains things that have definite qualities. The problem of opposites remains: how can the quality-less source give rise to qualities? Besides, Anaximander's solution was too vague. If the first principle is neither hot nor cold, does that mean it's lukewarm? And isn't "lukewarm" still a quality? Can we really conceive of something with *no* qualities whatsoever? As Jimi sings, "colors without names" lead to "confusion" ("Love or Confusion").

That being said, Jimi, and many other rock artists, *are* capable of using seemingly "non-musical" elements like feedback or distortion to musical effect. Burning and smashing your guitar may not seem like a particularly *musical* gesture, but to regard the end of Hendrix's Monterey finale as pure visual spectacle or a Who-inspired gimmick is not to appreciate the very powerful sonic effect he achieved. It comes through on the CD, even without benefit of watching the movie. So perhaps there's something to Anaximander's insight after all. On one level, musical notes are simply vibrations, and vibrations—motions—are not experiences.

As the philosopher George Berkeley observed, if a tree falls in the forest and no one is there to hear the air still vibrates, but no sound occurs. If a sound is a type of experience, vibrations are not sounds. And yet, they produce sound. So, the audible literally comes from the inaudible. (Maybe that's why we need stacks of Marshall amplifiers!)

Air as First Principle

In any case, Anaximander's successor, Anaximenes, returned to more familiar ground. Anaximenes proposed that air was the first principle, but with an important addition. He thought he could explain how air could become its opposite and, indeed, all of the other elements. Air becomes fire when it is "rarified" and becomes first water, then earth as it is "condensed." The different elements are simply different concentrations or densities of the one fundamental substance. In this sense, the material elements are not genuinely in opposition to each other; the only true opposites are the processes of condensation and rarefaction themselves.

Jimi also frequently refers to the air or airy motifs in his lyrics, mostly through allusions to flying ("Astro Man," "Dolly Dagger"), wings ("Little Wing"), angels ("Angel"), the sky ("Purple Haze"), atmospheric phenomena like weather or storms ("In From the Storm," "Midnight Lightning"), and flying spacecraft ("Third Stone From the Sun," "EXP," "Castles Made of Sand"). But Anaximenes's choice of air is arbitrary. If air can become any of the other elements, what makes it primary? Why insist that fire is rarified air? Why not say rather that air is condensed fire? Or that air is rarified water? What really matters for Anaximenes are the processes involved, and his emphasis upon the causal mechanisms by which things undergo transformation was an important advance in Greek scientific thinking.

To this point, the "problem of opposites" still persisted. To solve it, pre-Socratic philosophers had to find a way to unify, reconcile or combine the opposites, and that is just what Heraclitus (born around 560 B.C.) attempted to do.

Heraclitus's writings are aphoristic and obscure. In arguing that opposites like the hot and the cold, the wet and the dry, are one, he writes from an oracular and quasi-mystical (psychedelic?) perspective. Or, if you prefer, his writings are somewhat lyrical. Jimi does something similar. He sometimes juxtaposes water and fire, the hot and the cold, in his lyrics, effecting in essence a poetic ("Heraclitian") unification of the opposites.

In "Hear My Train a-Comin'," Jimi sings of "Tears [water] burnin' [fire] me down in my soul." A similar image is evoked in "In From the Storm": "It was a crying blue *rain* that's *burning* my eyes." In "Long Hot Summer Night" he wonders, "Where are you when there's a hot cold summer?" The song opens, "It sure was a long, long, long hot summer night" but "my heart was way down, in a cold, cold winter storm." In the first line from "Love or Confusion" he writes: "Is that the stars in the sky [flaming orbs], or is it, rain fallin' down?" A few lines later, he sings "My heart *burns* with feelin' / Oh, but my mind is *cold* and reeling." In "Night Bird Flying" he says "No *tears* will be shed . . . till the *sun* gets out of bed." Or consider these lines from Dolly Dagger: "Hey, *red hot* mama you better step aside / this chick's gonna turn you to a *block of ice*." "Voodoo Chile": "I float in liquid gardens / and Arizona red sand." In "Are You Experienced" he'll "watch the sunrise from the bottom of the sea." "Burning desire, puts some magic in my fire / I feel my body drowning in your sea of love" ("Burning Desire").

I don't mean to suggest that Jimi *only* juxtaposes the opposites fire and water, or the hot and the cold in his lyrics. In "Have You Ever Been (To Electric Ladyland)" he juxtaposes right and wrong: "Good and evil lay side by side / While electric love penetrates the sky." In "Power of Soul" he combines high and low, warning of "high flyin' rides" that "fly you too low." In "Ezy Ryder," "Today is forever." In "Voodoo Chile" Jimi's "a million miles away" but "at the same time I'm right here in your picture frame." And in Manic Depression: "You make love, you break love, it's all the same . . ." Many more examples could be given.

Unifying the Opposites

Heraclitus himself attempted to "unify" the opposites in a variety of ways, sometimes through deliberately provocative paradoxes. He writes, "Upon those who step into the same rivers, different and again different waters flow" (fragment 10.64 in *Philosophy Before Socrates*). On the one hand, this is the same river I saw yesterday or stepped into a moment ago; on the other hand, because the water in it is different, it is not the same. Thus, "We step into and we do not step into the same rivers" (fragment 10.66).

At other times, Heraclitus, like Anaximenes, observes that the elements can "transmute" into one another: "It is death to souls to become water, death to water to become earth, but from earth comes water and from water soul" (10.74). Heraclitus can be cryptic! But then, so is Jimi sometimes: "A stagecoach full of feathers and footprints pulls up to my soapbox door. Now a lady with a pearl handled necktie, tied to the driver's fence breathes in my face . . . Come around to my room with the tooth in the middle, and bring along . . . a president" ("My Friend"). Huh?

At still other times, he suggests that "opposites" depend on your point of view: "The road up and the road down are the same" (10.63) and "The sea is the purest and most polluted water: to fishes drinkable and bringing safety, to humans undrinkable and destructive" (10.53). "Now if 6 turned out to be 9, Oh, I don't mind." Whether the symbol "6" is a six or nine is a matter of perspective. (If you don't believe me, turn the page upside down and look again.)

Although Heraclitus thinks that opposites—and, indeed, all things—are in some sense "one" (10.47), he also, paradoxically, thinks fire is the primary element: "The kosmos, the same for all . . . was always and is and shall be: an ever-living fire being kindled in measures and being extinguished in measures" (10.77). Heraclitus thought that, like a flowing river or flickering flame, all things are in continual flux and motion. There is no stable, abiding material reality. What is constant is only the rational, predictable, law-like way in which this change occurs—the fact that the fire is "kindled in measures and extinguished in measures."

Heraclitus believed in a rational, ordering principle governing the universe, which he called the *logos* (word): "Listening not to me but to the *logos* it is wise to agree that all things are one (10.47)." The *logos* is, in some way difficult to discern, linked to fire. That's probably why, in fragment 10.63 above, it is "death for souls to become water." The soul is rational because it participates in the *logos*. Since the *logos* is fiery, the moist (drunk?) soul is irrational.

The important point is that with the introduction of the *logos* we have reference to something like natural laws which provide order to what otherwise would be sheer chaos: "This *logos* holds always . . . all things come to be in accordance with this *logos* . . ." (10.1). The *logos* renders the universe comprehensible by making it intelligible. Because (at least some) humans are rational, they have a *logos* within themselves, and this rational nature in humans enables us to grasp the rational nature of nature itself.

Hendrix certainly understood the importance of fire! Before the Experience Jimi went by the stage name Jimmy James and fronted a band called the Blue Flames. From his blazing Monterey finale where he famously dowsed his guitar with lighter fluid before setting it on fire, to the title of his brilliant hit "Fire", heat and combustion are motifs that recur often in Hendrix's work. In "House Burning Down" from *Electric Ladyland*, a song about race riots, he urges his listeners to "learn instead of burn," a seeming inversion of Heraclitus's association of knowledge and the logos with fire. In "Burning Desire" he says there's "magic" in his fire. "Burning of the Midnight Lamp" is perhaps my favorite Hendrix track of all time, and though it speaks of isolation and the melancholy of loneliness, according to Shapiro and Glebbeek "Jimi keeps his own flame of love – ultimately the lamp is a beacon. Jimi calls out to anyone who cares to listen." A beacon is a fire that guides—like Heraclitus's *logos*.

Eventually, the pre-Socratic philosophers abandoned monism. The problem of the one and the many proved just too intractable, and more pluralistic philosophies were explored. One of the first pluralists, Empedocles (around 492–432 B.C.) decided that earth, air, fire and water were equally primary, and that material reality was the result of a combination of these four elements, none of which were reducible to the others. Empedocles was becoming more like what we would call a chemist. But there still remains the issue of how these four elements combine to produce all of the other things that exist.

Creation and Destruction

Empedocles speculated that the world goes through alternating cycles whereby it is created and destroyed again and again. Relatedly, that there is some lyrical evidence that Jimi believed in reincarnation. "Belly Button Window" considers the perspective of the unborn child of an unwanted pregnancy. "If you don't want me this time around / Yeah, I'll be glad to go back to spirit land / and even take a longer rest before coming down the chute again / Man, I sure remember the last time, baby / they were still arguing about me then . . . / I ain't coming down this way too much more again."

Like Anaximenes, Empedocles thought there were two forces of attraction and repulsion, but instead of referring to condensation and rarefaction, Empedocles viewed the processes as akin to Love and Strife. When Strife is ascendant, the elements are utterly separated (or "segregated"); all of the fire is by itself, all of the water is separate and collected together elsewhere, and so on. But when Love enters, the four elements are brought together, mingle by chance, and produce myriad worlds. Some worlds evolve where the random combinations of the elements can't support life. But some can. Our world, fortunately, is one such world. Empedocles thought, however, that Strife was once again entering the world, and that the stable world order we enjoy and require is destined eventually to come apart.

Empedocles might be right; it certainly seems like Strife is growing. Jimi's era was deeply polarized, and ours can hardly be considered much better. Though Jimi's music was not often very political, towards the end he gave us "Machine Gun," probably the most violent song in his catalog, and surely his most potent statement of opposition to the Vietnam war. "Izabella" is another sad song of war. And we've already noted Jimi's lament about the destruction and vandalism associated with race riots in the 1960s in songs like "House Burning Down." As an impoverished youth growing up in Seattle, a former paratrooper and a black man touring the South on the chitlin' circuit, Hendrix certainly understood the threat of violence. He remarked on the ludicrous suggestion that white Southern cops might actually provide security for him.

Which brings us back to Hendrix's career-making performance at Monterey. That set is often remembered for the fact that it was literally incendiary. Not only did Jimi mock rape his amplifier and torch his guitar, he also smashed it to smithereens. But what is usually lost as we recall these attention-grabbing antics is Jimi's verbal introduction to "Wild Thing" where he very sweetly says that he could stay on stage all night and just say "Thank you, thank you, thank you." He wants to grab the audience and kiss them but, he laments, he just can't do that. So, he continues, he will instead sacrifice something very dear and precious to him— something he really loves. His guitar was an offering, and despite the dramatic way in which the offering was made, at least according to Jimi, it was motivated by love. In the spirit of bringing together rather than tearing apart, he also said he was going to play "the English and American combined anthems."

Love and Strife

For Empedocles, Love and Strife, though opposed, are like yin and yang, two sides of reality, and neither separation nor combination can occur without the other. On the cover of *Axis Bold as Love*, the members of the Experience are superimposed over a religious poster of Vishnu. Vishnu is the "preserver and protector" and one aspect of the Hindu trinity whose other deities are Brahman the Creator and Shiva the Destroyer. But it matters that Jimi and the band are depicted as Vishnu, not Shiva. Jimi's is a "Message to Love." Empedocles makes it seem as if, in the fullness of time, Strife will prevail, and there's nothing we can do about it. The universe periodically undergoes cyclical transformations on a cosmic scale, and humans can only watch or anticipate the trends.

But perhaps there is hope. If opposites can indeed give rise to opposites, maybe the world's conflict and despair will eventually give place to peace, and moreover, maybe there's something we can *do* to help make love ascendant. Not that we will; there are no guarantees, and for all the references in his music to rainbows, angels, comic-book heroes and flying saucers, politically, Jimi seems to me a realist. But his "Message to Love" is that we can make a difference. "Earth Blues' conveys the challenges and the opportunities brilliantly: "Well, I see hands and tear-stained faces / reaching up, but not quite touchin' the promised land / Well, I taste tears and a whole lot of precious years wasted / saying to the Lord, 'please give us a helping hand'."

Perhaps referring back to the riots of the "long, hot summer" of 1967, Jimi sings, "You better hope that love is the answer / Yeah, better come before the summer / Well, everybody can hear the sound of freedom's bleeding heart / Sirens clashing with earth and rock and stone."

But disillusionment, injustice, and violent protests notwith-standing, "Yeah, they're talking about getting together, yeah / Together for love, love, love . . . / Everybody. Every sister. Every lover. / To feel the light that's shining bright, baby. Everybody. We got to live together."

Or, as he puts it elsewhere, "With the power of soul / anything is possible."

So in a way, Korner was right. Jimi was a catalyst. But for love, not strife.s

A Historical Note

JOHN-THE-BOSS

The history books will tell you that mid-1960s Britain was "swinging" and that everyone was groovy. This is not true. If you grew up in the provincial towns, as I did, it was still the 1930s. Life was drab and grey. My mother would iron paper bags and store them away for . . . well, I never really found out why. But it was all part of the make-do-and-mend culture they had been inculcated into since the deprivations of the Second World War.

The Sixties didn't happen in the north of England, where I grew up, until about 1988. So this myth of the Swinging Sixties has only got a foothold in the annals of history because the one place that was swinging was the west end of London and in Britain, if it happens in London, it is widely assumed to be happening everywhere else, especially by people in London. All the press and media is focused there, so it blows up everything into a big thing, when in reality it isn't.

This still happens today, even in the age of global media. London is still in love with itself and it still thinks it's everywhere and the rest of us know they're wrong. However, in 1966 when Jimi Hendrix arrived in London, he was catapulted into this colorful, elite world of hip London life. And he fit right in because there was a cultural seedbed prepared for him. For about three years, the blues boom had been happening. Blues was hip, it was cool, and increasingly it was commercial. It inspired bands that would become popular worldwide.

It was the perfect moment for Jimi to arrive in the UK. Perfect. The ground had been prepared by Cream, by John

Mayall, by the Yardbirds, by the Animals. Amplified, electric blues was everywhere. So when Jimi plugged in, it was a sonic revolution, yes, but also sort of familiar. It was a quantum blues leap, but was still rooted in the music which had turned on the Rolling Stones and all the other bands who would soon cross the Atlantic and with some chutzpah, sell the music of America back to itself. White UK got it at a time when white America didn't.

The UK was also a liberal place for a black guy, compared to most of USA at the time. This isn't to pretend racism didn't exist. It very much did. But it hadn't been enshrined in the law, the way it had in parts of America. Racism in the UK is less intense and virulent than it was, and still is, in the USA. It manifests by small acts of discrimination, exclusion, and nastiness. The signs in windows which said "No blacks, No Irish, No dogs" is classic British bigotry. They won't say it to your face but passive aggressive to the last, they will put a polite notice in their window just so you know where they stand.

If you tried to rent a flat in the UK at the time, and you were not white, mysteriously it would have always just been rented out before you arrived. So sorry. And yet, perversely, we're a mongrel nation full of generations of immigrants and those of us who embrace that, embraced Mr. Hendrix as another beautiful color in the rainbow of life, so much so that being a wild-haired black guy played very much in his favor. He was exotic and exciting in equal measure. He was 'other' and as such totally distinctive and utterly memorable to our country.

And then we got to the music. Oh my lord, the music. The first release was "Hey Joe" backed with "Stone Free." Released on 16th December 1966, it was a Christmas gift to us all. It peaked at #6, three months later "Purple Haze" peaked at #3. In this country he had five Top Twenty singles. In the USA, just one. The first album, released in the musically tumultuous summer of 1967, was only kept off the top by *Sgt Pepper's*.

We. Loved. Jimi.

Jimi's short career was based on his success and support in Britain. He had Chas Chandler, an English manager. He had an English band with Noel Redding and Mitch Mitchell. His records sold well here from the get-go. He toured here extensively, playing sold out small clubs because there was no regular gig network, This was before city and town halls were routinely used for rock gigs. So you'd play in a room above a pub, or if you were lucky, an old theater.

It was Paul McCartney who recommended to the organizers of the Monterey Pop Festival that Jimi should be added to the bill, where he was introduced by Brian Jones. Even the idea to set light to his guitar came from Keith Altham an English publicity guru. Monterey changed everything.

Obviously, post-Monterey, Jimi was soon to be acknowledged in the land of his birth but it was Britain, grey old Britain, full of class-based hang-ups and post-war blues, that set him on his way. And every one of us British acolytes of rock-'n'roll still feel immensely proud of that.

Bibliography

Alston, William P. 1967. Religion. Paul Edwards, ed., *The Encyclopedia of Philosophy*. Macmillan.

Aristotle. 1998. *Politics*. Hackett.

Baldwin, James. 1962. *The Fire Next Time*. Dell.

Bate, Jonathan. 2009. The Original of Laura by Vladimir Nabokov: A Review. *The Telegraph* (November 15th).

Batuman, Elif. 2010. Kafka's Last Trial. *New York Times Magazine* (September 22nd).

Berkeley, George. 1982. *A Treatise concerning the Principles of Human Knowledge*. Hackett.

Bloom, Allan. 1987. *The Closing of the American Mind*. Simon and Schuster.

Bloomfield, Michael. 1975. Michael Bloomfield, Reminiscences. *Guitar Player*, (September). Quoted in Waksman 1999.

Clecak, Peter. 1985. *America's Quest for the Ideal Self: Dissent and Fulfillment in the 60s and 70s*. Oxford University Press.

Cohen, Stefanie. 2014. The Man Who Keeps Legends Alive. *Wall Street Journal* (January 9th).

Crehan, Kate. 2002. *Gramsci, Culture and Anthropology*. Berkley: University of California Press.

Cross, Charles R. 2005. *Room Full of Mirrors: A Biography of Jimi Hendrix*. Hyperion.

Dalton, David. 1986. *Piece of My Heart: The Life, Times, and Legend of Janis Joplin*. St. Martin's Press.

Danto, Arthur C. 1964. The Artworld. *Journal of Philosophy* LXI.

Davis, Walter A. 2001. *Deracination: Historicity, Hiroshima, and the Tragic Imperative*. SUNY Press.

———. 2007. *Art and Politics*. Pluto.

DeCurtis, Anthony, and James Henke, eds. 1980. *The Rolling Stone Illustrated History of Rock & Roll*. Rolling Stone Press.

Descartes, René. 1999. *Discourse on Method and Meditations on First Philosophy*. Hackett.

Dickie, George. 1971. *Aesthetics: An Introduction*. New York: Pegasus.

Du Bois, W.E.B. 1994. *The Souls of Black Folk*. Dover.

Edwards, Gavin. 2016. One Man's Mission to Keep Musicians' Legacies Alive. *New York Times* (June 17th).

Estates Gazette. 2004. The Jimi Hendrix Experience. *Estates Gazette* 144.

Ethicist. 2016. What Should I Do With my Dead Husband's Journals? *New York Times* (September 7th).

Fabbri, Franco. 1981. A Theory of Musical Genres: Two Applications. In Horn and Tagg 1981.

Fricke, David. 2010. Jimi's Last Ride. *Rolling Stone*.

Frith, Simon. 1998. *Performing Rites: On the Value of Popular Music*. Harvard University Press.

Hamilton, Jack. 2016. *Just Around Midnight: Rock and Roll and the Racial Imagination*. Harvard University Press.

Harvard Law Review. Property Law—Right of Publicity—Ninth Circuit Upholds Washington Statute Recognizing Postmortem Rights of Individuals Domiciled Out of State—Experience Hendrix L.L.C. v. Hendrixlicensing.com Ltd, 762 F.3d 839 (9th Cir. 2014). *Harvard Law Review* 128:6.

Hayles, N. Katherine. 2005. *My Mother Was a Computer: Digital Subjects and Literary Texts*. University of Chicago Press.

Hegel, G.W.F. 1967. *The Phenomenology of Mind*. Harper Torch Books.

Heidegger, Martin. 1962. *Being and Time*. HarperCollins.

Hendrix, Jimi. 2013. *Starting at Zero: Jimi Hendrix in His Own Words*. New York: Bloomsbury.

Holub, Robert. 2015. *Nietzsche's Jewish Problem*. Princeton University Press.

Horn, David, and Philip Tagg, eds. 1981. *Popular Music Perspectives*. International Association for the Study of Popular Music.

Kirby, David. 2009. *Little Richard: The Birth of Rock'n'Roll*. Continuum.

———. 2015. *Cross Road: Artist, Audience, and the Making of American Music*. New American Press.

Kittler, Friedrich A. 1999 [1986]. *Gramophone, Film, Typewriter*. Stanford University Press.

Kundera, Milan. 1980. *The Book of Laughter and Forgetting*. Penguin.

Lee, Pey-Woan. 2003. Responses to a Breach of Contract: *Experience Hendrix v. PPX Enterprises*. Lloyd's Maritime and Commercial Law Quarterly 3.

Liu, Jennifer. 2014. Jimi Hendrix's "Star-Spangled Banner": The Epitome of the Countercultural Experience. *Medium* (October 6th).

Marx, Karl. 2000. Critique of Hegel's 'Philosophy of Right.' In *Karl Marx, Selected Writings*, ed. D. McLellan, Oxford University Press.

McDermott, John. 2015. Liner Notes for *You Can't Use My Name: The RSVP/PPX Sessions*. Sony Legacy.

McDermott, John, and Eddie Kramer. 1992. *Hendrix: Setting the Record Straight*. Warner.

McKirahan, Richard D., Jr., ed. 1994. *Philosophy Before Socrates: An Introduction with Texts and Commentary*. Hackett.

Mill, John Stuart. 2002. *On Liberty*. In *The Basic Writings of John Stuart Mill*. Modern Library, 2002.

Mitchell, Mitch, with John Platt. 1990. *Hendrix: Inside the Experience*. Harmony Books.

Montesquieu, Charles de Secondat, Marquis de. 2012. *My Thoughts*. Liberty Fund.

Montgomery, Scott L., and Daniel Chirot. 2015. *The Shape of the New: Four Big Ideas and How They Made the Modern World*. Princeton University Press.

Moskowitz, David. 2010. *The Words and Music of Jimi Hendrix*. Praeger.

Murray, Charles Shaar. 1991. *Crosstown Traffic: Jimi Hendrix and the Post-War Rock'n'Roll Revolution*. St. Martin's Press.

Niemeyer, Christian. 2011. *Nietzsche verstehen: Eine Gebrauchsanweisung*. Berlin: Lambert Schneider.

Nietzsche, Friedrich 1967 [1872]. *The Birth of Tragedy and The Case of Wagner*. Vintage.

———. 1969 [1888]. *On the Genealogy of Morals and Ecce Homo*. Vintage.

———. 1989 [1885]. *Beyond Good and Evil*. Vintage.

Nocera, Joe. 2015. "The Harper Lee 'Go Set a Watchman' Fraud." *New York Times*, July 24.

Oakeshott, Michael. 1996. *The Politics of Faith & the Politics of Scepticism*, ed. Timothy Fuller. New Haven, CT: Yale University Press.

Osto, Douglas. 2016. *Altered States: Buddhism and Psychedelic Spirituality in America*. Columbia University Press.

Palmer, Robert. 1980. Rock Begins. In DeCurtis and Henke 1980.

Perry, John. 2004. *Electric Ladyland*, volume 8 in the 33 1/3 series. Continuum.

Piven, J.S., Chris Boyd, and Henry Lawton. 2004. *Terrorism, Jihad, and Sacred Vengeance*. Giessen, Ger: Psychosozial-Verlag.

Plato. 1997. *Complete Works*. Hackett.

Plotinus. 1991. *The Enneads: Abridged Edition*. Penguin.

Reich, Charles A. 1995 [1971]. *The Greening of America*. Crown.

Roby, Steven, ed. 2012. *Hendrix on Hendrix: Interviews and Encounters with Jimi Hendrix*. Chicago Review Press.

Rose, H.J. 1959. *A Handbook of Greek Mythology*. Plume.

Rossi, Robert. "Jurisdictional Haze: Indiana and Washington's Unconstitutional Extensions of the Postmortem Right of Publicity." *Boston College Law Review*, Volume 57.

Roszak, Theodore. 1995 [1969]. *The Making of a Counter-Culture: Reflections on the Technological Society and Its Youthful Opposition*. University of California Press.

Rudinow, Joel. 1994. Race, Ethnicity, Expressive Authenticity: Can White People Sing the Blues? *The Journal of Aesthetics and Art Criticism* 52:1 (Winter).

Santosuosso, Ernie. 1970. Epitaph for Jimi Hendrix. *Boston Globe* (19th September).

Sartre, Jean-Paul. 1993 [1943]. *Being and Nothingness*. Washington Square Press.

Schopenhauer, Arthur. 1966 [1859]. *The World as Will and Representation,* Dover.

Shapiro, Harry, and Caesar Glebbeek. 1990. *Jimi Hendrix: Electric Gypsy*. St. Martin's Griffin.

Stein, Ruth. 2009. *For Love of the Father: A Psychoanalytic Study of Religious Terrorism*. Stanford University Press.

Stubbs, David. 2002. *Jimi Hendrix: The Stories Behind Every Song*. Carlton.

Taylor, Charles. 1991. *The Ethics of Authenticity*. Harvard University Press.

Tolstoy, Leo. 1995. *What Is Art?* Penguin.

Ventre, Michael. 2009. Hendrix Created Banner Moment at Woodstock. <www.today.com/popculture/hendrix-created-banner-moment-woodstock-2D80555766-woodstock-2D80555766>.

Wacks, Raymond. *Philosophy of Law: A Very Short Introduction*. Oxford: Oxford University Press, 2014.

Waksman, Steve. 1999. Black Sound, Black Body: Jimi Hendrix, the Electric Guitar, and the Meanings of Blackness. *Popular Music and Society* 23.

West, Cornell. 2001. *Race Matters*. Beacon Press.

Wittgenstein, Ludwig. *Philosophical Investigations*. New York: Macmillan, 1953.

Winthrop-Young, Geoffrey. 2011. *Kittler and the Media*. Polity

York, Ritchie. 1969. "I'm into Different Things," Says Jimi Hendrix. *Los Angeles Times* (7th September).

Ezy Wryters

THEODORE G. AMMON drives a 1956 Dodge Coronet Lancer, with push-button transmission, V-8 and dual exhausts to Millsaps College, Jackson, Mississippi, where he teaches philosophy. He's published some scholarly stuff, but mainly he plays his turntable and his 4,500-plus albums. Jimi rules.

RANDALL E. AUXIER is one of The Usual Suspects. (That's his current bar band.) He is experienced at writing about rock and roll. That haze of purple prose is collected in his *Metaphysical Graffiti: Deep Cuts in the Philosophy of Rock* (2017). He also writes on movies and TV, baseball, and really almost anything. When he gets bored of music and words, he wanders off to work at Southern Illinois University, Carbondale, where he is Professor of Philosophy and Communication Studies. Since childhood he has sacrificed chickens at the full moon. For dinner.

RICHARD BILSKER teaches philosophy and lives in Southern Maryland. His hobbies include tabletop roleplaying games, single-malt scotch (especially since the election), *Doctor Who*, playing guitar (most often poorly) and wondering whether he would be better off if he were a cat.

ROB BOATRIGHT is a professor of political science at Clark University in Worcester, Massachusetts. He usually writes about primary elections and campaign finance laws. During the 1990s he was the bass player for Chicago's premier new wave band, the Permanentz. Like all of the greatest rock stars, he plays guitar left-handed.

SAMUEL V. BRUTON is an associate professor of philosophy at the University of Southern Mississippi, and he has recently been writing about a range of philosophical topics almost as eclectic as Hendrix's musical influences: research ethics, American pragmatist Charles Peirce, race, and professional sports. He lives in Hattiesburg, Mississippi, with his wife Jennifer and plays professionally as a jazz pianist.

SCOTT CALEF is professor of philosophy at Ohio Wesleyan University where he's stone free to do what he pleases. Besides editing and contributing to *Led Zeppelin and Philosophy*, he has written for philosophy volumes on The Who, Bruce Springsteen, Metallica, The Beatles and Pink Floyd. They talk about him like a dog, talkin' about the clothes he wears. But they don't realize they're the ones who's square. In his humble opinion, side two of the original Hendrix *In the West* LP features the finest rock guitar playing ever recorded.

There are so many realities. **JASSEN CALLENDER** is a dog parent, husband, and son, obviously in that order, in addition to being a teacher of architects, painter of abstract things, designer of obscure buildings, and lover of literature and philosophy. Associate Professor; Director of Mississippi State University's Jackson Center in Jackson, Mississippi, author of some articles and one book; he grew up in a rural area where there was little to do besides listening to albums, cassettes, and 8-tracks over and over for hours on end. Often Hendrix. He is surprised, despite the proliferation of realities we live, how often we come back to the beginning.

MOLLY BRIGID FLYNN is an associate professor of philosophy at Assumption College in Worcester, Massachusetts, and an occasional movie reviewer for the Liberty Fund's Law and Liberty blog. While all the cool kids were getting properly socialized, she was memorizing *Singin' in the Rain* or reading Florence King's column in *The National Review*. She snuck into college on a lacrosse scholarship and now teaches philosophy as a contact sport.

RONALD S. GREEN teaches Buddhism at Coastal Carolina University where he also makes castles of sand that fade into the sea . . . eventually.

When he's not fussing with Pro Tools, waxing sentimental about the days of analog, kicking back with his wife Kathi and several pints of Guinness, or letting their cat Polonius out of the house at 3:00 a.m., **ERIC GRIFFIN** teaches Shakespeare and Renaissance Literature at Millsaps College.

DARYL L. HALE is Associate Professor in the Department of Philosophy and Religion at Western Carolina University. He has written on the ancient Stoics, Epicureans, and Cynics, with the latter giving him insights into current political shenanigans. He's still working on a manuscript on "Kant for Everyone" (yet another impossible task). His real joys in life come from his second (mostly summer) profession as a master carpenter, having studied with a master timber-framer and learned the rules of the craft. Through that tradition, he has grown to appreciate Jefferson's genius as architect, and also reinterpreted his wisdom as a follower of Epicurus.

DAVID MACGREGOR JOHNSTON teaches Philosophy and Film Studies on this here people farm at Northern Vermont University. His initial reaction to Hendrix's "Star-Bangled Banner" was conditioned by four years in military prep school. Studying philosophy in college was only one of the mind-expanding experiences, not necessarily stoned, but beautiful, that allowed him to appreciate Hendrix's virtuosity more fully.

CHRISTOPHER KETCHAM. Howl of a wildcat . . . Chris earned his doctorate at the University of Texas at Austin. He teaches business and ethics for the University of Houston Downtown. His research interests are risk management, applied ethics, social justice, and East-West comparative philosophy. He has done recent work in the philosophical ideas of forgiveness, Emmanuel Levinas's responsibility, and Gabriel Marcel's spirit of abstraction. So, as you can see he is quite experienced. Have you ever been experienced?

DENNIS LOUGHREY has a PhD in philosophy from the Australian National University. He came to philosophy because he loves clarity and precision, and all that. More, Dennis loves listening to the pioneering sounds of the 1960s. He would go as far as to say that he perceives music as a kind of ally. He has learned a lot from David Light, player with the Primitive Calculators, connoisseur and collector of music past, smart, keeps his music knowledge in his head.

FRANCIS MÉTIVIER is a French philosopher, pop philosopher, lecturer, and songwriter. He teaches philosophy at *Université de Tours*, France, and at the *Lycée Duplessis-Mornay* in Saumur, France. He is the author of *Rock'n'philo* and *Rock'n'philo, volume 2* (Paris: J'ai Lu) and Rap'n'philo (Paris, Le passeur éd.). His next book is *Ma guitare* (My Guitar), the story of his relationship with his Martin guitar. Rock'n'philo explains the ideas of the philosophers by illustrating them with rock pieces that he interprets himself, live. The concept is presented in France (notably at UNESCO, at "Fête de la philosophie" and "La nuit des Idées" in Paris; "La semaine de la pop philosophie" in Marseille) and abroad (notably at the festival "Popsophia," Italy;

"Festival philo," Belgium; and at "Rencontres philosophiques de Monaco," before Princess Caroline in Monaco). He dreams of playing *Rock'n'philo* in the USA, Canada, and England!

DAVID MORGAN received his PhD in theoretical physics from William and Mary in 1997, and he is currently the Associate Professor of Physics and Astronomy at the Richard Bland College of William and Mary. His writing on popular culture and the philosophy of science has appeared in *Planet of the Apes and Philosophy* and *Jurassic Park and Philosophy*. Dr. Morgan has taught, written, and presented extensively on the connection between science and music. When he's not teaching physics, he can be found playing lead guitar with multiple classic rock and metal bands in the Richmond, Virginia, area. Like Jimi Hendrix, his weapon of choice is the Fender Stratocaster.

JOHN-THE-BOSS (NICHOLSON) is from Teesside in the northeast of England and proud of it. He has lived a rock'n'roll life and is a writer with columns about soccer, food, rock music. and comedy. He's also a novelist with fifteen books to his name. He lives in a lofty Edinburgh apartment with five thousand vinyl albums and is also renowned as a t-shirt guru, the like of which the world has seldom seen.

JERRY S. PIVEN, PhD, has been listening to Jimi and riding broomsticks since he was a tween. He's taught at NYU, The New School, and Case Western Reserve University, where his courses focused on existentialism, metaphysics, and letting your freak flag fly. After the days melted down into a sleepy red glow, he could be seen most midnights at a very groovy place called Nighttown Jazz Club (you know, on the outskirts of infinity), where he'd land his kinky machine and sing a little Jimi.

CHARLES TALIAFERRO, professor of philosophy at St. Olaf College, is the author or editor of over twenty books. While he remains impressed by Jimi's guitar smashing, he has destroyed only one musical instrument in his life—a very old, broken and irreparable piano after a mediocre performance in college.

HANS UTTER is an intellectual dilettante—novelist, poet, painter, and professional musician. After mastering every Hendrix riff, he took a sojourn to India and was reborn as a sitarist. Caught in the intersection between neurosciences and philosophy he became an ethnomusicologist, and has taught and lectured at various universities around the world. He has performed and recorded with artists such as Public Enemy, Bianca, REO Speedwagon, and Jimmy Buffett.

Index or Confusion?

"Spanish Castle Magic," 84, 171

"Star-Spangled Banner," 19, 20, 25, 28, 44, 83, 163, 188, 191, 197, 198, 201, 202

"Still Raining, Still Dreaming," 174, 228

"Stone Free," 40, 42, 103, 118, 176, 238

"Third Stone from the Sun," 42, 111, 231

"Up from the Skies," 84

"Valleys of Neptune," 28, 229

"Villanova Junction," 19, 20

"Voodoo Chile," 3, 5, 8, 80, 163, 172,173, 232

"Voodoo Chile (Slight Return)," 7, 11, 31, 82, 172, 197

"Wait Until Tomorrow," 46, 48

"Who Knows," 164, 177

"Wild Thing," 235

"The Wind Cries Mary," 40, 48, 76, 78, 89, 111, 163, 171, 207

You Can't Use My Name: The RSVP/PPX Sessions, 182, 183

electric church music, 93, 96, 97, 208

Grandmother (Cherokee, Vancouver), 73

Hendrix's birth: November 27th 1942, 73

Hendrix's death: September 18th 1970, 10

Hendrix influenced w/ Band of Gypsys: Miles Davis, George Clinton and P-Funk, Bootsy Collins, Nile Rogers, Vernon Reid and Living Color, Lenny Kravitz, Prince Jimmy James and the Blue Flames, 234

"Letter to the Room Full of Mirrors," 80

Lost Writings of Jimi Hendrix, 215

LSD, 77, 121

Military Service, Fort Campbell, Kentucky, 74

Movie: *Jimi: All Is by My Side*, 61

"A psychedelic Uncle Tom," Robert Christgau, 164

race desertion, 81

Rock and Roll Hall of Fame Biography, 52

"Story of Life," 71

Hendrix, Leon, 184

Hephaestus, 5

Heraclitus, 88, 231, 232–33

Hinduism: Vishnu, Brahman, Shiva, 236

Hoffman, Abbie, 20

Holliday, Billie, 85

Holmes, Oliver Wendell, 185

Holly, Buddy, 51

Hooker, John Lee, 164

Howlin' Wolf, 57, 74, 77 ("Killin' Floor", 159, 172)

Hutcheson, Francis, 222

Ice-T: "Cop Killer," 47; "Freedom of Speech," 47; *Law and Order: Special Victim's Unit*, 47

idealism, 207

Isaiah (*Bible*): 93, 95

Isley Brothers, 163, 174, 182

Jackson, Michael, 63, 142

James, Elmore, 74

Jampol Artist Management, 142

Jagger, Mick, 44, 165

Jefferson Airplane, 41, 172

Jim Crow, 43, 92

Joey Dee and the Starliters, 182

Jones, Brian, 51, 68, 239

Jones, Elvin, 34

Nietzsche, Friedrich: 9, 29, 33, 131, 144; *The Birth of Tragedy* 7, 8, 27; *Beyond Good and Evil*, 33; *Ecce Homo*, 33
nihilism, 94
Noh drama 15, 16

Olympic Studios, 127, 129, 132, 135
Osto, Douglas: *Altered States*, 20

pacifism, 198
Palmer, Robert: "Rock Begins," 158
Pandora, 5
Pass, Joe, 173
Paul, Les, 173
Paul Revere and the Raiders, 41
Personalities Rights Act, 184
Pink Floyd, 128, (Atom Heart Mother: 130; "Fat Old Sun," 130)
Picasso, Pablo: *Guernica*, 201–02
Pixies: "Where Is My Mind?" 122
Plato, 57, 113 (*Republic*, "Allegory of the Cave," 117), 123, 150–51, 208, 209, 228
Plotinus, 208
Postmortem Right of Publicity, 184
Presley, Elvis, 64, 67, 68, 69, 158
Prince, 67, 182
Prometheus, 5, 7
psychedelic drugs, 20

Rabelais, 87
racist myth, 165
Ramones, 142
Redding, Noel, 76, 162, 172
Redding, Otis, 163

Reggae: (Jamaica), 158
Reich, Steve, 223
Richards, Keith, 44, 162
Rimbaud, Arthur, 36
Robbins, Tom: *Room Full of Mirrors*, 225–26
Rolling Stone, 58
Rolling Stones, 41, 158, 159; *Exile on Main Street*, 169, 238
Roberts, Billy: "Hey Joe," 39
Roby, Steven: *Hendrix on Hendrix* (*Circus, Melody Maker, San Diego Free Press, Disc and Music, Jazz and Pop, Rave, Rolling Stone*), 76
romanticism, 57
Rossi, Robert in *Harvard Law Review*, 184
Rudinow, Joel: "Can White People Sing the Blues?" 155

Sartre, Jean-Paul, 103, 104, 107; *Being and Nothingness*, 88, 103, 107; *Nausea, The Wall, No Exit:* 103
Saville Theatre, 77
Schopenhauer, Arthur, 29; 64, 66 ("Genius and Virtue"), 68
Sex Pistols, 142
Shakespeare, William: *Othello*, 46, 47, 57
Shapiro, Harry, and Caesar Glabbeek, *Jimi Hendrix: Electric Gypsy*, 121, 234
Shondells, 41
Simpson, O.J. 47
Sinatra, Frank, 91
"Six Feet Under" (death metal), 47
Slick, Grace, 40
Smith, Bessie, 58
Smith, Freddy, 173
Smith, Jimmy, 173

Squires, 174
Starting at Zero, 90, 91, 93
Stax Records, 162
Stein, Ruth: *For Love of the Father*, 31
Stockholm (destroyed hotel room), 44
stoics, 112
Stratocaster, 20, 39, 76, 81, 82, 84, 119, 121, 174
Stubbs, David: *Jimi Hendrix*, 228
Sumlin, Hubert, 172
Supremes, 158

Taylor, Charles: *The Ethics of Ambiguity*, 72
T-Bone Walker, 164
Teenset, 82
Thales, 227, 229
"Theme from *Shaft*," 162
Time: "Rock'n'Roll: Everybody's Turned On," 158
Tolstoy, Leo: *What Is Art?*, 192, 198–205
Tonight Show, 76
Townshend, Pete, 4, 164, 168
Tricycle: The Buddhist Review, 19
Tupac Shakur, 142
27 Club, 51

utilitarian principle, 194, 198

Valens, Ritchie, 51
Van Gogh, Vincent, 55
Vaughn, Stevie Ray, 84
Velvet Underground, 142
Vietnam War, 19, 20, 71, 83, 92, 101, 158, 160, 163, 202, 203, 205, 235
Von Tersch of *The Rolling Stone*, 177

Waller, Brian James (*see Bridges*), 54
Warhol, Andy, 62
Warner Brothers, 182
Watts Summer Festival 1970, 82
West, Cornell: *Race Matters*, 85
Wild Cherry; "Play That Funky Music White Boy," 160
Williams, Tony, 178
Wilson, Brian: *Pet Sounds*, 42
Winehouse, Amy, 51
Winthrop-Young, Geoffrey: *Kittler and the Media*, 131
Winwood, Steve, 80, 172
Wittgenstein, Ludwig, 149–50, 158, 187
Womack, Bobby, 163
Wood, Chris, 80
Woodstock, directed by Michael Wadleigh, 203
Woodstock, 17, 19, 20, 71, 83, 163, 192, 196
World War II, 92
Wray, Link, 127
Wundt, Wilhelm, 223
Wyman, Bill, 155

Yardbirds, 238
Yasgur, Max, 193
York, Ritchie, of the *Los Angeles Times*, 161

Zappa, Dweezil, 42
Zappa, Frank: *Weasels Ripped My Flesh*, 223
Zeitgeist, 56, 59, 66, 207, 212
Zeus, 5
Zevon, Warren/Bruce Springsteen: "Jeanie Needs a Shooter," 46

METAPHYSICAL GRAFFITI

Sob A Stereo

DEEP CUTS IN THE PHILOSOPHY OF ROCK

RANDALL E. AUXIER

FOREWORD BY LUKE DICK

Metaphysical Graffiti

Deep Cuts in the Philosophy of Rock

RANDALL E. AUXIER

FOREWORD BY LUKE DICK

"Dr Auxier's book covers two subjects he's spent his life immersed in—rock music and philosophy. . . . His analysis of The Rolling Stones' musical and interpersonal dynamic is nothing short of brilliant."

— ANDREW CALHOUN, singer-songwriter and founder of Waterbug Records

"What I like best about this book—aside from the rollicking prose— is the way the thought emerges from the music, rather than being imposed on it. The life, the politics, memory, philosophy, and melody are effortlessly and fully integrated. Metaphysical Graffiti *shows that profound thought can be a kind of music."*

— CRISPIN SARTWELL, author of *Six Names of Beauty* (2006) and *Against the State: An Introduction to Anarchist Political Theory* (2008)

"This wonderful book provides insight into two dissonant arts as only one written by a philosopher-musician can."

— NICOLAS MICHAUD, editor of *Discworld and Philosophy* (2016)

RANDALL E. AUXIER is a musician and professor of philosophy. He wrote *Time, Will, and Purpose: Living Ideas from the Philosophy of Josiah Royce* (2013).

LUKE DICK is a songwriter and co-editor of *The Rolling Stones and Philosophy: It's Just a Thought Away* (2012).

ISBN 978-0-8126-9964-7

For more information on Open Court books, go to
www.opencourtbooks.com.